1

Seeing and Savoring Italy

A Taste and Travel Journey through Northern Italy, Tuscany and Umbria

Pamela Marasco

E and I Publishers

3

Contents

Part 4: Travel

Bibliography

Index

Photo Credits: A.M. Marasco, P. Marasco

Cover Photo: Courtesy of Castello Gropparello

Acknowledgments

There are a small group of people in Italy and the US who supported my efforts and kept me believing that writing this book was possible. They range in age from 4 years old to friends and family well aged. Their recommendations on the content and focus of this book are gratefully appreciated and their encouragement and candid opinions have given me the insight and resolve to bring you a book that I hope will allow you to discover Italy in a unique and personal way.

My Italian family in Milano and Portogruaro, my friends in Perugia and Parma and my colleagues in Florence, Chianti and Emilia Romagna, have all been an invaluable source of information and support. Without their generous hospitality and willingness to help me learn about the authentic Italy this book could not have been written and my taste and travel journeys incomplete at best. The lasting memories and priceless moments I have had in Italy are due to them and would not have been possible without them.

A special note of thanks to my Italian teacher, Gina. She continues to be very patient and I am grateful to her in the present, past, future, imperfect and conditional tenses. And finally to Michael, whose Italian family became my family and whose love and support is never ending. Grazie mille a tutti!

Pamela Marasco

August 2010

7

Introduction

the noblest pleasure of all is the joy of understanding
. . . Leonardo DaVinci

The London Times once said that if we are what we eat who wouldn't want to be Italian. I would take that one step further and say if we are what we eat who wouldn't want to be Northern Italian. The geography and climate of Northern Italy make it one of the most culturally diverse and gastronomically active regions of Italy. The abundance and variety of food in Northern Italy is legendary and reads like a Who's Who of the culinary world. The prosciutti of San Daniele and Parma, Milano's risotto and osso bucco, the pestos of Genoa and the pastas of Emilia Romagna are classic foods of the North. Northern Italian favorites like carpaccio are featured on most fine dining menus and espresso laced tiramisu has so many global variations that I've stopped counting. The wine and food routes, *le strade dei vini e sapori*, of the 8 regions that loosely define Northern Italy, extend from the Alpine ranges of the Dolomites to the fertile plains and rolling hills of the Emilia-Romagna Apennines and from the sun drenched Ligurian Riviera to the Venetian shores of the Adriatic. All along the way you can taste the historical landscape of a region of Italy whose food is at the gastronomic epicenter of the world.

This book is based on my experiences traveling, eating, cooking and shopping in Northern Italy, Tuscany and Umbria with my Italian family and friends. It is a travel journal of taste based on my experiences eating, cooking, shopping and traveling over 10 years and 10,000 miles and reflects Italy as I have come to know it. Only sites and experiences that have been the most significant and memorable to me are mentioned in this book. The people you will read about are real people although in some cases I only use their first names to protect their privacy. Hotels, inns, agriturismos, country houses and restaurants are mentioned in the context of my travels. All accommodations and eating establishments should be further researched by the reader for suitability based upon their travel needs. I would advise the reader to check all travel costs and schedules prior to departure as seasonal and exchange rates may apply.

I have included samples of some of the most memorable meals I've had traveling through this region of Italy, meals that I often have again and again. They are in no particular order and the list is by no means comprehensive. They are classic dishes that are reflective of the region and in my opinion should not be missed. So when you are face to face with *il menu* and not sure what to choose, choose to eat any of these dishes and you will not be disappointed.

See and Savor More: The 8 Regions of Northern Italy are Lombardy, Emilia Romagna, Liguria, Piedmonte, the Veneto, Friuli-Venezia Giulia, Trentino-Alto Adige and Valle d'Aosta.

FOOD

Chapter 1   A Gastronomic Treasure

My first experience of Italy was by way of a road trip with my Italian cousins through Tuscany. It was the fall of 1999. Fresh from reading Frances Mayes' *Under the Tuscan Sun*, with visions of vineyards and olive orchards dancing in my head, I jumped at my cousin Lidia's suggestion that we travel by car from Milano through Chianti on our way to Siena stopping to visit Monteriggioni where my cousin's husband Roberto was born. That trip was and will always be the singular most perfect experience I have of Italy. Not because everything went right, it didn't. We got lost, repeatedly. I fell down in a vineyard and got car sick a few times (the roads of Chianti are winding). The experience was so memorable because this is where I first discovered the heart and soul of Italy with my Italian family and began to see that Italy was far more than I could have ever imagined. Now after 10 years traveling, eating, cooking and shopping in Northern Italy, Tuscany and Umbria with my Italian family and friends, I've come to regard Italy as a far away friend that I look forward to visiting every year. And after 10,000 miles traveling in Italy by car, bus, tube and train Italy still continues to engage me in new and different ways. My travels in Italy have taken me from the front door of the cities in the guidebooks to back door visits of family homes and kitchens in small towns and villages where the formal *come sta* has become the more informal *come stai*. I've learned about the way Italians live and work, regional food and wine, language and cultural traditions. I've learned about how Italians think and what they like to

10

do but more importantly I've learned about the Italian view of life, seeing and savoring the food, wine, art and design of Italy.

My travels in Italy began unexpectedly. I am not Italian by birth but by design. What I mean to say is that certain people in my life have positioned me to become Italian. There was no Svengalian manipulation or sleight of hand but rather a subtle induction into a way of life that I happened upon incidentally. The transformation was gradual and began when I married Michael. My marriage to Michael was as much a celebration in Italy as it was at home and it was at that moment that my transformation began. It was at that moment that I became a part of a family in Italy. This one act and a family bond of love would take me on a series of trips to Italy that would change the way I view my life. In fact I didn't even know a transformation was happening until years later when I made my first trip to Italy to reconnect with Michael's relatives in Milano after his mother died. It was her dream to travel to Italy. She wanted to discover the family that Nonna had left behind. Nonna, Michael's grandmother, left Italy in 1919 for America. Like many Italian immigrants, circumstances of time and place, marriage and duty had caused Nonna to travel to the United States with her husband, Santo. Her first child, Michael's father, was born in America and America was to become her home for the next 70 years. Nonna lived with Michael's family and became an Italian-American, blending the cultural heritage of Italy with the American lifestyle she so enjoyed. But her heart was still in the Veneto, a region of Northern Italy located in the Venetian plain whose culinary and cultural traditions make it one of the most visited regions of Italy today. The oral traditions of life in the Veneto were kept alive in

11

Michael's family and everyone was influenced by them including me. Families in the Veneto wrote to families in the United States, over holidays and birthdays, through wars and liberations, at births and deaths. Letters and pictures were sent, money and presents exchanged and all the while it was the dream of Michael's mother to visit Nonna's family in Italy; a dream that would only be realized years later when her son and his family traveled to Italy. In the beginning I was following the unfulfilled dream of a mother who wanted to reconnect with her family's heritage. In the end, Italy for me would become much more.

My first real taste of Italy began in America with a gentle coaxing into Nonna's kitchen the day after I married Michael. I had been helping in the kitchen all the while Michael and I dated, helping to stir the polenta, chop the garlic; watching Nonna shape the gnocchi with the tines of a fork. I had been helping Michael's mother make her famous Italian Rum Cake, the centerpiece of many family celebrations. I had spent countless hours going over pictures, postcards and letters from relatives in Italy. But now things were about to get serious. Nonna was not an architect but just as surely as Brunelleschi designed the Cathedral Dome in Florence, Nonna had a design for me. I was married to her grandson, Michael who she loved very much and as with all grandmothers she had a special place in her heart for him. So teaching me to cook Italian was now a priority. One of my many lessons on the art of "*cucina alla casalinga*", home style Italian cooking, was learning Nonna's recipe for Hunter's Chicken (*Pollo alla Cacciatora*). It was one of the first recipes she taught me to cook. A classic Italian dish, most families have their own variation of the recipe

12

using red or white wine sometimes adding mushrooms and peppers. Nonna frequently cooked this dish on Sundays to serve at the afternoon meal that lasted for hours. She called the dish Stewed Chicken with Polenta because the sauce from the chicken was always served over hot polenta. Measuring ingredients for Nonna was "a glass of wine and olive oil to coat the bottom of the pan". "What size glass, Nonna, how much olive oil?" She would reply patiently "You know the small water glass and the pan we always use". I learned to cook this dish by watching her and helping in the preparation and along the way I began to learn about the background and traditions of her family in the Veneto and her life in Italy.

Now I realize that Nonna had a plan for me. She wanted me to know about her Italian family heritage and culture and she would teach me about it through food. Nonna always served her stewed chicken with polenta, a type of cornmeal that is cooked in water to make a kind of porridge. The regions of northern Italy especially the Veneto where Nonna came from were large producers of corn and so polenta became a common food often eaten by peasants who served it alone or with cheese (Parmigiano, Fontina) or milk. There was a special pot Nonna used to cook polenta.There was a special wooden spoon/stick *(mescola*)) Nonna used to stir the polenta and there was a special board Nonna used to serve the polenta which she then covered with a white tea towel to keep warm. As you can see, polenta had a prominent place at the family table. Polenta is still a very popular dish in the Veneto, a region in Northern Italy that includes some of my favorite taste and travel destinations. Here you can drive along the course of the Brenta River between Padua and

13

Venice, known as the Brenta Riviera (*Rivera del Brenta*) where architects such as Palladio designed country residences (villas) for wealthy Venetians who were looking for a diversion from the summer heat of Venice. In the Veneto you can create your own balcony scene *alla* Romeo and Juliet at No. 27 Via Capello in Verona and taste grappa at its birthplace in Bassano del Grappa, an authentic Italian river town at the foot of the Alps. And at the *Piazza dei Signori* in Treviso I listened to an outdoor concert of American classics by Gershwin after dining on peacock and *nidi di amore* at the home of my friend, Simone.

When Nonna died at the age of 89 she did not leave a material inheritance valued in dollars and cents but she did leave a gastronomic treasure chest full of traditional family recipes and memories that connected us to the rich, cultural traditions of Italy and the belief that sitting at the table in fellowship with your family and friends is a lost pleasure that must be found again. I have been on a mission to discover the gastronomic treasures of Italy ever since that first cooking lesson in Nonna's kitchen. That mission has taken me on a remarkable journey down Roman roads, past castles with Celtic altars and Etruscans ruins, through medieval walled cities and alpine lakes, visiting Renaissance chapels and Gothic cathedrals, into kitchens, vineyards and orchards, to experience the food of princes, popes, pilgrims and everyday Italians developing a taste for Italy and wanting more.

See and Savor More

Nonna's Hunter's Chicken *Pollo alla Cacciatora*

Nonna loved chicken so she would include every part of the bird including the "last part that went over the fence" when making this dish but I have made this recipe with just breasts, legs and thighs and it works well. I don't feel that you can make this recipe with just the light meat of the chicken. Combining light and dark meat gives the dish a richer flavor. Also Nonna always cooked this dish with the skin on the chicken and the chicken on the bone. I remove part of the skin and skim off some of the fat during cooking because generally the men I am serving this dish to are not sitting down at the table after a hard day of hunting and do not need the extra calories from the richness of the fat. The measuring of ingredients is according to my best guesstimate as Nonna never used exact measurements for this recipe.

- Wash a 3-4 lb chicken in cold water and pat dry. Cut the chicken into 6-8 pieces. Heat 2 T of olive oil and 1T butter (Nonna was from Northern Italy) in a large enough pan that can accommodate the chicken pieces without crowding them (I use a Dutch oven or enamel casserole pot)
- When the oil and butter begin to foam add 1 large onion thinly sliced and cook until softened. Add chicken pieces, skin side down. Cook chicken until nicely brown on one side and then the other. Add 1-2 cloves garlic being careful not to let the garlic burn (this is very important). Add a little salt (I use gray salt) and freshly ground pepper, as you like. Keep turning the

chicken over as it browns. Now you must add the wine - about 1/3 to 2/3 cup of Vino di Tavolo, an Italian table wine (red or white), Nonna used the wine she would be serving with the meal. Allow the chicken to simmer with the wine as the alcohol steams offs and the wine evaporates to just about half. This will happen fairly quickly. At this point add 1½ cups of Italian plum tomatoes, coarsely chopped with their juice. Adjust the heat to a steady simmer and cover the pan with the lid slightly askew.

- Slowly cook the chicken for about an hour or until the meat begins to fall off the bone. Some people add fresh sliced mushrooms to the pot the last 15 to 20 minutes of cooking but in our household the mushrooms were prepared separately and served at the table with polenta.

The term "hunter" in Italian cooking refers to the style of preparation of a whole meat carcass made with local rustic ingredients including tomatoes, mushrooms, onions, herbs and wine cooked over an open stove resulting in a stew of rich, robust flavors. I have seen this dish made with other meat including rabbit which is more typical of a hunter's meal. Chef-author restaurateur Pino Luongo has a recipe for Rabbit Hunter's Stew (Coniglio alla Cacciatora) in his book   A Tuscan in the Kitchen. Like mia nonna he doesn't believe in measuring ingredients saying "You don't need a prescription for cooking food, you're the person in charge. Don't be afraid to follow your feelings. Be flexible, be creative, abandon your inhibitions and have fun. When it looks good and feels right, you'll know it". A native of Tuscany, Luongo is known for his innovative interpretation of classic Tuscan

16

cooking and often riffs on classical Tuscan recipes and ingredients resulting in traditional and crosscurrent dishes like eggplant-chocolate mousse. All his books have interesting and informative descriptions with stunning and mouth-watering pictures. As do all Italians, he believes that "seasonality is key to Italian cooking". So make this dish in the fall during the height of the hunting season. Even if your *cacciatore* hasn't brought home the main ingredient you can connect to a time of the year that in Italy is truly magical. The colors of the autumn landscape in Tuscany and the Umbrian hills are deeper and richer than ever and the Emilia Romagna countryside is full of the fruits of the harvest. The bronze and brown porcini mushrooms, the deep wine colors of the *vendemmia* (grape harvest) and the earthy aroma of truffles create a taste for Italy in the autumn like no other time of the year.

Chapter 2   Eden Has a Taste

In the distant past it was a common belief that East of Asia Eden could be found. Countless merchant ships relentlessly searched for a place, a compass point, a tangible position on a map where Paradise lost could be rediscovered. The biblical location of Eden may have pointed to the East but the gastronomic location of the garden of earthly delights most certainly was to the West. If Eden had a taste it would be Italy. For no country is more perfectly constructed for the enjoyment of food and wine to the benefit of man than *l'italia*. The 16th century Italian writer, Teofilo Folengo wrote of a country with "rivers full of soup which ran together into a lake and a sea of stew in which plying to and fro were thousands of boats made of pastry with shores of tender fresh butter and on them hundreds of saucepans smoking to the clouds with ravioli, macaroni and other delights". Although these imaginative accounts of the culinary landscape of Italy are part of the diversional storytelling of a Renaissance poet, the foods you will taste while traveling in Italy are truly gastronomic wonders.

My travels in Italy have always been influenced by what and where I have eaten and where and with whom I have cooked. Both have made a strong impression on me and made my experiences traveling in Italy more meaningful. I knew that there was a strong relationship between food and my travels in Italy when I returned from my first trip. It began with a set of pictures taken when I was a novice taste traveler just learning about the hidden gastronomic codex that was to be my key to unlocking the pleasures of Italian food and wine. Most visitors to Italy take pictures of cathedrals and monuments, fountains, villas,

18

ancient Etruscan and Roman ruins, piazzas, museums, monasteries and abbeys, the inspiring landscapes, vineyards, mountains, rivers and lakes, the Vespas, Smart Cars, Ferrari and fashions. Now don't get me wrong, I've taken more than my share of pictures of all of the above but I realized that a sizeable portion of my pictures seemed to focus on FOOD. I had pictures of *pici* in Pienza and *polenta* in Bergamo, *cantucci* and *Vin Santo* in Siena, *salame*, *salumi* and *salsiccia* in Parma. As I returned to Italy time and again pictures of food became more a part of the scene. Why had I become so fascinated about the foods of Italy? I am not a foodie, gourmand or particularly large eater. I like to cook but I am not a chef. I also began to notice that as impressed as I was when I saw the frescoes of Giotto in Assisi and Leonardo's art and architecture in Florence and Milan, I spent an equal amount of time at the Ambrosian Gallery staring at Caravaggio's *Basket of Fruit* painted with a reverence usually reserved for saints. I also began to notice that this preoccupation with the foods of Italy was shared by other famous Italians like Giuseppe Arcimboldo, a 16th century Italian artist who liked to play with his food and arrange fruits, vegetables and flowers in unconventional ways turning his portraits upside down as a gardener becomes a bowl of vegetables with a carrot for a nose and onions for cheeks. It didn't take too many more trips to Italy for me to realize the pivotal place food has in Italian culture and living. The regional foods of Italy define the culture and traditions of Italy in a very unique way. As you travel from one region of Italy to another you discover the artisanal skills of *cucina regionale* where each regional specialty reflects the traditions of a time and place. The entire cuisine of Italy is based on traditional

19

regional cooking passed down from generation to generation. I've been able to see firsthand where the traditions of our Nonna's cooking came from and experience cooking these dishes in the kitchens of my Italian family and friends.

Traveling in Italy without taking the time to understand the traditions behind regional Italian cuisine will only allow you to experience Italy on the most superficial of levels. Most Americans think they know what Italian food tastes like, but without knowing the background, traditions and ingredients necessary to be authentic they don't. In America, Italian food is often narrowly defined and misunderstood. In some cases, Italian food has been commercialized often beyond the point of recognition. Introducing Americans to Italian food after the Second World War was fast and furious as GI's returning from the Italian front sought to duplicate the flavors of Italy at home. But when convenience won over tradition, often the only authentic interpretation of the foods of Italy was to be found in the kitchens of the Nonni (grandparents). As the years went by many of these food traditions were lost even within the Italian American communities. That's not too say that there are no true interpreters of Italian food and cooking to be found outside of Italy today. Certain restaurateurs, home cooks and chefs keep the bloodline of Italian cooking alive and value the artisan traditions of Italian cooking but for the truest interpretation of Italian food you must travel to Italy because only in Italy can you experience the traditions behind the food in the vineyards and orchards, markets and shops and at the table where centuries of culinary traditions are still a part of eating Italian.

Traveling in Tuscany you see the famous Chianina cattle graze in the stunningly beautiful *Val d'Orca*. The *Vacca Chianina* (pronounced kee-a-nee-na) cattle were praised by Virgil and were the models for Roman sculptures. At the table Chianina beef is served as *Bistecca Chianina* (aka *Bistecca alla fiorentina* or Tuscan T-Bone). It is legendary and considered to be the ultimate expression of Tuscany cuisine, simple, rustic and bold. The meat has exceptional flavor and is very tender with little fat. It is traditionally served with a drizzle of extra virgin Tuscan olive oil. Here as in all of Italy there is a connection between the food and the land. In Emilia Romagna, Bologna the city of medieval arcades and endless porticoes, lavish menus of Renaissance courts inspired generations of dishes still prepared today. This region of Italy is known for its fresh pasta but no less so for its pork, bread, cakes, biscuits, tarts, fruit, *aceto balsamico* vinegar and cheese (Parmigiano-Reggiano is made here). The cooks of this region not only pair pasta with the rich massive *Ragu' alla Bolognese* but also make the gentle tortellini modeled after Venus's navel. About 50 km N-NE of Bologna is the medieval city of Ferrara. For its beauty and cultural importance Ferrara has been listed by UNESCO as a World Heritage Site and is a perfect example of a taste and travel city. It is not typically on the tourist radar yet it offers a unique experience to taste the delicious flavors of history. Here you can experience my all time favorite pasta, *cappellacci* (big hat pasta). *Cappellacci,* a larger version of *tortellini,* are often filled with a mixture of pumpkin (*capellacci di zucca)* and parmesan cheese and served *al burro e salvia* with a delicate butter and sage sauce. Ferrara is on the Bologna to Venice train line so even if you do not have a car there are

33 trains a day originating from Bologna that connect you to the flavors and history of Ferrara.

Food eaten in its place of origin is very evocative. Eating a *bistecca* in Tuscany or *tortellini* in Emilia Romagna creates a mood that elevates the experience of eating. I refer to this as evocative eating and it is at the core of the taste and travel experience. If this sounds like a banner line for foodies, yes, it would certainly appeal to those who have a keen interest in food but a taste and travel trip isn't just about the food. Whatever your travel goals; relaxation and well being, the arts and music, shopping, adventure travel, a family vacation, they all can be enriched by combining them with a pleasure of eating food in its historical place of origin. The taste traveler mind set is to approach traveling with the intention of exploring all five senses because taste traveling in Italy is as much about what you feel as it is about what you will see. A taste and travel trip creates experiences that make travel more than just a "show and tell" tour so that you can open yourself to all that Italy has to offer and in my mind one should not be separated from the other.

See and Savor More

Teofilo Folengo was an Italian writer who lived during the Renaissance, at the same time as Machiavelli and Michelangelo. Folengo used the Italian and Latin language in a comical made-up language called Macaronic Latin, a mixture of languages often with bilingual puns. Another example of Macaronics is Spanglish, a mixture of Spanish and English or Franglais, a mixture of English and French.

Chapter 3   Italy on My Plate

Over the years many people have asked me what is the best place to eat in Italy. The best place to eat in Italy is at the home of your family. The second best place to eat in Italy is at the home of your friends. The third best place to eat in Italy is at "*un ristorante*" chosen by your family and friends. I say this because eating in this manner represents the most authentic Italian experience around the table. Your Italian family and friends want only to serve you the best and are the most generous of hosts. When accompanied by Italians in a restaurant, the proprietor is most eager to please because you are with Italians and are considered to be one of them. Just eating in Italy is an experience you will long remember, eating in this manner touches your very soul. I remember one afternoon I spent at an *enoteca* in Montefalco with my Umbrian friends, Luca and Luigi. The word "*enoteca*" literally means library of wines but an *enoteca* in Italy can mean anything from a wine tasting room in Chianti to a wine bar in almost any town or village where you can try regional wines with some *crostini*. Luigi is my wine mentor and I am his eager and accepting student. He is a sommelier and explained all the wonderful nuances of Umbrian wines over a bottle of Montefalco Sagrantino. This was "la dolce vita" squared as I basked in the glow of the Umbrian autumn gazing into a glass of perfection. That moment is what seeing and savoring Italy is all about, hidden and undiscovered treasures, slightly off the beaten path that provide lasting memories and exceptional culinary experiences. Finding these places in Italy is what this book is all about. With a little effort and a sense of adventure your travels in Italy can go way beyond the usual

23

tour bus experience. Now you may not have two handsome Italian friends to drink wine in the piazza with, yet, but I hope this book will inspire you to discover Italy in a very personal way that creates lasting memories that only get better as time passes. In order to do that you must first learn the fundamentals of Italian food. Knowing about the foods you will taste in Italy will heighten your travel experience and make it more meaningful. Although the breadth and depth of Italian food is beyond the scope of this book, I have chosen six categories that are most representative of what you will want to eat when traveling in Italy. They are pasta, rice, cheese, cured meats and sausage, condiments and sweets.

Pasta

I have had many memorable meals on my plate in Italy that have centered on pasta. After all pasta may be the poster child of Italy. Italians are passionate about their pasta. Their feelings for making, eating, cooking and buying pasta are defended with strong emotions that run run as deep as the Medici-Pazzi rivalries of Renaissance Italy. North versus South, dry versus fresh, *fatto a mano* or machine rolled Every Italian has their opinions about the art and science of making pasta. The average Italian citizen eats over 90lbs of pasta per year and pasta is the first food given to babies when they're ready to eat. The first course *il primo*, served in a traditional Italian meal is often pasta and the foundation of regional Italian *casalinga* home style cooking has always centered around the making of pasta. But the pasta in Italy is much different than the pasta most Americans are used to. The many shapes and sizes of pasta have caused it to become trivialized by most Americans who often choose pasta on how it looks rather than how it cooks and pairs with a particular sauce. Many factions quarrel and quibble and complicate this simple unleavened dough made from flour, water and sometimes eggs. The conflict often begins with the origins of pasta. Did pasta originate in the East or the West?

The long standing urban myth that Marco Polo introduced pasta to Italy after returning from China is hotly debated by Italian pastaphiles. Evidence found in Etruscan tombs suggests that these ancient Italians enjoyed pasta and Apicius, Italy's first top chef, mentions a layered, lasagna-like dish in his book of recipes from the 1st century AD. References have been cited of a manuscript of a will found in Genoa two years before the return of Marco Polo that leaves the heirs a chest full of dried pasta. Another point of contention is how to determine the quality of pasta. In other words, how do you buy good pasta? My friends from Perugia, Pinota and her son Luigi who has a doctorate in agronomy, gave me my best lesson yet on pasta. Not all pasta is created equal. Good quality pasta is roughly textured because the rougher the outside of the pasta thebetter the sauce will adhere giving a more uniform and consistently delicious flavor to each bite. Italians regard sauce as a "seasoning" or condimentrather than serving the pasta drowning in the sauce. In Italy just enough sauce is added to coat the pasta (a scant ¼ cupper portion) with a spoonful on top so diners can see the beauty of the sauce. The exception to this is lasagna which in the North is preparedwlth plenty of béchamel sauce almost like a sandwich with more fillingthan bread. When you are in Italy you maywant to bring home a few packages of *pasta secca* (dry pasta).

25

The Italians perfected the art of making pasta in the 16th century to createa food that could be stored for long periods and provide them with a meal in times of famine. Artisan pasta makers seek to preserve the traditionalways of making pasta by using perforated bronze plates that mold the pastaand by allowing for slow drying times. Pasta *lunga* (long shaped pasta likespaghetti*)* and *pasta corta* or *tagliata* (short shaped pasta like penne) arethe two main types of dried pasta with a variety of regionalsizes and shapes.Today artisan pasta makers are choosing their own signature pasta shapes and design bronze dies for their production.Dried pasta has always been more typical of southern Italy because it keeps well in the hotter, drier climate of the south. In Italy the dry,packaged pasta, boiledand eaten with a sauce, typical to what we buy and eat in the States iscalled *pasta asciutta* from the Italian adjective *asciutto,* meaning dry orlean.P*asta fresca*, fresh pasta, is traditionally handmade (*pasta a fatto*) readyfor immediate use. This type of pasta is often made with eggs (although not always) and a softer flour. My cousin Lidia, as do most Italians, buy *pasta fresca* from the local *pastaficio*, a shop that sells fresh pasta. Making fresh pasta can be time consuming and working Italians often shop at their local market for their favorite pasta. *Pasta ripiena* refers to stuffed pasta like tortellini or ravioli. Short, thicker pastas like grooved penne or rigatoni are better with a full, meaty sauce while long, thinnerpasta like spaghetti are best served with smoother sauces using oil. When Italians speak of pasta (noodles) they usually refer to a specific kind of noodle i.e. spaghetti, pici, tagliatelle,tortellini served with some type of sauce, *sugo* or *salsa.* A *ragu'* is a meat sauce and in Italian-American communities a sauce is sometimes referred to as gravy. In Italy *la pasta* refers to a pastry and *il pasto* is the meal.

26

Rice

Pasta is not necessarily the first course of choice in Northern Italy. Rice or *riso* is the pasta of the North and Milano and other Northern Italian cities make use of its versatility to create regional dishes using the *superfino* Carnaroli, Arborio or Vialone Nano varieties. Although many look at Milano as a somewhat pragmatic city based on industry and commerce, Milano has a rich gastronomic history with a reputation for food production of the highest quality. The rich alluvial soil along the lower plains of the Po River in Lombardia produce some of the finest rice in the world and the types of *riso* grown here are the best for making risotto. Creamy in texture and delicate in taste, *risotto* is the signature dish of the North. The addition of *zafferano* (saffron), in Milanese risotto brings a golden color and flavor that distinguishes it from other risotto dishes like Piedmonte's *Risotto al Barolo,* made with red wine. Pelligrino Artusi, the godfather of Italian cooking, remarked a little more than a century ago, that the preparation of *Risottto alla Milanese* is left best to the Milanese. I would not argue with him. You MUST have risotto in Milan.

Cheese

Formaggio can be found on the Italian plate from antipasti to dessert. There are at least 451 different kinds of cheeses produced in Italy with local rarities that can be found nowhere else, creating an opportunity for the perfect taste and travel experience. Like wine they reflect the region of origin. In Northern Italy flavors and aromas range from the alpine flowers of the Alto Adige to the lush pasturage of Reggio to the earthy fields and woods of Tuscany and Umbria. Each cheese is

27

fiercely protected by national consortia who control the origin and production methods with traditions that go back centuries.

The cheeses of Northern Italy, Tuscany and Umbria have their own bloodline that begins with the ancient Etruscans who were thought to have a "recipe" for the making of Parmigiano cheese. Ancient cheese graters have been found at the Monte Bibele Etruscan-Celtic site near Monterenzio (BO). Known as the cheese of "knights, serfs, saints and kings", the process of making Parmigiano cheese has not changed in 700-800 years. The Romans adopted the Etruscan recipe for Parmigiano because the great wheels of cheese traveled well and could be used to feed their legions. In 14th century Italy, Boccaccio's Decameron tells the story of a group of seven women and three men who flee from plague-ridden Florence to a villa in the countryside of Fiesole. To pass the time, each member of the party tells one story for each one of the nights spent at the villa. Eight days into their confinement they must have been fantasizing about the pleasures of food as they tell a story about a country where "there was a mountain made entirely of grated Parmigiano Reggiano cheese, on which lived people who did nothing but make macaroni and ravioli and cook them in capon broth". In the North the undisputed king of cheeses is Parmigiano Reggiano but Parmigiano's rise to fame was not without a power struggle. The cheese wars of Emilia were finally won by the cheese who had gained the greatest prestige. Parmigiano Reggiano was proclaimed king and the other cheeses of the region were lumped together and named Grana Padano after the Padano Plains of the Po River Valley. Both cheeses are now appreciated for their firm, granular texture and are used for grating or in bite size morsels from

28

antipasto to dessert. While Grana Padano, like Parmigiano, can only be made within a certain region of Italy, that region is enormous, spanning 32 provinces in northern Italy, from Lombardy across the country to the Veneto. Parmigiano-Reggiano can only come from the cities of Parma, Reggio Emilia, Modena, Bologna and Mantua. Looking behind the brand, here are some interesting facts about the "king of cheeses"

- The natural rind of Parmigiano Reggiano cheese is edible and is used to flavor soups in Italy
- The crunchy texture of Parmiagiano cheese is from tiny salt crystals due to the brine bath that the cheese is soaked in
- Wheels of cheese can weigh up to 75lbs and may need to be cut with a saw
- Parmiagiano Reggiano cheese is so valuable that trucks carrying the cheese have been hijacked
- Because of the high content of calcium in Parmigiano Reggiano cheese, Russian cosmonauts have brought the cheese on their space flights to combat bone loss in space
- The trademark of the world's most famous cheeses, which is still valid today, was designed in 1612 by Bartolomeo Riva, Treasurer of the Farnese estates of Duke Ranuzzio I
- Parmesan (the cheese in the Green Can) is Americanization of the word Parmigiano. In Italy Parmigiano Reggiano is aged for a minimum of 18 months and for as long as four years. The standard US curing time for Parmesan is 6 -10 months.

29

The other great cheese from the North that should not be missed is blue veined Gorgonzola. First written about in the 11th century, Gorgonzola can be either *dolce* (young and creamy with a milder sweeter flavor) or *picante* (the firmer, shaper aged version). Describing the flavor and aroma of Gorgonzola dolce one ad man wrote "the perfume permeates the air and conjures memories of that soft, voluptuous texture, a warm, persistent and satisfying embrace, velvety smooth and a distinct personality that accentuates instead of dominating; with age, the creamy white color becomes slightly darker, the supple texture transforms ever so slightly, perhaps dryer but sensual just the same, a more distinct personality arises still complimentary but less yielding". The sensual texture and flavor of an artisan Gorgonzola dolce is a fashion food statement with the appeal of an Italian model from the catwalks of Milano. My cousin Lidia uses Gorgonzola dolce to make a wonderful sauce that she serves with gnocchi. To soften the edgy flavor of the cheese, she first soaks the crumbled Gorgonzola in milk. Lidia's *Salsa al Gorgonzola* uses 4 oz of soft, fresh Gorgonzola dolce cheese and allows it to come to room temperature. She then soaks the gorgonzola in 1/3 cup of milk. The gorgonzola milk mixture is warmed in a saucepan with 3 T butter until the cheese melts and is of a creamy consistency. Make this just before you are ready to serve the gnocchi. Some recipes add ½ cup of heavy cream to the sauce and bring it up to medium heat if the sauce has been sitting for awhile. The success of this sauce depends on the sweet, creamy, buttery texture of the Gorgonzola dolce which is not the same as Gorgonzola or blue cheese.

Ten years ago when I first traveled south from Lombardy and sat at the bountiful tables of Tuscany I began a love affair with a cheese that continues to this day. I am partial to Pecorino Toscano cheese because it was the first cheese I tasted in Italy at my cousin Lidia's table. She served *le pere col pecorino*, pecorino served with pears and chestnut honey and I instantly fell in love. Shy but with the taste and flavor of the Tuscan countryside, Pecorino Toscano is my favorite cheese in Italy. There are various types of pecorino cheese, but in my mind the pleasant and inviting nature of Pecorino Toscano make it very special. Pecorino Toscano should not be confused with Pecorino Romano a hard, sharp, salty cheese produced exclusively from the milk of sheep raised on the plains of Lazio and in Sardegna used primarily as a grating cheese. Pecorino Toscano is the Tuscan relative of the more well known Romano which because of its stronger flavor is preferred for some pasta dishes with highly flavored sauces. Both are sheep's milk cheeses (*pecora* means sheep in Italian) and both have PDO (Protected Designation of Origin) status but the similarity stops there. Best eaten at its source, Pecorino Toscano can be difficult to find in the states preferring to remain under the Tuscan sun. Eating a Tuscan pecorino surrounded by vineyards and olive orchards is evocative eating at its finest. The characteristic flavors and aromas of the grass, herbs and wildflowers on which the sheep graze create a taste of Tuscany that is incomparable. A taste of a good Pecorino Toscano is like languishing in a field of Tuscan wildflowers. The mild creamy texture has a slightly tangy flavor with hints of fragrant meadow grass. It is a perfect cheese to serve at the end of a meal or with the proverbial glass of wine and loaf of bread.

31

Pecorino cheese on display at Azienda Zazzeri in Pienza

Pecorino Toscano is a fresh, young cheese typically to be eaten in 30-60 days. When it is aged it is referred to as *pecorino stagionato*. *Stagionato* comes from the Italian word for season (*stagione*) and in this case means aged. Italian cheese makers sometimes age the cheese in old wine barrels or wrap it with myrtle and chestnut leaves that give the cheese a unique flavor. Although there are other areas in Tuscany that produce pecorino, the town of Pienza, near Siena is home to some of the finest. The clay soil of the Val d'Orcia produces lush fields of grass that give a particular taste to the milk produced by the sheep that graze on it and in turn produce the cheese. There are many cheese shops in the Pienza that offer tastings and you can stroll the stone paved streets sampling from one to another. Taste travelers in Tuscany can stop at a local *alimentari* (grocery store) and buy 100 g of *Pecorino Toscano*, 100 g of the *salumi locale* (cured meats, Italian deli meats), a couple of *panini* (bread rolls) and *una bottiglia vino di rosso locale* (a bottle of local red wine) and drive into the Tuscan countryside for a picnic to remember. And if your travels happen to take you across the border to Umbria, there is a very nice Pecorino of Norcia to be had there.

Whether enjoying the buttery rich alpine cheeses of the Val d'Aosta in a creamy *fonduta* (fondue) or the earthy yet delicate flavors of an Umbrian *Caciotta ai Tartufo*, (semi-soft sheep's milk cheese infused with black truffles) taste travelers in Northern Italy, Tuscany and Umbria can sample the best of the best. If at all possible try to schedule a visit to a *caseificio* (cheese factory) to see methods of production and the art of Italian cheese making. Tours should be arranged in advance as hours and days may be limited. It's good to have an Italian insider with you as these factories are off the beaten path so you will need very good driving directions (I recommend a GPS). Also English speaking guides may not always to available so inquire beforehand.

I could not leave a section on Italian cheeses without mentioning a cheese used in one of my favorite Italian dishes, *insalata caprese*. The simplicity and perfection of an *insalata caprese* begins with sun ripened tomatoes, fresh basil and the best extra virgin olive oil you can afford. Slices (1/8th inch thick) of buffalo mozzarella cheese are nestled among the tomatoes and fresh basil leaves for a salad that pops with the flavors and aromas of summer. Although this cheese comes from Campania in Southern Italy, it is a favorite all over Italy. *Mozzarella di bufala* is made from the milk of the water buffalo not the American buffalo or bison. No one seems to know for certain how the water buffalo got to Italy but they have been used as draught animals for centuries in Southern Italy where cheese made from their milk has been produced since the 1700's. Production in and around Naples was briefly interrupted during World War II, when retreating Nazis slaughtered the area's water buffalo herds. *Fiore di Latte* is another Italian mozzarella cheese. It is not a protected controlled production cheese like *mozzarella di bufala* and can therefore be made anywhere in Italy (authentic, traditional Italian buffalo mozzarella cheese can only be made in Campania, Apulia and Lazio). *Fiore di Latte* is made from cow's milk and is most likely to be the type of fresh mozzarella you will buy in the States. It often is sold as *bocconcini* (small round balls of cheese) and packed in salted water and has a longer shelf life. The *mozzarella di bufala* sold in the States will most likely have traveled from Italy so you will need to verify freshness. However there are mozzarella cheese makers here in the States who have their own herds of water buffalo and are making some very good *bufala* style cheese. I prefer to use these if I cannot get fresh Italian *mozzarella di bufala.*

Look for regional cheeses as you taste travel through Italy. Like wine their flavor and aroma are a product of the *terrior*; the land, the air, the soil of the region. In Italy, cheese is served freshly grated at the table or brought to the table in a covered cheese dish with a lid to preserve its fragrance and flavor. Covered cheese dishes make a nice gift to bring back home to remind you of the special place cheese has at the table in Italy. Another way to experience cheese in Italy is after the meal before dessert. A selection of regional cheeses are often served with fruit or a savory-sweet chutney, wine jelly or mostarda or drizzled with honey.

Extra Virgin Olive Oil

The plates of Italy have always been drenched with liquid gold. Italian olive oil is one of the gastronomic treasures of the world. According to the Italian Trade Commission, Italy produces nearly one third of the world's olive oil, distinguished by the superior class of *extra vergine.* And yes, being extra virgin is really better. Artisan extra virgin olive oil tends to be higher in heart healthy compounds with high levels of monounsaturated fats and low levels of polyunsaturated fats, high in antioxidants, vitamins and with as much calcium as milk.

The flavor profiles, colors and aromas as well as the way the olive oil pairs with the foods of Italy create an unforgettable experience. If you can arrange a visit to a *frantoio* (site of production of olive oil; olive press) you must go. Look for a *frantoio* that lists *Vendita Diretta - Olio Extra Vergine di Oliva,* here you can buy oil to take home with you. To me it is as desirable as a Prada purse so be sure to leave room in your suitcase for a bottle or two of artisan Italian olive oil.

Salumi, Salame and Salsiccia

No taste of Italy is complete without a sampling of regional *salumi, salame* and *salsiccia.* Every region of Italy has its own unique variations and takes great pride in the preparation. That means that traveling down the road in Italy tasting the varieties is a little like following the yellow brick road to Oz. You will be tempted to taste just about everything trying to get home and end up saying OH MY! But before we go further a definitional diversion is necessary. Cured ham like prosciutto or bresaola (air dried filet of beef), pancetta and speck

35

are referred to as *salumi*, whole cured cuts of meat. *Salame,* known as salami in the States is encased (*insaccati*) ground meat and *salsiccia* is sausage. There are literally hundreds of different types of cured meats, sausages and *salame* to be found all over Italy. Regional variations in meat, seasonings, aging and preparation account for the varieties of flavors and textures. You will find a gastronomic panorama of all manner of Italian *salame*, sausages and cured meats hanging from the rafters of *salumeria* in every town and village.

Depending on where you travel, you can have access to a variety of Italian *salame* but trying them under the tutelage of your Italian family and friends is a whole different thing. On a recent trip to Italy I had dinner at a friend's house in Parma. He is a university professor and was very happy to further my "Italian education" on the art and science of the *Salame di Felino*. *Salame di Felino* comes from the hill town of Felino, near Parma in Emilia Romagna and is highly regarded for its delicate flavor. It is thought to be the oldest *salame* linked to a specific region. *Salame di Felino* is made from lean ground pork (75% lean) seasoned with sea salt, black pepper, garlic and white wine. The *salame* is aged under the same climatic conditions that create the world famous *Prosciutto di Parma*. My Italian friends and family specify that *salame di Felino* "should be cut at a 60° angle no thicker than a grain of pepper contained in the *salame* itself". According to them this keeps the salame intact and makes for a nice presentation as an antipasto. This *salame* should not be confused with *finocchiona*, from the Florence and Chianti region. *Finocchiona* is made from finely ground pork flavored with black peppercorns, garlic, wine and fennel seeds. Traditionally, wild fennel is used and gives this *salame* the aroma of the Tuscan countryside. *Finocchiona* has an interesting but unsubstantiated legend associated with its origins. It is said that many years ago, a thief had stolen a fresh salami near the town of Prato. He hid it in a field of wild fennel. When he came to retrieve his ill gotten gain he found that it had absorbed the unique flavor of the wild fennel in which it had been hidden and *finocchiona* was born. *Salame* from Milano is made from meat that is ground very fine with a close grained texture speckled with grains of fat resembling the rice that Milanese cuisine is so famous for. Although there are several DOP (Protected Designation of Origin) salami made in the region (including the delicate and distinctive *Salame Brianza* produced in the provinces of Lecco, Como and Milan) you would expect the commercial center of Italy to be more pragmatic in its production of *salame* and it is. Mass produced and commonly found, *Salame Milano* although less artisanal in its preparation is very popular. Along with *Salame Genovese*, it is what most Americans know as "salami".

The most famous of the *salumi* or cured meats of Italy comes in the form of cured hams known as *prosciutto crudo* from San Daniele, Parma and Tuscany. These are among several regions of Northern Italy where a savvy taste traveler can enjoy one of the most celebrated hams in the world. The prosciutto from San Daniele is made in the province of Udine located in Friuli Venezia Giulia. This region of Northern Italy borders along the lands of Slovenian and the Carnic Alps. Elegantly shaped, prosciutto from San Daniele are pressed to give them a characteristic, elongated "Stradivarian" violin

37

shape. *Prosciutto crudo di San Daniele* is valued for its sweet and delicate flavor and exceptional aroma which is said to be due to the Alpine air. DOP certification sets out strict rules regarding the genetic make-up of the pigs and their feeding. The only ingredient used to make *prosciutto crudo di San Daniele* is sea salt, and that only sparingly (the salt content in a properly aged Prosciutto di San Daniele is less than 6 per cent). But to taste a prosciutto whose trademark is a ducal crown you must taste prosciutto from Parma. In the land of the king of cheeses there is a line of food royalty with a history and tradition that goes far back in time to more than 2,000 years ago. According to the *Consorzio del Prosciutto di Parma* (the Italian Parma ham trade consortium) for a pig to qualify for its thighs to become *prosciutto di Parma*, it must be born of the large white Landrace, or Duroc breeds; raised in north or central Italy, preferably in Lombardy, Emilia Romagna, the Veneto or Piedmont, fed a specially regulated diet that is a blend of grains, cereals and whey from Parmigiano-Reggiano cheese, be a least nine months old and weigh approximately 150 kilos and may not have eaten for 15 hours when butchered. The meat must then be treated and seasoned using traditional methods carried out in a strictly delineated area of production within the province of Parma. Once again it's all about the air. It seems that the ham-flavored atmosphere in the town of Langhirano is ideally suited to the making of *prosciutto.* Here the hams are molded and massaged, smoothed and rounded and undergo a magical transformation that gives them a sweet flavor, velvety texture and a pale pink appearance that is the envy of every Italian cured meat. After 12 months of curing, a quality testing of the ham takes place. An inspector pierces each ham at five critical points with a porous horse bone needle, sniffing it after each puncture and inhaling the aroma. This helps determine whether the ham is of sufficiently high quality to be sold as Parma Ham. If it passes the test, the ham is then branded with the stamp of Parma's five-pointed ducal crown.

The other prosciutto, *Prosciutto alla Toscano,* is a raw aged ham produced entirely within Tuscany. Like all of the other DOP prosciutti, its production complies with a series of conditions and requirements contained in a code of discipline covering the breeding and raising of the livestock, the treatment of the meat and the aging process. Tuscan style prosciutto is savory and saltier than prosciutto made in other regions of Italy. Food historians write that *Prosciutto di Toscano* is saltier than that made in other regions in order to compensate for the lack of salt in Tuscan breads. A Papal Edit enacted centuries ago when the Papal State dominated Tuscany imposed a high tax on salt and as a form of protest Tuscan bakers began to bake bread without salt. To this day traditional Tuscan bread is made without salt and the seasonings and sea salt that each prosciutto maker uses to cure his meat perfectly match with the bland, mellow, yeasty breads of Tuscany. The prosciutti of Tuscany, because they are produced in small numbers, are harder to find than those of Emilia so taste travelers in Tuscany have the distinct pleasure of eating a piece of history that can be duplicated very little else.

And then there's *speck,* an Austrian-type of smoked prosciutto from the Trentino - Alto Adige (SudTirol) in Northern Italy. Bordered by Austria to the east and north and Switzerland to the west, this region of Italy is a cross cultural mélange of the culinary traditions of Austria-Hungary, Germany and Italy. There are many different dialects spoken here and the German language is considered equal to Italian, as is the Ladino language which is spoken in some areas. In many of the provinces the Italian name is listed along with its German counterpart (Bolzano-Bozen) and local specialties share both German and northern Italian traditions, as in *speck*. The Venosta Valley of the Alto Adige is to *speck* what the Langhirano is to *Prosciutto di Parma,* in other words the motherland, the place where all things come together to create the ideal conditions for the birth of a food tradition. The climate, the seasonings (salt, spices, bay, juniper, pepper, coriander, nutmeg and cinnamon), the smoking (juniper and pine wood), the cool mountain air of the Dolomites and the pride of the producers combine to make this one of Italy's most favorite and sought after cured meats. I had my first taste of *speck* in Cavalese, a town in the Val di Fiemme of the Alto Adige, where I also had a killer pork shank called *Stinco* (actually a roasted pork shinbone), *canederli,* a Tirolese bread dumpling similar to a large gnocchi and several bottles of Teroldego Rotaliano wine. No wonder this part of Italy is a popular destination for winter ski touring and summer trekking and a favorite taste and travel destination.

The cooking repertory of Emilia Romagna goes way beyond pasta. In Modena, well know for *aceto balsamico* vinegar, *cotechino,* a 3-inch thick, 9-inch long pork sausage (*salsiccia*) flavored with nutmeg, cloves and pepper is equally sought after. *Cotechino* has a gelatinous mouth feel and is somewhat of an acquired taste as is its graphically displayed cousin, *zampone*. *Zampone* has a similar filling to *cotechino*, but it is encased in a whole pork foreleg (pig's trotter). Considered a delicacy, *cotechino* is often served at New Year's celebrations with lentils to bring luck and good fortune (the lentils symbolizing coins). These sausages are not commonly found outside of Italy so if you are an adventurous eater who wants to experience a food preparation that dates back to a Renaissance city-fortress then eat on.

You can go right to the source for many of Northern Italy's traditional food products by traveling the *strada dei vini e sapori,* regional food and wine routes of Italy. These enogastronomic itineraries are designed to help locals and tourists alike learn about and taste authentic foods of the region. Farms, vineyards, dairies and orchards offer tastings and tours that allow you to get up close and personal with local food products. Visiting food museums like the Felino Salami Museum located in the commune of Felino18km from Parma and traveling the roads of wine and good taste are wonderful ways to see the countryside, visit production facilities, eat in local restaurants and go to shops and markets where the products are sold. Just be aware that these are off the beaten path so if you're not comfortable driving in Italy, don't have a GPS and can't speak some basic Italian you may want to arrange a tour through an agency.

Shops in Italy that sells *salumi, salame and salsiccia* are called a *salumeria.* They may also sell other food products typical of the region such as olive oil, vinegar and cheese. These shops are a good alternative to a sit down lunch or when you're on the road. Some *salumeria* even sell bread *(pane)* and now you have the makings for a fresh *panino (*sandwich*).* This is easy meal especially good when traveling with kids.

Condimenti

The art of cooking resides in the details, the added touches in food preparation and serving that take a simple list of ingredients and elevate them to create a memorable meal. No one does this better than the Italians who have perfected *l'arte della cucina* as evidenced by the worldwide love of Italian food and the hundreds of tourists who visit Italy each year simply to eat. One of the great gastronomic treasures of Italy that enliven Italian cuisine are *condimenti,* a special group of foods whose primary purpose is to add to the details and compliment the food. In the States we are given a choice of mustard, ketchup, relish and onions but in Italy a list of condiments reads like the lyrics of an Italian opera; *Mostarda di Cremona, Aceto Balsamico , Pesto Genovese, Nebbiolo Chutney, Miele di Castagno ,Salsa di Tartufo Bianco, Sott'aceti.* In Italy *condimenti* not only act as a seasoning and accompaniment for meats, they enhance the flavor of sauces, pair with pasta and complement cheese.

A favorite *condimenti* that seems to make its way to my plate again and again is *Pesto Genovese* from Liguria, a strip of land in northwestern Italy on the Ligurian Sea. The unique coastal microclimate and ideal soil favor the growth of a variety of basil whose sweet, pungent flavor is essential for authentic Ligurian pesto. Food historians trace the origin of pesto to ancient condiments made by grinding spices with a mortar and pestle and combining them with oil. The word 'pesto' literally means 'pounded'. According to <u>Culinaria</u>

42

Italy "the aromatic taste of the pesto is absolutely dependent on the quality of the olive oil and the basil". Cheap olive oil and limp basil will surely ruin a pesto. The making of a Ligurian pesto begins with the leaves of Genovese basil crushed by hand in a mortar (*mortaio*) using a wooden stick called a *pestello* (pestle). The movement of the wrist is of great importance. It should be a round movement to enhance the crushing of the basil leaves. Pour in some Ligurian extra virgin olive oil and then add some sea salt, fresh garlic, Parmigiano or Pecorino cheese and pine nuts (*pinoli*) and some more olive oil. Continue to mix. The result should be a creamy pesto, thick but not hard solid. The exceptional pesto of Liguria is traditionally paired with *trofie*, thin, twisted pasta made with flour and water or *trenette* a narrow, flat pasta. Both are typical of the region and both are meant to be tasted along the stunningly beautiful Ligurian Riviera.

Another *condimento* that should be on every taste travelers menu is *mostarda*. The *agrodolce* flavor of mostarda has been a favorite of Italian cooks since ancient times. Catherine de'Medici included a jar of *mostarda* in her dowry trunk when she left Italy to marry the king of France's son In 1533. *Mostarda* is a classic Northern Italian fruit condiment with a healthy kick from powdered mustard or mustard essence. Although you'll find it from Piedmonte to the Veneto and down into Emilia Romagna, the best interpretation of this favorite Italian *condimento* is from the town of Cremona in the Lombardy region of Northern Italy. A sweet and spicy blend of fruits (oranges, figs, pears) preserved in a simple syrup of sugar and white mustard, *Mostarda di Cremona* is traditionally served with *bollito misto* (boiled meats). It is also delicious when served as a condiment with cheese.

43

There is another *mostarda* I have tasted in Mantua. This *mostarda* is the secret ingredient of Mantua's delicious specialty, *Tortellini di Zucca (*Tortellini with Pumpkin Filling), my all time favorite Italian pasta dish. This *mostarda* is made with quince, mustard oil and sugar. There is a Tuscan version made with apples and in Piedmonte there is *cugna*, a jam made from reduced grape must which is spiced with ground mustard and mixed with fruit. There is also a memorable *mostarda* made in Parma and in Venice. Try them all and bring home a jar for yourself and a special friend.

In Italy vinegar is also thought of as a condiment. An ancient flavoring, residues of vinegar have been found in urns uncovered at archeological sites in the Mediterranean Basin. Most Italian vinegars begin with the fermentation of white or red wine and are used to enhance the flavor of foods and to dress salads including *panzanella*, a popular salad from Tuscany made with leftover Tuscan bread, tomatoes, basil, wine vinegar and extra virgin olive oil. This salad was made for me at Tenuta di Capezzana, where I shared an afternoon meal with the Contini Bonacossi family, the current owners of this estate farm that produces some of Italy's finest wine and olive oil. I had spent the morning with Benedetta, who guided me through the *frantoio* (olive mill) where I saw estate olives being processed and pressed. The *panzanella* was perfect and the company more so. The Wine and Culinary Center at Capezzana is the ideal place to get up close and personal with Tuscan cuisine in a setting that is right out of Renaissance painting. Italian wine vinegar is also used to prepare vegetables *sott'aceto*, vegetables preserved in vinegar. Assorted fresh vegetables (artichokes, carrots, small onions, eggplant, string

44

beans, peppers) are marinated in a mixture of water, vinegar, sugar, salt and seasonings, brought to the boil, then cooled and preserved in jars. Seasonings often include a blend of bay leaves, cloves, cinnamon, pepper, garlic and thyme resulting in an aromatic infusion of sweet and sour (*agrodolce*) that Italians love. But in the pantheon of Italian food products one type of vinegar stands above all others, *Aceto Balsamico Tradizionale*. A unique condiment that is often imitated but can never be duplicated. A true *Aceto Balsamico Tradizionale* is made according to a set of guidelines that go back to the noble families of Modena. It was so highly prized that Alfonso I, Duke of Ferrara, who took his ducal feasting seriously, even maintained his own *acetaia*, a loft where vinegar barrels were stored. Specific regulations on the production and aging of balsamic vinegar are strictly followed to this day. There are only two consortia that produce true traditional balsamic vinegar. One is from Modena and the other from Reggio Emilia. The grapes used to make *Aceto Balsamic Tradizionale* must come solely from province vineyards. After bottling, a numbered non-reusable label must be placed on each bottle in such a way as to prevent anyone from removing any of the contents without tearing it. Because of its elevated position in the hierarchy of Italian *condimenti,* only a few precious drops of *Aceto Balsamico Tradizionale* are needed on fish, meats, vegetables and even deserts. *Aceto Balsamico Tradizionale* is designated by age. Vinegars aged for 25 years or more carry the designation *extravecchio* and because you are taste traveling in Italy, you are in the enviable position of accepting an invitation to sit at the tables of Modena and Reggio Emilia and experience the benefits of old age.

In the US we don't often think of honey as a condiment but rather as a sweetener slathered over pancakes, biscuits or French toast but in Italy honey is so much more. I experienced my first taste of honey in Italy at my cousin's Lidia's apartment in Milano when she served pecorino toscano cheese and pears for desert after dinner one evening. She passed around a jar of *Miele di Castagno,* chestnut honey, and told me to drizzle it over the cheese. The mild grassy flavor of this sheep's milk cheese paired with the rich, wild flavor and molasses-like consistency of the chestnut honey was m*olto buono.* The honeys of Italy are used in a greater variety of ways and are more flavorful than the honey we are accustomed to in the States. Italian honey bees, *Apis mellifera ligustic,* are known to be very prolific with a strong disposition toward breeding. They are excellent housekeepers and comb builders, excellent honey producers and show a gentle temperament. Although American beekeepers have been using Italian honey bees since they were first imported to the New World in 1859, there are unique types of honey in Italy that can be found no well else. Such as *Miele d' abete*, the almost black pine honey from the Alpine regions and Apennine ranges in Tuscany and Romagna and *Miele di lavanda,* a aromatic honey made from lavender grown along the rocky Ligurian coast. Another unique Italian honey is *Miele di corbezzolo*, strawberry tree honey so called because during autumn the flowers of the tree (*Arbutus unedo*) produce a red fruit that resembles small strawberries. Found in central Italy and the island of Sardegna, this honey has a hazelnut brown color with a smoky aroma similar to roasted coffee. Yet as exceptional as these honeys are, there is a honey that I covet about all the rest, Italian Truffle Honey, a millefiori honey infused with *Tuber Aestivum*, the black summer truffle.

46

Much of this honey comes from the Italian region of Umbria, where the knobby black mushroom-like *tartufi* (truffles) are considered gastronomic gold. Italian truffle honey is a balance of earthiness and sweetness and is used in Italy as a glaze for meat, served with cheese, spread over fruit, cake or gelato. There should be a warning on the label of this honey that says "Extraordinarily Addictive".

Of the 85,000 beekeepers in Italy, many are small, traditional beekeepers like Paolo Pescia. A second generation Italian beekeeper, Pescia transports his beehives to seasonally flowering zones in the protected national parks along Tuscany's Etruscan coast .These artisan beekeepers often move their bees from place to place in a nomadic existence to follow the blossoms throughout the seasons to capture the essence of each honey. They take great pride in a product that reflects the botanical landscape of Italy. As a condiment, Italian honeys are used in a variety of ways and I would take every opportunity to savor the true meaning of "la dolce vita" by tasting as many as I possibly could.

Dolce

You'll want to say "*basta*" (enough) when your Italian plate is empty but resist and save room for dessert. Although you are most likely to see Italians eating fresh fruit and cheese at the end of a meal, they do like to indulge and celebrate special occasions with some irresistible sweets not only at the end of a meal but oftentimes for breakfast. In the morning it's not unusual for Italians to have a brioche or *cornetto,* a croissant-like pastry, plain or filled with chocolate (*cioccolato*), custard (*crema*) or jam (*marmellata*) with their cappuccino or espresso. A larger breakfast buffet served in some hotels or at a bed and breakfast will usually include a fruit tart or breakfast cake. This is not a sweet layer cake covered in icing but a simple cake often made with olive oil with the texture of a Bundt or tea cake.

Pastries in Italy are often bought at the local pastry shop, *pasticceria*. For special occasions and holidays, Italians often go to the *pasticceria* to buy delicacies to celebrate *il giorno di festa*. Many sweets are still made according to traditional recipes that are unique to the region. For example, *cantucci* are a specialty of Prato, a city near Florence and the secret of a good *ricciarelli* is only known to the Sienese, as is the making of *panforte,* a delicacy of Siena. *Panforte* is a dense, flat cake rich with honey, hazelnuts, almonds, candied citron, citrus peel, cocoa and spices. Almost a candy, it contains just enough flour to hold the fruits and nuts together. Although the name *panforte* translates to "strong bread", the strength of this confection is not only due to its spicy flavor but to its hard chewy texture. Christmas was once the traditional time to make this dessert, but now it is made and enjoyed year round. Another traditional Italian confection originally made during the holiday season but now enjoyed year round is *pampepato*, a spice cake with a history that goes back to the 15th century. This confection was so highly regarded that Duke Borso d'Este of Ferrara served a *pampepato* with gold pieces inserted in each cake at a ducal feast. Today *pampepato* is sealed in chocolate and packaged in golden cellophane and available at *pasticceria* throughout the city of Ferrara.

Although many kinds of Italian *dolci* are little known outside of Italy, there are many more that have become familiar all over the world. Biscotti, tiramisu, gelato, cannoli, zeppole and zabaglione are only some of the Italian sweets we enjoy as desserts. Tasting and traveling in Italy you can experience the authentic flavors of these delicacies with sweet dreams of many more *i dolci* to try along the way. Buona notte.

See and Savor More

Italian favors or *bomboniere* are traditional gifts presented to guests to celebrate a wedding and other special occasions. Sugared almonds and other sweets are put inside a bag made of tulle or satin and tied with ribbons. Italians love to celebrate special occasions with candies, cakes and confections and have been known to be somewhat lavish at their wedding celebrations. At the wedding celebration of Bianca Maria Visconti and Francesco Sforza, the bride not only had many jewels, money and riches of every kind as part of her dowry but her father also offered the city of Cremona itself! To commemorate this, the court's pastry chefs decided to make a new confection in the shape of the city's tower, the *Torione.* The nougat like candy made with honey and beaten egg whites was called *Torrone* and became an instant success. It is still very popular today, especially at Christmas with delicious variations, including the addition of hazelnuts, orange, lemon and even chocolate. A certain type of torrone made with pine nuts, had a flavor so wondrous it was considered worthy of the mouth of the Pope and therefore named *Torrone di Pape.*

Apis mellifera ligustica – the Italian honeybee

Chapter 3 Eat, Drink and Make Memories

There is no better place to eat, drink and make memories than in Italy where eating is an art. Although it has been said that you can't have a bad meal in Italy, I'm not sure that's completely true. As a tourist in Italy you are at risk of being misled to a lesser dining experience because most tourists have little appreciation for looking beyond the tour bus to discover Italy. I have been fortunate to taste and travel throughout most of Northern Italy, Tuscany and Umbria with my Italian family and friends and experience eating "like an Italian" with attention to locality and customs of cooking, tasting foods that are particular to each place. Remember as a taste traveler a food itinerary is just as important as a site itinerary. The taste and traveler mind set is to approach a trip to Italy with the intention of paring the flavors of Italy with the sites of Italy as one compliments the other. So we need to spend some time talking about what it's like to eat "like an Italian".

Italian meals are served in courses with a sequence of dishes to be eaten one at a time and savored; but portions are small and in Italy a reservation means you have the table for the evening. Not all Italians eat this way every day, at very meal and when they eat out. The evening meal at home is often a light variation of one or two courses and it is not necessary to order all courses at a restaurant. You can often split a pasta dish as a first course or have it as your only course. But to experience the Italian style of eating while in Italy is something that you should not miss.

The general courses at an Italian meal are as follows:

l'apertivo - Italians often begin the meal with an apertivo, a drink designed to "open the stomach" and aid in digestion; Italian *apertivi* are often extracts of aromatic herbs and roots blended with spirits in alchemic proportions like those used to make the Italian apertivo Campari. Or an *apertivo* can be as simple as a glass of *prosecco,* a sparkling Italian wine. An apertivo is often an accompaniment to *l'antipasto.*

l'antipasto - Prepares the palate for the courses to come and stimulates the appetite. One of my favorite is *affettati misti,* a variety of sliced cured regional meats arranged around a large platter sometimes served with olives or marinated vegetables. An antipasti of fresh seafood is referred to as *antipasto misto di mar;* the seafood is dressed simply with olive oil and lemon or if the seafood is fried and served as a mixed platter it is known as *fritto misto di mare.*

il primo – The first course in an Italian meal usually pasta, polenta, rice or perhaps gnocchi. Portions are small; just enough to satisfy; may also be a soup (*la zuppa*)

il second - The second course in an Italian meal. Meat, poultry or fish served alone on the plate accompanied by side dish; a *contorno;* like a vegetable (*la verdura*).

il dolce - Dessert usually fresh fruit and cheeses (*i formaggi*), sweets on special occassions *Frutta varia di stagione* (fresh fruits in season) or a mixed fruit cup, *macedonia di frutta* are very popular ways to end a meal in Italy.

un cafe' – Coffee, also known as *cafe' normale* always follows the meal and always means *espresso*! *Cappuccino* is only served for breakfast or before noon, never after a meal. While the adults and older children may want to try all the various types of Italian coffee, remember they are all STRONG. If you would like your coffee weaker, order a stretched espresso known as a *lungo* made with more water. A normal espresso takes from 18 to 30 seconds to pull, and fills 25 to 30 milliliters, while a *lungo* may take up to a minute to pull, and might fill 50 to 60 milliliters. A *cafè lungo* should not be mistaken for a *cafè américano*, which is an espresso with hot water added to it. Ordering a *latte* in Italy is ordering steamed milk. It is not the same type of drink as it is in the States. The milk is frothed and warmed to between 65° and 70° C and makes an ideal drink for young children. So when the adults are drinking their *espresso, macchiato or cappuccino* , ordering a latte for your child will make them feel very sophisticated. What do I drink in Italy? I order a *latte macchiato tepido*, warm milk stained with *espresso* usually served *al vetro,* in a glass but only in the morning. After dinner I skip the espresso but on occasion I might have a glass of *vin santo* and leave the after dinner *digestivi* of *grappa, amaro*, or *limincello* to harder souls.

You will most likely be having *un café'* at coffee or espresso bar. They are not a US style bar which in Italy is known as an "American bar" and generally found in hotels. Italians visit café bars throughout the

53

day, but especially in the morning to start the day with a pastry and coffee. Consider where you sit or stand. *Al banco* is standing at the bar while *à tavola* means sitting at a table, where you'll usually be expected to be waited on and charged two to four times as much. At an Italian caffe' or bar you can also buy snacks, *il giornale* (the newspaper), *una rivista* (a magazine) and if there is a black and white capital T displayed outside the store it stands for *il tabaccaio* - the tobacconist where you can buy stamps, bus and Metro tickets as well.

le bevande - Beverages. *Bevande calde* are hot (*calda*) drinks and *bevande fredde* are cold (*fredda*) drinks. Cold drinks are generally not served with ice (*ghiacco*). You need to ask for ice with your drink. Why ice is not commonly served in Italy with cold drinks as it is in the US I don't know. My Italian friends feel it isn't necessary *(non necessario)*. Many do not like it and my Italian family doesn't have room in their refrigerator to make ice. American soft drinks (*le bibite)* are expensive in Italy and discouraged by Italian parents although I have recently noticed more Italians drinking them especially Coca Cola Light. Taste travelers can try the more recognized Italian *bibite* (sodas) like San Pelligrino Aranciata (orange) or Limonata (lemon) or they can go native and try a Chinotto which looks like but doesn't taste like Coke or a Crodino. All are on the bitter side in keeping with the Italian taste. Water is not automatically served with a meal. You will need to order a bottle of mineral water, *una bottiglia d'acqua minerale*, with your meal. It is ordered non-carbonated, *d'acqua minerale naturale* or *d'acqua minerale senza gas* (without carbonation). Carbonated mineral water, *frizzata or d'aqua minerale gassata* (con gas) is what my kid travelers call "fizzy water".

54

il vino – In Italy wine is served with meals as an accompaniment to the food. Italians truly feel that a meal is not complete without wine. In Italian households children grow up with the tradition of table wine *(vino da tavolo)* served with the main meal. My husband's Italian American family allowed the older children, on special occasions, to have a taste of the wine served to the adults. In Italian homes older children may sip a small amount of wine with their meal and younger children may have experienced their first taste of wine mixed with water. This cultural tradition may or may not be part of your taste and travel experience. Allowing older children to taste the wine you are being served is, of course, your decision.

You may have noticed that the salad is not served before the main course of the meal. A salad (*la insalata*) is usually eaten at the end of the meal although I have seen fresh vegetables (celery, fennel, carrots, peppers) eaten *al pinzimonio* as an Italian raw vegetable antipasto with a dipping sauce of extra virgin olive oil, salt and pepper. A raw bar of fresh vegetables anointed with regional extra virgin olive oil; nothing is better to feed your head. You cannot help feeling better after eating this combination of the fruits of the earth. It is my favorite. Italians are not fond of limp, lifeless lettuce swimming in a sea of heavy dressing. In Italy if salads are eaten they are simply dressed with vinegar and oil and are eaten after the main course before dessert and are thought of as a digestive as the vinegar is a natural product with friendly yeasts and bacteria that aid in digestion.

Why do Italians eat in courses? I believe that they feel food should be served in a natural progression with one plate leading into another.

The apertivo and antipasto served before the meal (*il pasto*) prepare your palate for the meal to come. Remember Italians generally serve small portions so that you can taste and enjoy the foods. So a 5 or 6 course meal is not a feeding frenzy and you will not necessarily be over indulged and overstuffed as you do when eating the over the top portions you find in some Italian restaurants in the US. To do so would be unseemly in Italy. So you can begin with *gli antipasti*, the opener. You can stop at the primi if you decide that a pasta entrée is enough (*basta*) for you that evening. Or if you desire pasta as your only course you can say "*piatto unico*" meaning a one course meal and in this case, the only course you want is pasta. All ingredients in an Italian meal are perfectly orchestrated to completeness with a *digestivo* at the end to allow everything to settle in nicely. Also Italian's social life has always focused on the pleasures of the table, visiting and talking with their family and friends. So the meal has a natural flow that combines food and conversation. My Italian family and friends say "*Tutti a tavola per mangiare*" everyone to the table to eat and take time to enjoy the food and the company.

Having an authentic experience eating and traveling in Italy brings you face to face with *il menu*, something that most travelers in Italy find a little intimidating at first. In many of the larger towns and tourist areas *il menu* will be translated in English and the waiter, *il cameriere,* will speak some English. But seeing and savoring Italy will take you down the road less traveled so you need to be able to navigate around an Italian menu. Many menus in Italy are posted outside the restaurant or written on a chalkboard on the wall. Some are discussed verbally with you by the waiter. Don't panic if the waiter is speaking too fast for you to understand. You can ask him to speak more slowly by saying "*Non capisco l'italiano bene, parli piu' lentamente per favore*". "I don't speak Italian well, speak more slowly please".

You likely will not have to worry too much about ordering breakfast. Most accommodations in Italy include breakfast (*la colazione* or *prima colazione*) although it might not be what you expect. Italians usually grab a quick espresso or cappuccino with a *cornetto* or brioche. A more substantial Italian breakfast would include sliced cured meats, cheeses, bread and cakes. Some hotels in Italy now offer what is referred to as an "American" breakfast with eggs, juice and cereal. Lunch (*il pranzo*) in Italy is served from about 12:30 PM until about 4:00 PM. Inexpensive fast food Italian style, to eat in or take out, can be found all over Italy and pizza by the slice (*pizza al taglio* aka *Lazio style*) is sold at small free standing shops everywhere. The quality of fast food in Italy is exceptional, much better than our American counterparts. Look for a *rosticceria* or *girrarosto* for spit roasted meats, a *tavola calda* (translated to mean a hot table) similar to a self service cafeteria, a *tavola fredda* (cold table) or a *paninoteca* for a sandwich. Sandwich bars in Italy serve *panini,* crusty bread rolls filled with vegetables, cheese or cured meats like prosciutto. The *panini* in Italy bear little resemblance to the sandwiches you might be used to and does not come with mayonnaise, mustard, lettuce, tomato and sprouts. If you are looking for a more "traditional" sandwich you will want to order a *tramezzino*, made with a thin, soft white bread, with no crusts. Kid travelers like these more familiar sandwiches made with *Mortadella di Bologna*. Resembling the familiar American B-O-L-O-G-N-A, Italian mortadella is made from finely ground pork blended with

57

white pepper, peppercorns, coriander, anise, wine and pieces of pistachio (you may need to remove the larger pieces of pistachio before serving to small children). A specialty of Emilia Romagna, mortadella must meet certain guidelines to be considered a *Mortadella di Bologna* and is protected by its IGP (Protected Geographical Indication) designation, ensuring that authentic mortadella is free from fillers, artificial colors, flavors and preservatives. Most of the fat content in mortadella is the same type of fat found in olive oil and cholesterol levels are equal to a similar serving of chicken. When the guild of sausagers was found in Bologna in 1376, mortadella was already known by the Romans who flavored the sausage with myrtle (*mortella*) in place of pepper and blended the ingredients using a mortar and pestle (*mortaio*), giving mortadella its name and a place in the history of lunchboxes everywhere. One more word about eating a *panino in* Italy. As all food in Italy, the *panino* can be regionally translated with variations throughout Italy. In Ferrara, Emilia Romagna, their interpretation of the *panino* is known as a *piadina.* Although you can find a traditional *panino* here, the *piadina* is a specialty of the Romagna region. It's a flat bread cooked on a *testo,* or griddle and unleavened. During the Middle Ages Romagna was heavily influenced by the Eastern Byzantium Empire and this bread looks very similar to the pita bread of Middle Eastern and Greek cuisines although Italians would say "*piadina e piadina*" meaning a *piadina* is a *piadina* and that there is no comparison. *Piadina* are made with a variety of fillings both savory and sweet including the ever popular chocolate hazelnut spread, Nutella.

Italian's usually eat dinner (*la cena*) at 8 o'clock. 7:30 is considered early and dinner may be served as late as 10:00 or 10:30pm. Most Italian restaurants are either called a *ristorante* or a *trattoria* . A *ristorante* is considered to be a more formal type of restaurant while a *trattoria* is a small, informal family owned restaurant with a rustic casual menu showcasing the food of the region, generally less expensive than a *ristorante.* A *trattoria* is a good place to eat with children. They are family style eateries specializing in local cooking and are usually kid friendly. They will serve a more home style meal that is adaptable to a child's taste. An *osteria* was originally an inn (*locanda*) that provided food and lodging where you could get a simple plate of pasta and a glass of vino. Today the difference between a *ristorante, trattorie, osterie* and *locande* is becoming less distinct. Always check the menu which is generally posted outside.

Memories are made around the tables of Italy where taking the time to eat is still considered to be important. Italians make an effort to prepare a well laid table where there is beauty and grace in the smallest detail. Meals are an essential part of Italian life. Not that they obsess about food or over indulge. Italians truly value food and its preparation. It is evident at the table but begins with the growing of the food, the selling of the food at their markets and extends to the careful and considerate preparation of their food. They value the traditions and regional diversity of Italian cooking based on the geography of the land and the cultural traditions of the region. Combine this with the warm and generous hospitality of the Italian people, the freshest regional ingredients and some of the finest wine in the world and you can't help but eat, drink and make memories in Italy.

Here are a few helpful hints about eating in Italy

- cocktails before dinner are not as popular in Italy as they are in the US and they are expensive; an apertivo such as a Campari and soda or a flute of sparkling wine is more typically Italian; restaurants often have their own special type to offer
- *lo chef consiglia* means the daily specials and literally translated means "the chef's advice"!
- cheese is not as commonly served with all pasta as it is in the US but it is offered with certain types of soup
- bread is always served with Italian meals but butter is served only at breakfast; bread is part of the *pane e coperto* literally translated to mean bread and cover (tableware), a small charge usually 1-2 euro p/p will be added to the final bill, although some travelers think of this as a tip, you may leave a few coins (usually 1-3 euro) if you want but a mandatory tip (*la mancia*) is not considered necessary but given as desired for service that is exceptional
- the term *coperto e servizio* (cover and service charge) is also used and may be separate or included, if it is included as in *servizio incluso* or *servizio compreso*; a service charge for service at the tablet is included in the final bill generally 5-15% more like a mandatory tip
- Most often an Italian waiter will never bring the bill (*il conto*) until you ask for it, say "*il conto, per favore*"

See and Savor More

Like all eating in Italy, snacking is expressed locally and will vary from region to region. In Tuscany a mid-afternoon snack is called a *merenda* and may be a rustic loaf of bread with *prosciutto crudo* and some tomatoes. Snacks served in bars take on various names. In Venice small snacks called *cicchetti* (pronounced chi-KET-tee) are served in *cicchetti* bars. *Cicchetti* are served with a small glass of the wine which the locals refer to as an "*ombra* " a popular colloquialism in Venice that translates to mean "shade", referring to the shade of the bell tower in Piazza San Marco where *Gondelieri* would relax at the wine bars on the Square. You can taste and travel the *cicchetti* bars of Venice alla Rick Steves on a "*giro d'ombra*",a Venetian pub crawl, where you can snack on small servings of fish, crostini, tiny sandwiches and plates of olives. And then there is the "*spuntino*", a light snack or small antipasti or even a picnic lunch. As a young couple I can remember my husband and I enjoying a "spuntino" of thinly sliced prosciutto di Parma served with a ripe melon, a little bread and a glass of wine with his family outside on their patio almost every weekend in the summer.

Pinzimonio comes from the Italian words "*pinzare*" which means to pinch and "monio" taken from "*matrimonio*", combining the newly married vegetables and extra virgin olive oil in a happy union of flavors.

Chapter 4   At the Etruscan Table

We can learn a lot about seeing and savoring Italy from a group of taste travelers who found their way to Italy and never looked back. The earliest inhabitants of the Italian peninsula knew a good thing when they saw it and immediately began to take the fruitful groves, fertile fields and lush forests and cultivate them to their advantage. Most scholars agree that the food traditions of Italy began at the tables of the ancient Etruscans whose interest in food and ways of eating were the foundations of Italian cuisine. Once lost in the pages of history the material culture, language and habits of the "mysterious" Etruscans is now being resurrected and re-defined by talented and dedicated anthropologists and archeologists like those at the Luigi Fantini Museo Civico Archeologico in Monterenzio (BO). And what they have found is that this ancient civilization liked to eat and eat well. In fact the Etruscans may have been the original "foodies", establishing habits for dining that are still with us today. Excavations of an Etruscan settlement near Monterenzio show that the Etruscans knew how to make wine, loom linen and ate a variety of wild and domesticated animals including deer, rabbit, boar, chickens, pigs, fox, wolf, frogs and turtles. They were particularly fond of a small squirrel-like animal which they captured and kept in large clay jars called an *argilla*. The jars had holes and ledges like an ancient gerbil run in which the animals could be kept until it was time for dinner. I visited the Luigi Fantini Museo in September 2009 and met with staff anthropologist Margherita Benvenuti to tour the museum and learn more about how the Etruscans lived and ate, apparently very well. There were finely crafted ceramic and bronze cooking vessels and figs, pears, grapes, beans, eggs, garlic and lentils were on their menu. The Etruscans knew how to make cheese which they grated and mixed with wine then strained and diluted it with water. Cheese graters and strainers were found among the many food related implements during excavations.

Celtic tribes from central Europe, hearing of the "well laid tables" of the Etruscans were attracted to the region and around 350BC built a settlement alongside the Etruscan village and began to invite themselves over for dinner. This resulted in a peaceful co-existence, intermarriage and the building of an Etruscan-Celtic settlement at Monte Bibele. Overlooking the Idice and Zena Rivers, the strategic position and rich deposits of copper and iron attracted the Celts to this location but what kept them there was the food.

Numerous Etruscan tomb paintings depict the preparation and cooking of food. The Etruscans love of food is evident as there are a variety of ingredients and cooking tools including a ladle, rolling pin and cutting wheel that have been found on tomb paintings and vases. Murals show men and women dining equally at tables covered with embroidered linens attended by servants. Diners reclined on couches in a scene of conviviality more associated with Roman times. The Etruscans developed the habit of eating two main meals a day, the first in the morning and the second in the evening just before dark which became the accepted style of eating still followed in Italy today. In his extraordinarily detailed account of Italy's gastronomic history, The Food of Italy, Waverly Root writes that polenta, one of the classic dishes of Northern Italy, was inspired by the Etruscans who made a thick gruel or porridge which the Romans later called *puls.* The Etruscan-Celtic fusion may have given rise to a penchant for pork in Perugia, an Umbrian city with an arch whose base is made of Etruscan stone blocks. One of the food specialties of this region of Italy is *porchetta*, a suckling pig generously seasoned, often cooked on a spit (*girarosto*). It seems that pork was the "other white meat" for the Celts who raised pigs for food and shared their taste for pork with the Etruscans. In fact the region of Umbria (the land of saints and salamis) is well known for the butchering and preserving of pork. The butchers of Norcia in southeastern Umbria have a reputation as the ablest in Italy. Some even are called upon to travel to outlying communities during certain times of the year as itinerant specialists not only in killing and butchering swine but specializing in the curing of the meat. Taste traveling through Umbria undoubtedly means a stop at a *norcineria,* an Italian butcher shop. Just look for the wild boar's head above the shop entrance and follow your nose. *Prosciutti* and *salsicce* hang from the rafters and counter cases are filled with specialty salami. The fragrance of expertly seasoned meats and handcrafted cheeses fill the air. You cannot take any meat products home if you are from the States so take advantage of the opportunity to eat like a local. Ask for a *panino* of *prosciutto crudo* with a slice of *caciotta,* a traditional Italian farmhouse cheese from Tuscany and Umbria that is popular throughout Italy. Made from a blend of sheep (70%) and cow's (30%) milk, *caciotta* has a creamy mild to sharp flavor depending on its age. Find a spot on a hillside, open a bottle of Sagrantino wine and spread a cloth on the grass for a picnic in the Umbrian countryside. Then raise a glass to the "mysterious"

Etruscans whose tables influenced the foods of Italy and the rest of the Western world.

See and Savor More

Etruscan artifacts at the "LUIGI FANTINI" ARCHAEOLOGICAL MUSEUM Monterenzio (BO)

Luigi Fantini was a famous cave explorer and pioneer of Bolognese prehistoric research. The museum that bears his name houses artifacts discovered at the nearby Etruscan-Celtic settlement of Monte Bibele and the necropolis of Monte Tamburino, whose finds are considered to be the most important Celtic collection in Italy. It is also the Center of the Department of Archaeology of the University of Bologna.

Chapter 5 La Via del Pane

If you want to eat a piece of history eat a piece of Italian bread. Every region has its own special type of bread (*pane*) with traditions that date back hundreds of years. Nearly 300 regional breads are produced in Italy with local ingredients and customs that make each one unique. The celebrated *La Via del Pane* (the Way of the Bread), a gastronomic itinerary through the Bolognese hills, is but one of the many indications of the important role bread has at the Italian table. Traveling along *le strade dei sapori* of the Bologna Appennino region you can taste the local mountain bread made with flour from ancient water mills *(mulini)*. The tradition of bread baking in the region is embedded in the land. Food journalist, Waverly Root, when writing about the foods of Emilia Romagna refers to a book, *Mangiari di Romagna* written by Marcello Caminiti, Luigi Pasquini and Gianni Quondamatteo in which the authors describe the cuisine of the region as "bread, wine and whatever goes with bread". So needless to say I have had many wonderful meals in Italy that included the most delicious of breads.

There is the signature bread of the Emilian region with a whimsical history that dates to the Renaissance court of Ferrara. During the Renaissance Ferrara was a center of commerce and learning where the arts flourished around a brilliant court that included three of Italy's most influential women, Beatrice d'Este, Isabella d'Este and the notorious Lucrezia Borgia, now wife of Alphonso I, Duke of Ferrara. Everyone in Renaissance Italy wanted to be invited to Castello d' Estense for evenings of amusement. The Este family were renown patrons of the arts whose A list included Da Vinci, Titian, Raphael and Petrarch. There are many accounts of sumptuous Renaissance banquets at the court of the Duke of Ferrara and at one such banquet the bread of Ferrara was destined for a place in culinary history. *Coppia ferrarese*, (*ciupe'ta*, in the local dialect), is a type of bread made from lard, olive oil and malt with a central portion called the knot or ribbon with two twisted pointed breadsticks attached. The history of *Coppia ferrarese* dates to the 15th century Renaissance banquets at the court. The officer of ceremonies wanted to create a bread shaped to astonish the guests at the banquets of the Dukes of Este. He suggested four rolls joined by a soft central core with a shape that resembles a coupled set of horns. Legend has it that this captivating shape was meant to resemble femininity and masculinity, the Italian version of yin and yang. Whatever the inspiration for these rolls, with a soft inside and crusty exterior, they are one of Ferrara's culinary specialties and the skill of the bakers of Ferrara is well known throughout Italy today for this unusual treat. *Coppia ferrarese* bread "ciupeta" has received IGP status (Protected Geographical Identification), a designation given by the EU to products of excellence, typical of Italian food quality specific to a particular region for example, *Mortadella di Bologna*. The designations promote the authentic characteristics and reputation (yes, in Italy food has a reputation) of certain agricultural products such as cheese, meat, salumi, vegetables, fruit and olive oil. The uniqueness of *Coppia ferrarese* is said to be found in the quality of the water and the ingredients, as well as the humidity of the air, leavening method and the correct temperature of the oven. I've eaten this bread all over Ferrara but never better served than at *Ristorante La Romantica (Via*

67

Ripagrande 36), a restaurant that used to be the stables of a 17th-century merchant's house. The restaurant serves typical Ferrarese cuisine including my favorite pasta, *cappellacci di zucca.* This is a white table restaurant more suitable for adults or families with older children however I have eaten here with a baby and younger children on a "tummy tour" of Italy and the restaurant was most accommodating. In fact Ethan, a seasoned " tummy tour" traveler and aspiring chef, commenting on the bread, whole heartedly agreed with Riccardo Bacchelli, an Italian writer from Emilia Romagna who said that *coppia ferrarese* is the "best bread in the whole world".

The other regional bread from Romagna is a flat bread made with flour, lard and salt. The dough was traditionally cooked on a terracotta dish called a *testo* (*teggia* in the Romagnolo dialect) which was placed over hot coals. Today flat pans or electric griddles are often used to make this classic flat bread. Filled with local cured meat, soft cheese and greens or slightly cooked vegetables the bread is folded in half to make the Italian *piadina*. In Italy you can buy a *piadina* from a street vendor, in a caffe or at a *piadina* bar where they are eaten for lunch or a snack. The *piadina* vendors of Emila-Romagna say that a *piadina* must be eaten no more than three minutes after it has been cooked or else it will lose its fragrance.

The refined bread of Ferrara has a distant country cousin in Tuscany where the bread is more rustic and often served when it is a day old. Elizabeth Romer in her book The Tuscan Year writes about the *contadini* traditions of the Tuscan people where everything is used and nothing is wasted and where the virtues of *gravitas, pietas and simplicitas* still influence the everyday lives of Tuscan families. Home produced products like bread, oil, vegetables and cheese are still very much a part of Tuscan cooking and the cultivated products of the farm are still grown and cooked by a people with a deep affection for the traditions of the land. The bread of Tuscany is made without salt and the making of bread in Tuscany has a tradition that goes back to ancient times. Why salt less bread? The answer may lay with 12th century political economics. The maritime city of Pisa controlled the salt trade and decided to raise the price of salt to exercise their power over rival Florence. When the price of salt rose, the Florentines protested by baking their bread without it and the tradition remains to this day. However there may be another reason for Tuscany's salt less bread. The highly seasoned meats, spicy salamis, strong flavored cheeses and love of wild game and pungent pate´ would be lost on salted bread. Case in point, the traditional Tuscan *crostini*, *crostini di fegato*, a liver pate´ made with chicken, wild boar or calves liver that goes so well with the neutral flavor of Tuscan bread. Tuscan white loaf bread, *pane toscano*, is the perfect base for the full bodied rustic flavors of *crostini* spreads. But the most traditional way to eat a slice of bread in Tuscany is toasted or grilled, rubbed with fat cloves of garlic, drizzled with extra virgin olive oil and sprinkled with coarse salt. In Tuscany this is called *fettunta*. It is one of the truest forms of Tuscan cuisine; simple, rustic food make with the freshest ingredients that reflect the *terroir* of the land. The pure flavors of warm Tuscan bread anointed with a green golden stream of extra virgin olive oil release an aroma and flavor that connects you to a historical timeline of food and culture that goes back thousands of years. *Crostini* served with tomatoes is *bruschetta*. Like a good man a good *bruschetta* it is

69

difficult to find. First of all you have to get the name right. The correct pronunciation is *"broo-sketta"*. Bruschetta (*bruschette* pl.) comes from the Italian verb, *bruscare*, meaning to roast over coals. These small slices of toasted bread with fresh tomato, garlic and olive oil are as popular in Italy as they are in the States. However, in many restaurants outside Italy, the underlying simplicity of this dish is often compromised by lesser ingredients resulting in a soggy or exceedingly dry piece of tasteless white bread topped with mushy tomatoes. In Italy, the bread is artisan, the tomatoes are fresh and the olive oil is extra virgin. While taste traveling in Italy, past disappointments will fade into the Tuscan sunset as you taste one of Italy's most famous antipasti.

Another classic use of bread in Italy is as a supporting ingredient in soups like *ribollita* and in the Tuscan bread salad *panzanella.* Both are made with day old or stale bread. This follows the thrifty Tuscan esthetic of *la cucina della fattoria*, home style farmhouse cooking, where bread was made once a week in huge loaves and when it had gone stale it was used as an ingredient. I can remember Nonna saving and using day old bread to make bread crumbs to use in her recipe for *polpette* (meatballs) and *ribollita* is vegetable soup made with stale bread. Onions, celery, carrots, tomatoes, Tuscan black cabbage (c*avolo nero)* and Tuscan white beans or *cannellini* are made into a minestrone on the first day then eaten and saved for the next day when the soap is reheated or reboiled (*ribollita* means reboiled). Bread is toasted, rubbed with garlic and placed in the bottom of a deep sided bowl. The leftover soup is then poured over the toast and Tuscan extra virgin olive oil is drizzled on top. Although called a soup, *ribollita* is thick enough to be eaten with a fork and very filling. A true Tuscan *ribollita* will always be made with salt less Tuscan bread and *cavolo nero,* Tuscan black cabbage or black leaf kale. Also known as Tuscan kale, *cavolo nero* is a leafy cabbage that doesn't form heads, but whose leaves rather resembles palm fronds. It is always available in Tuscany but may be difficult to find in other parts of the world. *Cavolo nero* is a good source of vitamins K, A and C as well as significant amounts of manganese, copper, fiber, calcium, iron, B vitamins and many other positive elements. Eating *ribollita* in Tuscany in the fall is a rite of passage for taste travelers in Italy that is not to be missed.

In Tuscany the recycling of bread has been taken to new heights with a dish known as *panzanella,* Tuscan bread salad. Served during the summer months, it is a delicious, refreshing salad with a wonderful texture and flavor that is unique. Calling *panzanella* a bread salad is like calling a diamond a piece of coal. The ingredients used to make a *panzanella* transform simple day old bread into an *antipasto* or satisfying *primo piatto* bursting with the flavors of fresh tomatoes, cucumbers, garlic, onions and basil dressed with Tuscan extra olive oil and wine vinegar. The magic begins when the bread becomes flavored with the oil and the flavors begin to meld. The olive oil used to make a *panzanella* should be fruity and peppery and preferably Tuscan. My perfect *panzanella* was eaten at the table of Tenuta di Capezzana, northwest of Florence. The scent, aroma and flavor of this highly acclaimed oil elevate the simpliest of ingredients into a work of food art.

I discovered the versatility of bread in Italy when I visited the town of Bolzano in the Trentino-Alto Adige region of Northern Italy. This region of Italy once known as the *Sudtirol* (South Tyrol) is bordered by Austria, Switzerland and the Italian provinces of Lombardy and the Veneto. It is dominated by the Dolomites, a mountain range of the Southern Alps with vertical reefs of rock that cut through the picturesque villages and rolling green pastures like a knife. Traveling through the Trentino- Alto Adige region of Italy is a cultural road trip through alpine meadows, snow capped mountains, chalets and ski resorts that begins with an Italian opera and ends with a Swiss yodel. If Dorothy were traveling down the yellow brick road that leads to the Italian Oz, she might be saying, at this point, "I don't think we're in Italy anymore". Here you will experience Italian food but with a distinctly alpine accent. The foods of the region are a combination of German, Austria-Hungarian and Swiss cuisine. This distinctive mix of cultures results in some of the most satisfying dishes you will taste when traveling in Northern Italy with unique food and wine that you will love. And if you like beer, look no further. My Italian cousins only drink German beer and when in Italy there is no better *birra* than to be found in the *brauhaus* and *birreria* of the Trentino-Alto Adige. The bread of the Trentino-Alto Adige takes on a dual personality, first as a rustic caraway rye and then as an ingredient in the making of *canederli*, a bread dumpling that often incorporates *speck,* a regional smoked *prosciutto.* My cousin Lidia had been talking about these "Alto Adige gnocchi" since we left Milano. They are made with leftover bread soaked in milk combined with eggs, flour, dry bread crumbs and nutmeg, formed into small balls and boiled in salted water then served with butter and cheese or added to a *brodo* (broth). You can make

72

them with spinach or other ingredients and they are sometimes filled with fruit for a delicious dessert. It seems that the love for *canederli* (*knodel* in German) is nothing new. Scenes of a women eating *canederli* are found in fresco paintings from the year 1200. In the chapel at Schloss Hocheppan, a castle above the vineyards of the river Adigio, there are frescos of a woman in a green dress below the Virgin Mary and Christ Child eating a Tyrolean *knodel* ! These frescoes date back to Roman times and are considered to be among the best examples of Romanesque style to be found anywhere in the world.

One of the happiest meals I've had in Italy was in the town of *Bolzano* (*Bozen* in German) with my Italian cousins at the table of Hopfen and Co. on Piazza Erbe 17 for a dinner of dumplings, *wurstel*, *stinco* and kraut. Hopfen and Co. is a Tirolean pub serving typical Tirolean food (*cucina tipica tirolese*) and original *Bozner Bier.* The fresh Bozen beer comes directly from the cellars (unfiltered) to your glass and is a perfect accompaniment to the hearty fare. We ordered an assortment of *wurstels* (sausages) served with sauerkraut and Eric, the adventurous one In our group, ordered the infamous *Stinco di maiale alla griglia*, a grilled pork shank (shin bone) of monumental proportions that gives new meaning to the term "living large". However the bill for this truly spectacular meal was very reasonable in keeping with my Italian cousins' taste and travel mantra "*mangia bene a buon prezzo*", eat well at a good price. The check at the end of the meal for 8 people was much less than expected and included mugs of cold beer and apple strudel.

The breads of Italy are truly unique and in large part define Italy's regional cuisine. Breads universal role as the staff of life makes it an ideal way to experience a country's cultural traditions. From the rustic simplicity of the farmhouse kitchen to the exquisite gastronomy of the Renaissance court, bread has been a symbol of the foods of Italy.

See and Savor More

If you are traveling in the *Sudtirol* you will need to be tri-lingual. Although you are in Italy, because of geographic boundaries and historical alliances, the South Tyrol is mainly German-speaking. As you cross the border you will begin to see not only a change in the scenery but a change in the language. The official languages of the region are German and Italian however there is a third spoken language called Ladin. Ladin is a Romanized version of the Germanic dialects that were once spoken here and today the language clings to existence with fewer than 100,000 speakers left. It is not uncommon to see menus written in German and Italian and local sites identified in all three languages. Road signs have to be bi-lingual (tri-lingual where Ladin is spoken) and normally the first name identifies the majority population in the area. "*Bën uni*" means *"Benvenuti"* or 'welcome' in the Ladin language. If you plan on traveling in Alto-Adige region of Northern Italy, cut and paste the following table into your travel guide for an example of the 3 languages of the *Sudtirol*.

The Three Languages of the SudTirol			
German	**Italian**	**Ladin**	**English**
Straße	*via, strada*	*streda*	street, road

You can make your own *Canederli* (Tirolese Dumplings) *Tiroler Knödel* by trimming any dry brown crust from bread. Cut the soft inner part into regular-sized cubes and combine with the following ingredients

- ⅝ lb stale bread
- 1 ¾ lb speck (smoked raw ham) or pancetta
- 1 ¾ oz salami
- 1 oz butter
- 1 sprig parsley
- 1 clove of garlic
- chive
- 3 eggs
- milk
- 2 tablespoons all-purpose flour
- 1 pinch nutmeg
- meat broth
- salt and pepper

Cut the stale bread into small cubes, toss in a pan in hot butter and then transfer to a bowel. Dice the speck or pancetta with the salami, add to the bread, lightly season with salt and pepper, add the chopped parsley, chives, garlic, mix well, add the beaten eggs with the milk and leave to rest for about an hour. Then mix adding the flour so as to form a homogeneous dough of the right consistency to produce dumplings. Boil some salted water in a large pot, and with wet hands prepare balls 2 inches in diameter, drop in the boiling water and leave to cook for about 10-15 minutes. Drain well using a slotted spoon and transfer to the tureen containing hot meat stock.

Because of its peasant roots *panzanella* was often referred to as the "poor man's lunch" or "poor man's dinner". Today *panzanella* is anything but a meal for the "poor" especially in restaurants outside of Italy where the charge for a *panzanella* salad can be pricey. Here is an authentic *panzanella* recipe inspired by my visit to Tenuta di Capezzana. Do not use stale American bread for this recipe. It is not a substitute for the firm, artisan quality Tuscan bread. American bread becomes fluffy when soaked and quickly turns to mush.

My Perfect *Panzanella*

Ingredients (this recipe will make several servings)

- 10 oz loaf of coarse Italian country style bread, sliced thick and left to dry
- 1 cup of fresh basil leaves, torn into pieces
- 1 small to medium red onion, sliced thin
- 3 large ripe tomatoes cut into cubes

- 2 Tablespoons of red wine vinegar; more or less to taste
- 1/3 cup Tuscan Extra Virgin Olive Oil
- sea salt and freshly ground pepper to taste

Break the slices of bread into medium sized pieces and place in a bowl of cold water getting them wet through, but not leaving them to soak, for a few minutes. Do not allow bread to become soggy. Gently squeeze any excess water from the bread. Place the bread pieces in a serving bowl and toss all ingredients together with the bread except the oil and vinegar. Dissolve salt to taste with the vinegar in a small bowl and sprinkle it over the bread mixture. Drizzle olive oil over all, add pepper and toss well. Serve immediately although some Italian cooks recommend leaving the *panzanella* sit for awhile before eating.

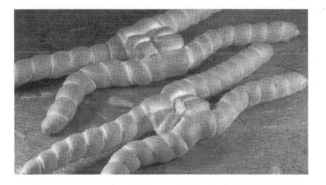

The twisted bread of Ferrara *"coppia ferrarese"*

Chapter 6 Leonardo and Alice

Leonardo and Alice. These are not the names of two characters from a 14th century Italian novella or a recently discovered secret diary of Leonardo da Vinci. Leonardo and Alice are the names of two flavors of *gelati* at Riva Reno Gelateria on Via G.Mazzini 12 in Ferrara. With typical Italian *sprezzatura* ice cream becomes an art form and as such takes on a personality that requires more than a mere labeling of chocolate or vanilla. Designer gelateria can be found all over Italy and like fashion and art people take pause, gaze and in this case take a lick. If they're at Riva Reno Gelateria you may even hear comments like "You can feel the ingredients". The creamy, velvety texture, intense flavors and exclusivity of product have brought Riva Reno gelato many accolades including the Best Gelateria in Italy awarded by Golosaria Magazine in 2008 with more glowing reviews in Gambero Rosso, the Lonely Planet and the Michelin Guide. You can taste *Leonardo* (mascarpone with chocolate and hazelnut topping) and *Alice* (prounced ah-lee-ch-ay) (pine nut cream with toasted pine nuts) in Ferrara or at Riva Reno Gelateria shops in Milan, Turin, Venice and Florence. Other Riva Reno specialties include *Otello* made with chocolate, egg cream, Marsala wine, Barozzi chocolate and coffee cake, *Morena* a white cream gelato topped with candied sour cherries and syrup and *Zafferano al sesamo* with saffron cream and carmelized toasted sesame seeds. More traditional flavors are always available. You can combine scoops of vanilla with chocolate chips (*Stracciatella*), pistachio, hazelnut, coffee, coconut and chocolate in a cup or a cone. Most gelateria will offer both so depending on your preference, when ordering, ask for either "*una* coppa" (a cup) or "un cono," (a cone). Unlike an ice cream cone in the States, the ideal cone in Italy comes with two flavors (gusti) of gelato like nocciola (hazelnut) and ciccolato (chocolate). It's also popular to order 3 flavors in a single cone or cup and they don't necessarily have to go together!

Designer gelato reaches new heights In the Tuscan hill town of San Gimignano. In "la citta' dalle belle torri", the city of the beautiful towers, there is a 13th century octagonal cistern in the middle of the Piazza della Cisterna and a gelateria that serves some of the best artisan gelato in Italy with innovative flavors like Cream of Fina® Saint (cream with saffron and pine nuts), Champelmo® (pink grapefruit and sparkling wine), Dolceamaro® (cream with aromatic herbs) and Vernaccia Sorbet made with regional Vernaccia wine. The gastronomic creations at Gelateria di Piazza in San Gimignano are limited only by the imagination of master ice cream maker Sergio Dondoli. His cups and cones are award winning creations with names like Sangue di Bue (Blood of Ox), said to have been inspired by Sergio's first Armani leather jacket. It was a reddish brown oxblood color; his gelato, dark chocolate with cherry jam and chili pepper.

The many faces of gelato can be found all over Italy. Like espresso and pasta gelato is associated with Italy in the minds of people all over the world. There isn't one taste traveler who doesn't take the Tour del Gelato, discovering Italy one lick at a time. If you happen to be traveling to the Lake region of Northern Italy visit the town of Sirmione where Italian families go to get away from the oppressive Lombardian heat of August and sample 101 flavors of gelato. Located on the south shore of _Lago di Garda_, Sirmione is an easy drive from Milano and a popular summer destination. An Italian Riviera for families, Sirmione is a wonderful blend of sophisticated charm and playfulness. Located within the town is the 13th century medieval fortress, Castle Scaligera (_Rocca Scaligera_). This castle is not a museum but a space that kids can explore to find their "inner Shrek". You enter the castle over a drawbridge across a moat into a courtyard surrounded by turrets that your kids can climb (with adult supervision) for a spectacular view of the lake. After exploring the castle you can walk into the town center to have all the gelato your heart desires. The streets of Sirmione are lined with ice cream shops (_gelaterie_) with an almost endless selection of flavors displayed in fantastic swirls of color with names that capture your imagination so that one scope is never enough. There are also sites to attract adults such as the grottoes of Catullus located at the tip of the peninsula, the 2,000 year old ruins of a Roman villa resembling a series of caves. Be aware that you won't get beyond the city gates of Sirmione driving. You will have to meter or ticket park your car and walk into the town. Car traffic is limited in the historical center of town as the cobblestone streets are very narrow and often filled with people walking.

Taste travelers in Italy have often been heard muttering, "so much gelato, so little time". The creative combinations of flavors of gelato will far exceed your ability to try them all. But try you will because they are irresistible. So whether you are in Milano at _Chocolat_ near _Castello Sforzesco_ and the Cardona tube station or in Florence trying to decide if gelato from _Perche No_ (Why Not) is better than gelato from _Vivoli_ don't overlook the less well know gelateria shops that are

80

on almost every corner in towns and villages throughout Italy. There are a few secrets to ordering and eating gelato in Italy. I refer to it as the Gelati Code. Like a sequel to a popular novel involving an Italian codex it has its own language with a hidden meaning that requires some deciphering. As I mentioned before, gelati flavors range from the simple to the sublime. Here are just a few suggestions from your gelato sommelier

- *fragola* - strawberry
- *lampone* - raspberry
- *limone* - lemon
- *mandarino* - mandarin orange
- *melone* - melon
- *albicocca* - apricot
- *fico* - fig
- *frutti di bosco* - "fruits of the woods," like blueberries and blackberries * a personal favorite
- *mela* - apple
- *pera* – pear
- *pesca* - peach
- *mandorla* - almond
- *cioccolato noir* - dark chocolate
- *cioccolato latte* - milk chocolate
- *stracciatella* - chocolate chip
- *bacio* - chocolate hazelnut combination similar to the Perugina Baci Chocolate candy

- *gianduja* **or** *gianduia* - another milk chocolate hazelnut combination of a traditional flavor from the Piedmont region from Italy
- *zabaione*- based on a dessert of the same name, made with egg yolks and sweet Marsala wine
- *amarena* - a cream base with sour cherries kind of mixed in
- *zuppa inglese* - based on English trifle
- *liquirizia* - licorice

When ordering *gelato* in Italy it is not uncommon to pay first. This seems backwards to us but when ordering at some bars or *gelaterie* in Italy you pay first at a cashier then receive a receipt that is taken to the counter where you place and receive your order. It goes something like this. Go up to the cashier and say, "Un cono con due gusti, per favore," or "A cone with two scoops (flavors), please." then pay for your gelato. You will be given a receipt showing the paid amount. Hand your receipt to the counter person and tell them the flavors you want.

See and Savor More

During the Early 16th century, an Italian architect named Bernardo Buontalenti discovered a way of freezing a mixture of churned, sweetened milk and egg yolks and so the art of making gelato was born. A native of Florence, Buontalenti is said to have delighted the court of Caterina dei Medici with his creation.

Chapter 7 The Polenta Capital of Italy

There are many places in Northern Italy that you can travel to taste polenta but none is more traditional than the town of Bergamo, 50km north of Milano. Bergamo is actually two towns, the modern Bergamo Bassa and Bergamo Alta, the medieval hilltop town that can be reached by funicular railway. Bergamo Alta "Upper Bergamo" sits 1200 ft above the plains below and was ruled for three and a half centuries by the Venetians, who built homes with wrought-iron balconied terraces and encircled the whole city within gated defensive walls.

Bergamo has been called "the polenta capital of Italy" because it is here that polenta has achieved greatness. A traditional recipe of Bergamo is *polenta coi osei* . *Osei* in Italian means small birds such as thrushes, sparrows or finches. At one time this dish was made with *osei*, grilled, stewed (in *umido)*, or skewered and sautéed, served on a slice of polenta. Today this somewhat unsettling preparation has been replaced with a sweet confection known as *polenta e osei* "tiny little bird cakes" made with a génoise in the shape of half-sphere that are gilded a golden yellow to imitate the color of the polenta and stuffed with almond paste and chocolate mousse. My cousin Lidia wanted me to taste this cake that commemorates a local custom no longer practiced but one of which I was familiar from the stories Nonna had told me when I was younger. Nonna said that when she was a girl she and her family would travel to the hills near their village with nets that they would stretch across the hilltops. Tiny song birds *(uccelli)* would fly into the nets and become entangled. Nonna and her sisters would catch the birds, break their necks and then grill the songbirds, serving them over polenta (remember most peasant families didn't have access to meat).The hunting of songbirds is now outlawed in Italy but the centuries old custom is commemorated by the making of *polenta e osei* remembering a time when meat was scarce and tiny little songbirds fed your family. I left Bergamo with several of the tiny little bird cakes and the sweet taste of knowing about a tradition that connected my family to a town high above the Lombardian plains and to a food that was still eaten the same way as it was 2,000 years ago.

Before I left the region there was one more polenta dish I wanted to taste. In the mountainous valleys of the Vatellina near Bergamo and Brescia you can find polenta's rustic cousin *polenta taragna* . Almost unknown outside of Italy, this hearty polenta is made with a combination of cornmeal and buckwheat flour. The buckwheat flour adds an earthy flavor and a darker yellow color to the dish. Usually served with sausages, game, cured or darker meats, this Lombardian specialty is sometimes called "black polenta" and is unique. I found what I was looking for at Ristorante Bernabo', located at Piazza Mascheroni 11 in Bergamo Alta. Several of my cousins, including myself had the *polenta taragna*. One of my cousins ordered the *stracotto d'asino*. Yes I did say *asino* as in ass. *Asino* in Italian means donkey. *Stracotto di'asino* is donkey stew and really quite good once you get past the fact that you are eating donkey. My cousin Lidia ordered it as a *ragu'* to be eaten as a sauce with a steaming plate of polenta. Donkey and horse meat are somewhat common in Italy and other European countries and the killing of horses for human consumption is not universally looked at with aversion. There are many markets, including larger grocery stores in Italy where a horse head is mounted above the meat counter. I have never eaten horse meat, nor do I plan to, but after traveling in Italy I realized that your culinary viewpoint is a product of your culture and tradition. Countries with a long standing history of siege or starvation viewed horses as a food source of last resort. Eating a pot roast of horse or an equine fillet may have fallen out of favor and for most countries is considered taboo. However during World War II, due to the low supply and high price of beef, New Jersey legalized the sale of horse meat until the end of the War and Harvard University's Faculty Club had horse meat on the menu for over one hundred years, until 1985.

The traditions of eating horse and donkey can be left in the past but the tradition of making polenta must be preserved. According to the handbook of the Order of the Knights of Polenta (*Ordine dei Cavalieri della Polenta*) *"No other food requires such a precise ritual, such particular utensils, perfect measuring of water, salt, and flour, such scrupulous and attentive care: if today we wish to make "good" polenta, we must follow that ancient ritual, use the same equipment, the same ingredients, use the same proportions and carry out the same ancient gestures."* The making of polenta does require some attention with constant stirring so it doesn't stick to the bottom of the pan and polenta purists recommend that you set aside at least one hour for some vigorous and almost continual stirring of the polenta. But sometimes I'd rather be out riding my Vespa than cooking polenta Nonna's way. There are many good techniques and shortened cooking methods for making polenta today included, dare I say it, pre-cooked polenta for cooking in *pochi minuti*. Even my Milanese family and friends in Italy buy "instant polenta" in a box when they want to make polenta the easy way.

See and Savor More

This recipe for *Stracotto d'asino* (Donkey Stew) is very similar to what my cousin had in Italy. All measurements are metric as this dish is strictly European. Substitute beef for donkey meat as eating donkey in the US is prohibited.

Ingredients:

1 kg donkey meat

2 onions

2 bay leaves

2 juniper berries (optional)

2 tablespoons tomato sauce

Extra Virgin olive oil, as needed

1-2 garlic cloves

lt red wine (I would adjust this to 1 cup)

salt, pepper

Preparation: Cut the meat into chunks. Add the garlic and vegetables, which have been previously chopped, together with the olive oil and butter into a saucepan and sauté for a few minutes. Then add the meat and brown it, turning it over frequently. Add the wine and few ladlefuls of beef stock and then tomato sauce. Cover the saucepan and cook the meat over a very low heat, adding a few ladlefuls of stock as needed, until it is completely cooked. Halfway through cooking, season with salt and pepper. In order to obtain an excellent 'stracotto', the heat must be very low and the meat should be cooked for at least four hours.

Chapter 8   A Slice Of Italian Life

See and savor Italy, a slice at a time. No one food better reflects the lifestyle of everyday Italians than pizza. They often grab a slice at the corner bakery, fast food bar or autostrada cafe. As in the States, pizza is a popular choice with Italian families for a casual family meal and for couples looking for an inexpensive night out. But pizza in Italy is nothing like the pizza at your typical American pizzeria. Pizza in Italy is made by a *pizzaiolo*, a trained pizza chef, according to traditional recipes and standards that began with a pizza made for a Queen. In 1889 Margherita Maria Teresa Giovanna of Savoy, wife of Umberto I, King of Italy was part of a taste and travel journey that brought her to the city of Naples. In her travels she saw the peasants eating a large flatbread which she tasted and loved. She asked a local chef to make this regional specialty for her and the rest is history. The local chef named the pizza after the Queen and Pizza Margherita became the matriarch of the classic Italian pizza. Lightly crisp with a thin, chewy crust and a hint of smoke an authentic Italian pizza is baked in a wood fired oven. The extremely hot wood fired oven requires only a few minutes (less than two) for the pizza to cook. My friend Luca says that if a pizza takes longer than ten minutes to order it's not a true Italian pizza.

Although Naples is the traditional home of pizza, authentic Italian pizza can be found all over Italy. You can be assured of that because of the VPN. According to the *Associazione Verace Pizza Napoletana*, an organization of pizza-makers dedicated to "protecting one of the most ancient and most important gastronomic traditions" of Italy, a true Neapolitan pizza is made from a specific kind of wheat flour and yeast, 14 inches round and no thicker than 1/3 centimeter at its center. The tomato base must be made from the San Marzano variety of tomatoes, the olive oil extra virgin and the cheese topping must be mozzarella made from the milk of the water buffalo. All ingredients must be from the Campania region. If restaurants in Italy advertise Pizza Napoletana but aren't complying with the rules they could be in big trouble. I told you that Italians take their food seriously.

The local *pizzaiolo* who made the first Margherita pizza used *Mozzarella di bufala,* a type of mozzarella cheese never before used as an ingredient. Today *mozzarella di bufala* is the soft moist cheese oozing with milky flavor that makes Pizza Margherita so unique. The history of the mozzarella is ancient but it wasn't until 1570 that it was mentioned in a cook book from the papal court. Today the cheese is so favored that mozzarella bars like OBIKÀ *(pronounced Oh-bee-KA),* Neapolitan for "here it is", serve fresh hand-pinched mozzarella with salumi, pasta and in salads or slathered on wood oven baked bread. On the seventh floor of La Rinascente, the venerable Milanese department store in Milan Centro, you can experience a flight of mozzarella cheese at the bar or at bistro style tables with a view that overlooks the spires of Milan's Duomo. There are OBIKA´ mozzarella bars in Turin, Rome, Florence, London and New York City and are a dining event that should not be missed.

In Italy a pizza is meant to be for one person and and you typically order your pizza according to the toppings. Each pizza has a name that determines what is on the pizza. For example

- *Margherita* - tomato, fresh mozzarella and basil
- *Marinara* - tomato sauce, oregano and garlic but no cheese
- *Funghi* - mushrooms
- *Quattro formaggi* - a four cheese pizza often made with a combination of fresh mozzarella and three local cheeses
- *Quattro stagioni* - a pizza that represents the four seasons each with a different topping with sections of artichokes, salami, or *prosciutto cotto*, mushrooms and tomatoes on each of the four quarters

In my mind pizza in America has been over thought and over wrought to the point that it is all but unrecognizable to Italians who visit the States. Luca told me that the pizza in the States "frightened him"! My Italian antennae went up when I read a Chowhound Blog about corn on pizza. I admit I'm somewhat of a pizza purist but is it because we've never tasted an authentic Italian pizza that we feel compelled to twist it and turn it into an unrecognizable mass of dough with toppings of every shape and form. Or do some of us look at it as a blank canvas to express our inner Jackson Pollok. Now I know you should eat what you like and culinary creativity should be applauded but sometimes less is more. Some of the recipes mentioned in the article sounded like Wolfgang Puck's California Pizza on acid. Traveling in Italy with my Italian family and friends has led me to believe that the classic Margherita pizza and a few variations are all you need and VPN guidelines should be followed. Corn, ketchup and mayo on pizza, if that's what you like OK, just don't call it a pizza.

Eating pizza in Italy is an experience that shouldn't be missed but even in Italy there are bad pizze although most of the pizza I have eaten in Italy has been outstanding. By American standards even *pizza a taglia,* pizza sold by the slice at bakeries, fast food take out bars and autostrada cafes are good. But be sure to take some time to look for a small neighborhood pizzeria off the beaten path where the wood fired oven casts a warm glow. Here you are likely to find the best slice of Italian life. If you are in Perugia, *Il Segreto di Pulcinella*, Via Larga 8 serves authentic Pizza Neapolitan. If you are in Navigli, the trendy canal zone south of Milan, pizza restaurant Solo Pizza, Towpath Naviglio Pavese Milan 6, serves wonderful Neapolitan pizza. I recently celebrated a family anniversary here with my Italian cousins. We had a great pizza, wonderful wine and a Neapolitan cake for dessert. We toasted our guests with a bottle of Cormons Ribolla Gialla Vino Spumante from Fruili. The aromatic nose and persistent bubbles kept reminding me that in Italy any meal no matter how simple is a celebration of family and friends and should be savored.

So experience a slice of Italian life. When in Italy eat pizza and eat it often. The tantalizing aroma of a pizza baked in a wood fired oven brought to your table bubbling on top waiting to erupt is about as authentic as you can get. Simple yet sublime. Anyone for a Coca Cola Light!

See and Savor More

The technique of cooking with wood fired ovens is centuries old. In Italy the ancient Etruscans pounded grain into mash and baked it on stones buried in the ashes, creating a smoky tasting flatbread, the prototype for today's pizza.

Italian flour makes the difference in the way a pizza in Italy tastes. In Italy they grind the flour very slow. That way the wheat isn't destroyed. In America, they grind the wheat very fast, which destroys it. Americans also bleach the flour and may add protein. A pizza made with American flour and cooked in a pizza oven in Italy would burn in two seconds.

Chapter 9 Michelangelo's Sandwich

8 km from the marble quarries of Carrara is the town of Colonnata, situated among the Apuane Alps of Northern Tuscany. Marble from this region has been used since the time of ancient Rome. The Pantheon and Trajan's Column are made from Carrara marble as are hundreds of monuments and sculptures in Italy and throughout the world. A monument in the Capitol Rotunda in Washington DC features portrait busts of the leaders of the woman suffrage movement sculpted from an 8 ton block of Carrara marble.

For thousands of years the quarrymen of the region have eaten seasoned lard (*lardo*) aged in marble tubs (*conca*) excavated from the work site. The work was hard and the *Lardo di Colonnata* would provide them with the calories needed to carve and transport the marble blocks that would be used for many of Italy's most famous monuments and sculptures (Carrara was the source of the marble used by Michelangelo). Today the cured lard of the quarryman's sandwich is an artisanal delicacy served as an antipasto. The technique used for making *Lardo di Colonnata* remains unchanged since ancient times although today there is a regulatory board that guarantees that the ingredients are prepared and processed according to strict guidelines to ensure an authentic and safe product. The *lardo* is made from a layer of fat from the back of pigs native to Tuscany called the Cinta Senese or Sienese Belt pig because of the white band around their chest (*cinta* means sash in Italian). Sienese Cinta pigs are said to have a higher percentage (57%) of oleic or "good" fat as opposed to the normal pig's 50%, which makes the meat tastier, healthier and of a fine intense red color. Cinta pigs were raised in and around Siena as early as the 14th century. A Cinta Senese is depicted in a famous fresco by Ambrogio Lorenzetti (1338) in Siena's *Palazzo Comunale* (town hall) titled *L'Allegoria del buon governo* (the good/wise government). In the contra fresco *il cattivo governo* (the bad government), the pigs are missing. The regulatory Board for the Protection of *Lardo di Colonnata* determines production standards including the weight of the pig at time of slaughtering. The pork fat is placed in the large tub like *conca* excavated from the marble. The marble vessel is rubbed with garlic and the *lardo* is layered with salt, fresh herbs and spices such as rosemary, oregano, sage, cloves, peppercorns, anise, nutmeg or cinnamon. After 6 to 10 months of aging in the cool, dry mountain air the *lardo* emerges as an aromatic, glistening white block to be thinly sliced and served over warm toast. It was at my friend Luca's house that I first tasted *Lardo di Colonnata*. I admit I was a little skeptical but I could not pass up what surely must have once been Michelangelo's sandwich. Luca cut a thin slice of the *lardo* and served it over warm Tuscan bread. The color was a gleaming white and the texture smooth and creamy. It melted in my mouth full of the flavor of aromatic spices and herbs, almost like an incense. Some have described the flavor as "intoxicating". I describe it as delicious. I'm glad I tasted it but my elevated LDL and triglycerides could not have stood much more unless I went to work in the quarries.

You can travel to Colonnata to visit the quarries and taste this unique delicacy or you can find it in many of the shops and restaurants in the area. It is difficult to duplicate the taste and flavor of *Lardo di*

Colonnata outside of Italy as it is an artisanal delicacy and the recipe is unique to the specific maker and influenced by the mountain air. There is nothing like it in the states but mention is made of a recipe for Tuscan creamed bacon in <u>Culinaria Italy</u>, a wonderful coffee table/reference/recipe book that is a food stylist dream. It is called *Crema Paradiso* and uses firm back bacon, black peppersorns, wine vinegar, garlic and fresh rosemary ground together then kneaded on a marble slab until a light, delicate cream is formed. I suppose if the marble is from Carrara all the better. The recipe advises to spread the *crema* on hot toast and serve with a Chianti wine. Michelangelo's Sandwich would have been made with thinly sliced *lardo* accompanied with bread, raw onions and tomatoes.

See and Savor More

Cinta Senese or Sienese Belt Pigs

Chapter 10 Chianina Bistecca

If there was one food experience that defines a taste and travel trip to Tuscany then that experience would be seeing and savoring the famous *Bistecca alla Fiorentina* aka Tuscan T-bone. I'm not a big meat eater and rarely eat steak but it would be a pity not to experience the truly spectacular Florentine *bistecca* while taste traveling in Tuscany. The beef comes from cattle raised in Tuscany's *Val di Chiana*, 50 km south of Florence and is renown throughout Italy. The rough pastures and rolling hills of the *Val di Chiana* (*Valdichiana*) have been the home of the Chianina (pronounced key-a-nee-na) breed for at least 2000 years. The Etruscans and the Romans used the ancestors of todays animals in processions and for sacrifices to their gods and the impressive stature and appearance of these Italian bovines made them a top model for Roman sculptures. I have seen these cattle grazing in the fields of Tuscany and Umbria and they are magnificent. They are massive and striking with a snow white coat and a wide well-rounded rump. Breeders and ranchers talk about their "unsurpassed capacity for lean meat production" producing a meat that is firm, lightly marbled and delicious with more protein, less fat and less cholesterol than other beef. Young animals can weigh up to 1540 pounds and are perfectly constructed to provide the large cuts of meat needed for a *bistecca di manzo della Val di Chiana alla fiorentina*. Anotherwords they are perfectly constructed to rise to the heights of culinary stardom.

Two of the most perfect afternoons I've spent in Italy have centered around a *bistecca alla fiorentina* including a great photo op of Chianina cattle in a field across from the *Abbazia Sant' Antimo* in Tuscany. Another was at the home of my Umbrian friends, Pinota and Antonio, eating a *bistecca* under the vine covered pergola in their garden overlooking a valley with the city of Perugia in the distance. Sounds like almost heaven, well it was. First and foremost the company of my Italian friends and their family was the centerpiece of the afternoon. The gracious hospitality of Italians in their home is an exceptional experience. Then there is the setting. My friend's home outside Perugia is set in a garden with an outdoor pavilion that included a Tuscan style wood burning oven and grill where the *bistecca* was prepared. I've had *bistecca alla fiorentina* in many restaurants in Tuscany but having one prepared by your Italian friends in the garden of their home is truly memorable.

What could top that wonderful afternoon in Umbria? It was to be a singular moment in time when food and family are one. An experience cooking with my son and 4 year old grandson at a Tuscan farmhouse outside the town of San Casciano in Val di Pesa. The house had a rustic Tuscan kitchen and just outside the kitchen door was a small patio enclosed by a brick wall surrounded by bushes of lavender and rosemary. The patio overlooked an orchard of olive trees with a vanishing point to the village below. At one end of the patio was a brick grill. One evening we decided to go into town to buy a *bistecca* to

97

cook outside. The aroma of the meat grilling in the open air, the flames dancing on the grill and the laughter of my grandson combined to make that meal the most memorable meal I've ever had in Italy.

Some people call *bistecca alla fiorentina* inspirational and after my experiences cooking and eating *bistecca* in Italy I can see why. There is even a festival, *Sagra della Bistecca*, in August in the town of Cortona in Tuscany to celebrate this epic beef. Preparing *bistecca alla fiorentina* is almost ritualistic with varying opinions on how it should be prepared and cooked .The Italian epicurean Artusi, whose famous 19th c book *La Scienza in Cucina* (Science in the Kitchen) strongly believed in the less is more approach to cooking a *bistecca* when he wrote "if you dress it beforehand with oil or other, as many do, it will taste like snuff and will be nauseating". The noted Italian cook book author Marcella Hazan believes this too saying "I have seen cooks rub the steak with oil before putting it on the grill, but the scorched oil imparts a taste of tallow to the meat that I prefer to avoid". She rubs the steak with ground peppercorns prior to grilling and rubs a lightly crushed and peeled clove of garlic over the bone on both sides after the steak is cooked to taste while still hot on the grill. I have seen a recipe for a *bistecca* that has been marinated in olive oil, salt, pepper and rosemary for a hour before grilling but no Italian would consider that. When ordering this steak in a restaurant in Italy it will be priced according to weight and cut *tagliata* style on a slight angle ½ inch (1 cm) thick pieces at the table. It was served to me this way at the restaurant of Fattoria Castelvecchi in the Tuscan hills outside of Radda in Chianti. Right off the grill on a wooden board carved at the table it was everything I had hoped for and more. The carnivores at the table were well satisfied.

Chianina cattle have been given IGP status and are protected under a European Union designation of regional quality just like Parma ham, Mortadella from Bologna or Parmigiano Reggiano cheese. Under the rules of the breed's consortium, the cattle must be born in Italy and the calf must be naturally nursed by the mother and then fed on preservative-free grass from the pastures of the central Appenini mountains. Slaughtering is done in the second year. All animals must be registered at birth in the official records and tagged, tattooed or branded for life-long identification. Don't miss a rare opportunity to eat a steak of mythic proportions and when you get home you can try this recipe for *Bistecca alla fiorentina* from my friends Pinota and Antonio.

See and Savor More

A traditional recipe for *Bistecca alla fiorentina*

1 Chianini beefsteak on the bone 1½ - 2" thick (my friends say 2 fingers thick) at least 2-3lb. This will serve 2-4 people (yes these steaks are huge). You can use a T-Bone Porterhouse cut as a Chianini *bistecca* is almost impossible to find in the US. Allow the steak to come to room temperature before grilling. The grill should be set at 4". My friends build a hardwood fire in the old manner of oak and olive but charcoal could be used as well (make sure the coals are glowing bright red but without flames). Lay the *bistecca* on the grill until a crust has formed (about 5- 7 minutes) then turn (ONLY ONCE). Continue to grill for about the same amount of time depending on the

99

thickness of the meat; another 5-7 minutes for rare; 12 minutes for medium rare. Italians generally grill their steak to feel "springy" to the touch that is to say rare to medium rare. Here are some hints

- turn the meat ONLY ONCE and DO NOT PIERCE with a fork
- don't salt the meat before cooking; season the steak after cooking with a coarse sea salt, a drizzle of olive oil I (use the best you can find) and pepper as desired
- gas grills do not yield the same results
- let the meat stand for 10 minutes before cutting to retain all the juices and cut at the recommended angle as discussed above
- stand the meat up on its bone the last few minutes of cooking to ensure meat is cooked around the T part of the bone

The connection between the Chianina *bistecca* and *alla fiorentina* (Florentine steak) refers to the San Lorenzo Night Festival in Florence when people use to roast Chianina calves.

Grilling a Bistecca in San Casciano in Val di Pesa, Tuscany

Chapter 11 A Taste as Old as Water

Lawrence Durrell, expatriate British novelist and travel writer, when writing about olive oil described it as "older than meat, older than wine, a taste as old as water". Despite its ancient origins, less than 30 years ago olive oil was relatively unheard of in the US. It was barely mentioned in the early editions of the Betty Crocker Cookbook and wasn't looked at as an ingredient in cooking until 1973 when Marcella Hazan published her classic book on Italian cooking. Today olive oil is as ubiquitous as salt, so much so that we might take it for granted. Not so in Italy. In Italy olive oil is still thought of as a gift of the gods. Around 1100 AD, olive groves began to flourish in Italy and Tuscany became renown for the cultivation of olives. Vases and amphora filled with oil were traded throughout the Mediterranean and by 1400 Italy had become the greatest producer of olive oil in the world, offering extraordinary oil that graced Renaissance tables throughout Europe. You have an opportunity to travel to the olive orchards and *frantoio* (olive mills) of Italy to taste oils that are still an expression of the ancient *terroir* of the region. Just like wine, olive cultivars are influenced by the character of the land. They respond to the soil and climate in which they are grown as well as the cultivation, harvesting practices and methods used to process the olives and produce the oil.

There are over 2,830,000 acres of land dedicated to growing olives in Italy with 14 different olive growing regions. Each has its own unique oils. With the exception of Italian wine no other product of Italy is as distinctive as Italian olive oil and many of the best are of protected origin (DOP) just as Italy's finest wines. A taste traveler in Northern Italy, Tuscany and Umbria can experience regional flavors that range from the delicate, fruity oils of the Ligurian Riviera to the pungent, peppery oils of Tuscany to the soft, buttery flavors of Umbrian oils from olives that were there before the Etruscans. Italians know that good olives make good oil and that the choice of the cultivar, ripeness of the olive at the time of picking and growing region all result in different flavor profiles. The olives used to make Ligurian oils are picked from December to February when they are fully ripe resulting in a mellow, aromatic fruity oil. The olives used in the production of Tuscan oils are picked in the fall of the year before they ripen. This results in an oil with a more pungent, peppery flavor. That classic Tuscan zing gives Tuscan oils a slight bitterness that goes well with the strong, savory flavors of Tuscan cooking. Tuscan oils are said to have a higher level of heart healthy polyphenols because the olives are picked earlier in the year. Higher levels of polyphenols also extend the shelf life for some Tuscan oils up to two years. However the *piccante* flavor of Tuscan oils may not appeal to everyone. Some tasters describe the slight bitterness of the oil as a "throat grabbing sensation" resulting in an "olive oil cough". Tuscan oils like many Super Tuscan wines are blended with other regional oils to create artisan oils with complex flavor profiles or to enhance the stability of other oils.

Italians also know that being extra virgin is better when it comes to olive oil. Extra Virgin olive oil is the freshest olive oil you can buy with the time from tree to milling in 24 hours or less. It is the first pressing of the oil and the highest quality oil you can buy. No chemicals

102

solvents are used to treat or rectify the oil and it is never subjected to heat to extract the oil. A benchmark of Extra Virgin olive oil is a low level of acidity (measure of oleic acid in oil). Extra Virgin olive oil has an oleic acid level of not more than 0.8%. A higher level of acidity (due to extreme ripeness of the olives or that the olives may have sat around too long before pressing or other damage) indicates an oil of lesser quality. In comparison, virgin olive oil has an oleic acid level of 2% and some are over 3%. Less than 5% of all the oils in the world are extra virgin. For flavor, taste, aroma, culinary uses and health benefits extra virgin olive oil is absolutely better.

A lot of what I learned about olive oil in Italy is about the same as how I learned about Italian wine, that is to say, through experiencing it with my Italian family and friends in the region of origin. One of the best lessons I received on Italian olive oil was at Tenuta di Capezzana outside the village of Carmignano northwest of Florence. I have mentioned this estate farm before when I described an afternoon meal that began with a perfect *panzanella* at the Contini Bonacossi family table. Today the Contini Bonacossi family are the resident owners of an estate of vineyards and olive groves that date from the 15th century when it belonged to the Medici family. But the history of olives and vines goes back even further. After a guided visit through the Capezzana winery and olive press, Benedetta Contini Bonacossi, took me into a room with documents that date back to 804 telling of how wine has been made at Capezzana for the last 1200 years. Under Benedetta's tutelage I learned that the olives are processed within 12-24 hours of picking. I visited the estate's modern, continuous cycle olive mill, which uses both modern technology and traditional

103

methods. The oil is left to decant in the old *"orciaia"* (oil jar room) next to the olive mill, in the traditional manner, which makes it possible to avoid a second centrifuge process. Extraction and processing of the oil are done with care to retain the optimal flavor and aromas of the ancient olive stock. The extraction process, together with the short time between picking and pressing ensures an oil that is of low acidity and has a higher number of useful substances such as tocophenols and polyphenols, which are important for the conservation of the oil and also for health. There is a one to one relationship between the olive trees on the estate and the oil they produce. One olive tree produces one bottle of oil. So when you buy a bottle of Tenuta di Capezzana Extra Virgin Olive Oil it's like having a bottle made just for you.

See and Savor More

6.5 Million olive trees can't be wrong. That's how many olive trees are cultivated on more than 10,000 farms in Italy producing olive oil on an area of roughly 55 thousand hectares of Tuscan land according to the *Consorzio per la tutela dell'olio extrvergine di oliva toscano* IGP.

Misconceptions about Extra Virgin Olive Oil

- "Olive oil is nothing more than an ingredient in a recipe". The Italians approach to food is more than utilitarian. They value their food and the traditions that surround it. They feel it enhances their lives

- "I just buy my oil off the shelf at the grocery store". Not all oil is created equal. Oil off the shelf is often exposed to light, heat and changes in humidity and temperature that adversely affect the quality of the oil. So if not conserved properly, the money that you spend may be wasted

- "These oils are too expensive". A good quality Italian Extra Virgin Olive Oil costs 40 cents a tablespoon and is high in polyphenols and heart healthy compounds

- "What's the difference where I buy my oil". Made in "the hills of Tuscany" does not always mean a true Italian oil. It may refer to where the olives were pressed not necessarily where they were grown. There is an enormous amounts of imported oils that are blended with Italian oils. Although there are some wonderful blended oils (not to be confused with infused oil), unscrupulous producers buy cheap, foreign oil blend it with local oil and call it locally produced and label it "Made it Italy", When you buy an artisan Italian oil your purchase helps to ensure that the traditional flavors of Italy are protected. When you buy a knock off product, it undercuts the ability to produce a genuine product and soon the product is eliminated because there is no market. Know your distributor and/or producer

Unlike wine olive oil does not improve with age. Once olive oil is exposed to heat, light and air, the oil will start to deteriorate. To maximize the quality of extra virgin olive oil store in a cool, dark place (57 -61°F) in a cupboard not on a window ledge or near the stove. Olive oil will generally remain fresh for 12-18 months and if stored properly, a bottle of quality extra virgin olive oil can last up to two to three years. Although some sources say that olive oil can be stored in the refrigerator, temperature fluctuations cause condensation and water and oil don't mix so when the oil returns to its previous consistency the flavor may be damaged. Save the cruets and the decorative bottles with the nice pouring spouts for serving not storing your oil. Preserve your oil in the original bottle with should be darkly colored glass or a tin container. Tightly cap bottles to prevent the oil from oxidizing. Exposure to air will cause the oil to become rancid. Use decanters when serving extra virgin olive oil at the table not for storing oil for an extended period of time.

Olive Oil Dipping Dishes by Mary Judge Designs

There are many containers and accessories for serving olive oil today including dishes for tasting and dipping that enhance the beauty and aroma of the oil.

Chapter 12   The Mythology and Mystique of the Wild Boar

The inward glow of food and wine has been part of the Tuscan landscape for 3,000 years when the ancient Etruscans first began cultivating the land of Eturia. Tuscany is a land of vines and olive orchards where fields of sunflowers color the landscape and the scents of rosemary, lavender and thyme fill the air where . . . whoa what was that? A sharp crack pierces the brisk autumn air. The harsh cries of many men resound through the forest, the barking of dogs, another sharp crack in the distance then loud cheers. The serenity of the Tuscan countryside changes in November, the time of the year to spend a healthy day in the country for a wild boar shoot. Seeing and savoring Italy during this time of the year is invigorating. The deep colors of the autumn landscape open the estates and reserved hunting areas in Tuscany and Umbria for organized wild boar hunting. An ancient sport, the boar hunt in Italy goes back to Roman times where the fierceness and strength of the boar made it a worthy opponent. Images of wild boars, alone or as part of a hunting scene have been discovered decorating a wide range of historical objects. There is a marble statue of a wild boar made by Florentine sculptor Pietro Tacca (1577-1640) that sits in the Uffizi in Florence as testimony to its hallowed position in Italian folklore.

Today the Tuscan love of wild game and their preference for rustic cooking makes *cinghiale*, wild boar, a popular dish throughout the region. In fact, *cinghiale* is so popular in Tuscany that it is considered by some to be (unofficially) the national dish. Eating *cinghiale* in Tuscany follows a food tradition of a time when hunters (*cacciatore*)

107

went into the chestnut forests and mountains to hunt the wild boar and bring it home to feed their families. Wild boars still roam the forests and vineyards of Tuscany and in autumn local hunting clubs continue the hunt. I have driven through Tuscany in November and heard the sounds of hunters shooting in the distance. It was unusual at first to be so close to the origin of the food we find on our tables. In the US we are so removed from the process of providing food and the thought of hunting as a source of food seems archaic and unnecessary. Yet hunting in Italy, as in most of Europe, follows an ancient tradition and the seasonal sport of hunting is not considered to be politically incorrect or inhumane. Today boar is also raised commercially, usually in fenced in sections of forest and boar meat is readily available year round.

Italians take great pride in the preparation of wild boar and consider it to be a specialty. There are many recipes that use the meat of the wild boar with stewing or braising being preferred as the meat can be tough if not properly cooked. In Tuscany and Emilia Romagna boar is often prepared as a stew (*scottiglia di cinghiale*) or *alla cacciatore* (hunter style) and served with *pappardelle.* The rich thick noodles are a perfect background for the strong, robust flavor of wild game so you often find this type of pasta served *con lepre*, with wild hare as well. Italians also like sausages, prosciutto and salami made from wild boar meat. I have eaten wild boar in Italy many times and like it very much. It has a strong flavor but not unpleasant rather rustic and bold. Shops in Italy that sell wild boar meat often display a stuffed wild boar's head outside their store front that can be quite startling to see at first. If you are unsure about eating wild boar and would just like a taste look for a *sagra* in Tuscany. These seasonal food festivals celebrate regional culture and cuisine with music, dancing, games, exhibits and of course food. In April the town of Rapolano Terme, Siena hosts a food festival with a variety of wild boar dishes to taste. In the small medieval Tuscan town of Suvereto, 90 km from Florence, the *Sagra del Cinghiale* (Festival of the Wild Boar) is held every December with exhibitions and medieval pageantry with food stands and local restaurants serving wild boar. There's also a *Sagra del Cinghiale* in Certaldo. Capalbio and Chianti and . . . well you get the idea. Wild boar is very popular in Italy. The traditions surrounding the eating of a particular food is a reason to celebrate in Italy so if you happen upon a sign along the road that says "*Sagra del Cinghiale*" or "*Sagra del whatever*" you should stop and go.

See and Savor More

In 1962, five copies of Tacca's sculpture of a wild boar were cast by the Florence foundry, *Fonderia Ferdinando Marinelli*. One of these was donated to the University of Waterloo in Canada. The four other copies of the boar are located in Sydney, Australia, Sonoma California, on the south side of the Straw Market in Florence and in Victoria, British Columbia. Copies of replicas of *Porcellino* (piglet in Italian) can be found in Sutton Place Park in New York City and various public places worldwide and on internet sites where it is sold as garden ornament and has become a popular addition to any outdoor setting.

A Recipe for *Pappardelle al Cinghiale* from Italy

Ingredients

4 lbs of mixed wild boar cuts, such as leg or loin meat

2 chopped garlic cloves

1 large carrot, chopped

1 stick celery, chopped

1 tablespoon, chopped fresh flat leaf parsley

1 tablespoon, chopped fresh thyme leaves

A few sprinklings of dried red chili flakes (I added this)

1 cup dry red wine

1 can of chopped Italian plum tomatoes

1 cup light meat stock

Olive oil

Salt & fresh ground black pepper

Pre-heat an oven to 350 degrees C. Cut the meat into bite-sized pieces. In a large frying pan warm 1 tablespoon of olive oil, add the garlic and cook gently for a couple of minutes to flavor the oil. Add the boar meat, increase the heat and brown on all sides. Season to taste with salt and pepper. Add the carrot, celery, parsley, thyme and chili, stir well and pour in the wine, lower the heat and cook until the wine starts to evaporate, about 10 minutes. Add the tomatoes and about half the stock, cook for a couple of minutes than put all the contents of the pan into a casserole or other ovenproof dish and cook in the oven for approx 2 hours. Check about every half hour and if it is drying out add some more stock , the aim is to cook the meat but retain a good quantity of sauce, the meat should be cooked to the point where it is really tender and falling apart. Cook Pappardelle or other wide ribbon pasta, mix with the sauce and serve with freshly grated Parmigiano Reggiano cheese.

Wild boar sausage can be used in a variety of ways. It is easy to roast, sauté, and grill or remove it from the casing and crumble to use in the same way as bulk sausage to make a stuffing. Most cooks I know saute onions, sausage and celery to combine with 4 cups of a seasoned stuffing mix, following the package directions. Adding apples and sage after the sausage is cooked.

In the United States, there are free-ranging Wild Boar humanely harvested from all over South Texas and the Texas Hill Country with local producers selling various cuts of meat. These animals feed on wild berries, nuts, roots and other natural vegetation and are said to be very flavorful.

A shop in Umbria that sold wild boar meat

Chapter 13 Cooking in Emilia

The food of Emilia Romagna is legendary. *Ragu´ alla Bolognese*, the quintessinal Italian meat sauce was born here. Eating a *ragu´* in Emilia is not to be missed when traveling through this region of Italy. It only takes one bite of an authentic *Bolognese Ragu´* to know that you are miles away from the jarred red sauces on the grocery store shelves. It is often duplicated but seldom replicated with the same flavors as in Italy. *Cappellacci* is another regional favorite. The ring-like triangular pasta with a point gets its name from the shape of a hat worn in medieval times and is delicious served *al burro e salvia* with a butter and sage sauce. The *tortelli con zucca*, favored by the Mantuan Court of the Gonzaga, filled with pumpkin, Mantovan mostarda (spiced jam) and crushed amaretti cookies are sublime. Lucrezia Borgia's hair is said to have been the inspiration for the origin of *tagliatelle*, another legendary pasta whose ribbon like strands are perfectly suited to pair with the rich sauces of Emilia Romagna. Pasta lore has it that this famous pasta from Emilia Romagna was "invented" on the occasion of the marriage between Alfonso d'Este and Lucrezia Borgia. The duke's cook dedicated his creation to the bride, enriching the pasta dough with eggs, making it softer and glossier with a few drops of oil, then cutting it into narrow strips "like the long blond tresses of her hair". So when I was invited to cook in the Emilian kitchens of Castello Gropparello near Piacenza with my friend Rita, the current owner, I jumped at the chance. Castello Gropparello is part of the itinerary of the *Strada dei Vini e dei Sapori piacentini,* wine and flavor routes of Piacenza in Emilia Romagna. These gastronomic itineraries can be found throughout Italy and allow you to get up close and personal with the authentic food and wines of a particular region. Seeing and savoring Italy can be no better.

One of the most ancient strongholds of its area, Castello Gropparello still preserves the fascination of a medieval fortress and the fantasy of a fairy tale. At first you are attracted to the rugged beauty of the landscape that surrounds the castle with origins that go back to the VIII century where you can experience history and fables, take part in medieval jousting tournaments and perhaps catch sight of fairies, pixies, elves and druids. But Gropparello Castle is more than a place for those seeking medieval adventures and childhood fantasies. The gastronomic festivals and exceptional regional dishes prepared in the Castle's Medieval Taverna reflect the great heritage of Emilia Romagna cooking at its best. Rita and I would cook a *modiovalo taverna* menu typical of Piacentini cuisine to be served with wines from the cellars of Castello Gropparello. *Colli Piacentina* wines including a lush red 2005 Mont'Arquato Duca di Ferro (Iron Duke) Gutturnio Riserva DOC were to be paired with baked stuffed vegetables, *maltagliati* pasta with zucchini and pine nuts, *faraona* (guinea fowl) with olives and a Piacenza tart with plum jam. Quite an ambitious menu but I was in good hands. Rita, Chiara (her daughter) and their staff soon had me feeling like I was back in Nonna's kitchen being shown the way of the Italian Jedi. Rita helped me understand the mysteries of Italian pasta; you need to use the right flour (0 durum wheat flour), make a mountain (the flour) with a fountain (the eggs, oil and water) in the middle and mix by hand. I learned to brown the garlic with the skins on in butter and oil to flavor the zucchini ragu´, to use whole rosemary sprigs when sautéing the *faraona* and the

113

proper way to fold and cut the pasta dough to make *tagliatelle*. But something else happened to me that September afternoon in the kitchens of Gropparello. I remembered that there is more than cooking that happens in an Italian kitchen. There is a spirit of conviviality, joy and a sincere desire to preserve and transmit the cultural heritage of Italy through food. The food in Italy still defines a people with a tradition of good eating and there are still many Italians who want to take the time and effort to make the food they eat meaningful. So the kitchen becomes a study in good eating where traditions are passed down from one generation to another and a way of cooking is taught that brings families and friends together at the table. That is one of the reasons why cooking in Emilia was such a memorable experience. The warm and gracious hospitality of Rita and her staff, the totally delicious food, the evocative atmosphere of the Castle and the countryside are what create the magic of Castello Gropparello. And if by chance you see a pixie, druid, wizard or witch well all the better. I absolutely love this place and want to return to experience more.

One of the most flavorful ways of enjoying Emilian pasta is in a bowl of steaming broth. Not a weak watery hint of a taste of bouillon but a rich concentration of flavors resulting from a long and gentle simmering of vegetables, meats and the bones of chicken or beef. These broths or *brodo* (in Italian) are the basis for many Italian dishes including *risotto* but they also are the vessel for pastas such as *cappelleti,* a smaller version of *cappellacci* or *tortellini* made with a meat and cheese filling and served with a capon broth. Marcella Hazan, the doyenne of Italian cooking describes the best Italian *brodo*

114

as being "light bodied and soft spoken helping the dishes of which it is a part to taste better". This is surely true of the *brodo* of Emilia Romagna which has brought many a famous chef to their knees. Some brodos in Italy grow up to be bollitos and become part of a legendary Emilia Romagnan dish known as *bollitto misto.* Although not confined to this region of Italy, *bollitto misto* is typical of Bologna, Modena and Parma. Because of the heartiness of this dish it is often eaten during the cooler months and is a popular Italian "comfort food". A *Bollitto Misto* (mixed boiled meat platter) is meat in a *brodo* that has developed from a slowly simmered boil of various cuts of meat; beef, chicken and others and may include veal breast, a beef tongue and ham. *Cotechino*, an Italian pork sausage, a specialty of Modena, is also part of this dish but it is boiled separately and served alongside the *bollitto.* Even if the *bolitto* is made according to another regional recipe (there are versions of this dish associated with the Milanese and it is also very popular in Piedmonte), the meat is often eaten with a *mostarda,*an Italian *condimento* from Cremona or Modena in Emilia Romagna.

It's only natural that taste travelers In Italy often want to attend a cooking school. Combining a cooking class with a taste and travel trip to Italy is like icing on a *torta*. There are many cooking schools in Italy to choose from. A recent Google search resulted in 1,410,000 hits with vivid pictures of mouthwatering pasta paired with ruby red wines and decadent desserts located in villas and Tuscan farmhouses "immersing" you into the *d'arte della cucina* of Italy. Culinary vacations and gastronomic adventures are becoming the trip d'jour as travelers search for more than than a three hour tour. But hands on

115

can sometimes mean hands off and you may be one of the many, rather than one of few, in a stage-designed kitchen more suitable to the Food Network. So what do you look for when you want to combine traveling, eating and cooking in Italy. Look for an evocative site where you can imagine the history of the food being prepared and eaten. Incorporate the experience of cooking into the experience of traveling. Choose to prepare a particular type of food unique to the region to bring home an "edible souvenir" of recipes to share with your family and friends. Unless you are a professional chef, let discussions on techniques, ingredients and equipment be a sidebar to the fun, creativity and conviviality of the moments spent in the kitchen. To do this find a one or two day class during the middle of your travels after you have had a chance to spend some time in country. Choose a class that provides accommodations on site or nearby so that after a day in the kitchen you can relax at the table and comfortably retire. Don't expect to remember every detail of the preparation of the food, there usually are printed recipes with instructions that you will take home. Take plenty of pictures. This is something you are going to want to remember.

See and Savor More

There are two Corsi di Cucina that I attend and work with on my taste and travel trips to Italy, one in Emilia Romagna and one in Tuscany. You can e-mail pam@cositutti.com for more information.

Here is the menu I prepared at Castello Gropparello with Rita. It includes foods typical of Piacentini cuisine and was served with wines from the castle cellars.

il Menu

Baked Stuffed Vegetables

*Maltagliati with Zucchini and Pine Nuts

Faraona (Guinea Fowl) with Olives

Piacenza Tart with Plum Jam

Colli Piacentina 2005 Mont'Arquato Duca di Ferro (Iron Duke) Gutturnio Riserva DOC Wine

Pasta drying in the kitchens of Castello Gropparello

Chapter 14 Milanese Gold

The Milanese gold I'm referring to is not found in the chic boutiques and designer shops of the *Quadrilatero d' Oro,* Milan's high fashion shopping district but rather in the home style cooking of Milanese housewives that has been handed down from one generation to another. The sophisticated reputation of the industrial North would lead you to believe that the cooking of Milan is very haute cuisine. Yet the foods of Versace and Prada, Missoni and Fendi are grounded in the same *casalinga* "home style" cooking found throughout Italy, cooking that is simply done and locally interpreted.

The classic dish that is the gold standard for Milanese cooking is *risotto.* When prepared as it should be, the creamy yet toothsome flavor of *Risotto alla Milanese* is without equal. The rich alluvial soil along the lower plains of the Po River in Lombardia produce some of the finest rice in the world and the type of *riso* (rice) grown there is perfect for making *risotto.* Arborio and Carnaroli rice are cultivated in the Po Valley and both are used to make *risotto.* However because Carnaroli rice retains liquid, holds its shape better and has a larger grain it is preferred over Arborio. In fact it has been said that Carnaroli rice will turn any amateur cook into a great chef. With the addition of saffron (*zafferano),* the rice from the plains of the Po becomes perhaps one of the best examples of Milanese cuisine that can be found in the world. Today there are hundreds of variations of Italian rice dishes with a book written entitled the <u>Top 100 Italian Rice Dishes</u> with riffs on the classic *risotto* that includes recipes for Rose Petal Risotto and Champagne Risotto. Even in Italy the *vecchio risotto*

Milanese (old version of the recipe) has been updated or enhanced with the addition of pork sausage, mushrooms, truffles and seafood. In the Silver Spoon cookbook (*il cucchiaio d'argento*), Italy's most successful cookbook often referred to as the bible of authentic Italian cooking and the Betty Crocker Cookbook of Italy, there are recipes for Blueberry Risotto, Carrot Risotto, Black, Green and Strawberry Risotto!

I'm often asked if any other rice can be used to make a risotto? According to my Italian family and friends, the best rice for making risotti is an Arborio or Carnaroli and if you are from Verona or Mantua, Vialone Nano. These types of rice are well balanced with good absorption and low loss of starch, qualities necessary to make a good risotto. Rice used to make risotto has a 'pearl' in the center of the grain. During cooking the outside starch of the rice grain is released and dissolves into the liquid and the interior absorbs the liquid and swells. Other types of rice do not behave like this and quickly become sticky. Risotto should never be gluey; it is always moist and creamy with a slight *al dente* bite. In Italy risotto is served as a *primi* (first course) alone on individual plates or a shallow bowl. Eat the risotto around the edges of your plate first so as to keep the mounded center hot to enjoy each bite.

In Milano *osso buco*, braised veal shank, is traditionally served with *Risotto Milanese*. The Milanese prepare *osso buco in bianco*, without tomatoes seasoned with cinnamon, allspice and a bay leaf. At the end, the dish is finished with a *gremolata* (*gremalada* in Milanese) a mixture of Italian parsley, garlic and grated lemon peel. Tuscan style

119

osso buco, Ossibuchi alla Toscana, is made with tomatoes. There is also a version from Piedmonte which may be the second best place to eat *Osso Buco* because of the full bodied red wines of the region that pair well with this dish.

My visits to Milano will invariably begin with a *risotto* and end with a *cotoletta alla Milanese*, a panned breaded veal cutlet fried in clarified butter. Sometimes referred to as *costoletta alla Milanese*, this dish presents itself as a simple yet sublime interpretation of Milanese cooking. With a history that dates to the 12th century, the success of this dish depends on the quality of the meat and in Italy that means milk feed veal. A *cotoletta* is a tasty crunchy cutlet, made from a veal chop and a typical *secondo* (second course) at the Northern Italian table. A true *cotoletta* is made with the rib bone attached but there are variations including the "elephant ear" *cotoletta a orrechio di elefante*. In this version the bone is removed and the meat is pounded very thin before it is lightly breaded and cooked. It is huge and often fills the plate.

I first learned to cook *risotto alla Milanese* from my mother in law, Marian by way of her mother in law, Epifania. Epifania, our *Nonna*, was from a town in Northern Italy on the border between Lombardia and the Veneto with her extended family living in Milano. In this part of Italy rice was favored over pasta and because France dominated this region of Italy for many years, you will find butter as the primary cooking fat. Both are used to make *risotto.* At the time, these women would not have been thought of as gourmet chefs although the food they prepared is now being served by top chefs in upscale

120

restaurants. When Nonna passed away she was 89 years old. She had no inheritance to speak of, no strong box full of stocks and bonds, no vacation homes or lavish jewelry. What I received was a small lined notebook of family recipes, a gastronomic treasure chest that included a recipe that has been described by food historian Waverly Root as a "preparation which seems to be made of grains of gold". A legacy of food and family that after all is said and done proved more valuable and long lasting. Molto grazie, Nonna.

See and Savor More

The iconic Silver Spoon Cookbook, *Il Cucchiaio d'argento* has sold over 2 million copies since it was first published in 1950 and contains over 2,000 traditional recipes. Published by *Editoriale Domus*, this cookbook is said to be a true representation of what everyday Italians like to eat both at home and when dining out. There are 11 pages dedicated to the cooking of *risotto*.

My Family Recipe for *Risotto alla Milanese alla Nonna e Maria*n requires time and attention. Think of it as the Diana Ross method of cooking as in the old school song "You Can't Hurry Love". Well you can't hurry a *risotto*. For a perfectly prepared *risotto* you will need a large (4-6 qt) heavy based pot sturdy enough to stand up to the constant stirring required to make a classic *risotto*. An enamel or non stick finish will prevent the *risotto* from sticking while it cooks. Sauté 1 large onion finely chopped in about 5 T of melted unsalted butter in the pot (you can use part butter and part extra virgin olive oil). After the onion is softened and has taken on a golden color add 2 cups of risotto rice. Nonna used arborio rice but also carnaroli when she

121

could get it. Stir rice into butter, onion mixture until thoroughly coated but not brown. The "pearl" in the center of the rice becomes more apparent as the rice cooks meaning you are ready to slightly increase the heat and add 1 glass of white wine (Nonna never measured anything but most recipes take this to mean about ¾ cup to 1 cup), stirring the *risotto* as the wine is being absorbed. Some chefs believe the wine should be warmed as cold wine will shock the rice and it will flake on the outside and stay hard at the core. Nonna never refrigerated her wine so it was always at room temperature. A pinch of saffron can be added at this time or it can be infused in 6 cups of chicken broth that has been simmering on the stove in another pan. The saffron will give the *risotto milanese* its classic golden color. Some cooks add the saffron just before the end of the cooking process in order to maintain its delicate flavor. At this point you will begin to slowly add the simmering chicken broth to the *risotto*, a ladleful at a time (about ½ cup at a time) and cook the *risotto* over medium heat stirring constantly until it has absorbed the added broth. When the broth has been absorbed, add another ladleful and repeat the process (towards the end you may only need to add ¼ cup of the broth at a time). Continue like this until the rice can absorb no more. Add most of the liquid at the beginning to avoid an overcooked *risotto*. When is the *risotto* done? When the rice is of a creamy consistency yet the grains remain separate and al dente to the taste. Different types of rice vary in the way they absorb the liquid so Nonna would say "just keep stirring until it is done". Every *risotto* will be slightly different. But remember, you will be adding a handful of grated cheese and a pat of butter at the very end. The cheese will thicken up the *risotto* a little so don't allow all the moisture to be absorbed or you

122

will have a paste. Cheese should be a grated *grana* cheese such as Parmigiano Reggiano or Grana Padano.

There is a very nice recipe for *Costoletta alla Milanese* in The Silver Spoon Cookbook. *Costoletta* means "little rib" in Italian because the meat is taken from the rib chop. There are many variations of this including using a pork cutlet but the classic dish is always simply prepared with the meat dipped in milk, then eggs, then breadcrumbs sautéing the chop in melted butter in a frying pan until a golden brown crust forms and the meat is pink on the inside.

Chapter 15 Has Anyone Ever Eaten Peacock?

One day as I was reading my hometown newspaper I came across the reader's Q and A section where someone asked the unlikely question "Does Anyone Know if Peacock Tastes Good"? I looked at it with some trepidation not knowing whether to reply. Answering it might have caused people to think I was part of some underground gourmet society like Brando and Broderick in the film <u>The Freshman</u>. But as a matter of fact I knew the answer to the question and the answer was "I do"!

On a recent trip to Italy, visiting our Italian cousins, we ate peacock at a friend's house in Treviso, a Northern Italian city located in the Veneto. In Italy peacock is called *pavone* and prepared similar to pheasant. It was a Sunday afternoon and we were served a wonderful meal that lasted 4 hours at the country home of an Italian book editor who raised peacocks on his property. When we drove up to the *fattoria* (farm), that looked more like a villa, there were peacocks roaming the grounds. Little did I know they would be part of the afternoon meal. The meal consisted of several courses including a *brodo* make of peacock with *nidi d'amore,* little love nests of pasta filled with ground veal floating in the broth. This was followed by braised peacock, then goose and an Italian style meat loaf. *Fantastici.* The *pavone* meat was served on the bone and the legs were quite large, much bigger than a turkey. The meat was dark and very flavorful and did not taste gamey at all. In the beginning we were not told that we were eating peacock. I suppose our hosts weren't quite sure how *gli americani* would react.

In Italy there is a culinary tradition of eating of all types of birds and although chickens, hens, capons and partridges were more commonly found at the table, eating peacock although not unheard of was reserved for the cultural elite. Served at lavish Renaissance banquets or at the dining tables of 16th century cardinals and popes, peacock was a popular center of the plate item among the aristocracy. The Italian scholar and cookbook author Platina, who dined with the Gonzagas in Renaissance Mantua, described peacock as "more suitable to the table of kings and princes than the lowly and men of little property". Bartolomeo Scappi (1500-1577), *cuoco segreto*, private cook, to five pontiffs mentions roasted peacock as one of his favorite recipes often prepared with an extravagant use of spices. Once cooked, he suggests that the bird be reassembled with metal rods and have its feathers reattached *come se fosse vivo,* "as if it were still alive" for a spectacular display. The elaborate, ancient and eccentric preparations of peacock make eating it seem decadent and disturbing. Yet I felt neither during that meal in Treviso. It all seemed very natural and rustic and homey, sharing in the bounty of the family farm at the table with my Italian family and friends.

The kindness and hospitality of our hosts lasted long into the day. After dinner we were taken on a personal tour of Treviso. We walked through the streets of the city on a rainy autumn afternoon with colorful umbrellas to see the canals and *pescheria*, city fish market. Situated on a small islet in the middle of *Canale Cagnan*, the market is connected to the rest of the city by two small bridges. Fishermen still bring their fresh catch to the open air stalls of the market to be sold daily. Treviso is hidden treasure of the Veneto and if you are

125

taste traveling in the area should not be missed. It is only about an hour drive from Venice whose historical influence is still seen in the art and architecture of the city and in its food. Ancient Venetian walls still surround the city where the typical regional cuisine of Venice is enhanced by vegetables from the farmlands of Treviso including the red wine colored, white ribbed lettuce, *Radicchio Rosso di Treviso*. A protected agricultural product given IGP (*Indicazione Geografica Protetta*) status, *Radicchio Rosso di Treviso* can only be sold as such if it is produced around Treviso, under the supervision of the *Consorzio Radicchio di Treviso*. Often served in Italy as part of the antipasto or as an *insalata* after the main course, *radicchio's* characteristic bitterness is said to stimulate the appetite and digestive system and acts as a tonic for the blood and liver.

When we returned to the table later that afternoon we were treated to a wonderful selection of sweets and confections typical of the region and original poetry written by our host's son, Simone. It was difficult not to feel as if you were sitting at the table of Renaissance kings and princes with the food, wine and company of this wonderful family from Treviso. I have come to find that sitting at the tables of Italy makes everyone feel like a king or a prince. The Italian view of eating and the care and preparation of their food has always focused on making the experience of dining special whether at a *festa*, local *ristorante* or around the kitchen table at the end of the day. As unique and unforgettable as the experience of eating *pavone* was, the most memorable part of the day was sharing it with my Italian friends from Treviso. If you were wondering whether I answered the Q and A question in my hometown newspaper? I did. Did they publish it? No.

126

Chapter 16 The Chocolate Valley

The gastronomic geography of Italy seems to have an underlying aroma and flavor of chocolate. The taste of chocolate can be found on the lips of Italians from Perugia to Torino into the Chocolate Valley of Tuscany where chocolatiers like Venchi, Slitti and Amedei pair tradition with innovation to create unique chocolates that rival any Super Tuscan wine. There is a Capital of Chocolate in the Umbrian town of Perugia where chocolate festivals draw crowds from all over the world. Past EuroChocolate Festivals have featured chocolate sculptures made from blocks of Perugina chocolate weighing 1,100 kilos each and a unique chocolate tasting session in a totally dark environment to "experience the sound, fragrance, shape, and taste of chocolate from another point of view" was a popular attraction at a recent festival. And in the city of Torino you can buy a Chocopass, a set of coupons that allows you two days to indulge your chocolate fantasies at over twenty participating shops and cafes. You'll be able to taste the famous Giandujotti, a rich velvety chocolate confection of cocoa paste and Piedmonte hazelnuts launched as the first paper wrapped chocolate candy in 1865 at the Carnival of Turin and since acclaimed as the finest chocolate candy in existence. Taste travelers to Tuscany's Chocolate Valley between Florence and Pisa can visit the laboratories and workshops of artisan chocolatiers like Mannori and Bettazzi in Prato, Catinari in Agliana, Corsini in Pistoia, Cioccolato & Co. in Massa Cozzile, Slitti in Monsummano Terme, Amedei in Pontedera, De Bondt and Salza in Pisa. They are all capital points on the map of Northern Italy's chocolate itinerary. These artisan chocolate makers take the concept of seeing and savoring Italy to another level.

 Like a fine wine and extra virgin olive oil the chocolates of Tuscany are defined by the *terroir* of the region, a sense of place that imparts a unique quality to a product. Wine and chocolate are natural companions. Both have complex flavors, similar components and subtle nuances. Both are meant to complement each other and like any good relationship both contribute to your good health. But as in any good relationship you have to pair them carefully to get the most out of the match. Generally lighter chocolates go well with lighter wines; darker chocolates with full-bodied wines. The flavor profiles of Italian chocolate are limited only by the imagination of the chocolatier. Chocolate beans (typically from South America or Africa) take on the flavors of Tuscan lavender, olive oil, aged *aceto balsamico* vinegar and rosemary to make artisan chocolates that capture the spirit and soul of Tuscany. I admit I'm under the influence of Italian chocolate as I'm writing this chapter and my endorphins are at a fever pitch but indulge my chocolate fantasy a little further as I tell you the story of another famous Italian chocolate from the town of Perugia, the Chocolate Capital of Italy, where the aroma of chocolate has been wafting over the ancient Umbrian hills for 80 years. The Italian devotion and commercial success of the Peugina Chocolate Company may have to do as much with the history of their most popular chocolate, the Baci Kiss as with the taste of their chocolates. Both capture the imagination. The story of the Baci Kiss began with a secret love affair and a chocolate confection created by an Italian chocolatier named Luisa Spagnoli. In 1907 Spagnoli created a

128

whipped chocolate candy blended with chopped hazelnuts, coated in dark chocolate. Her creation, originally called *cazzotti* (little punch), was later renamed Baci (meaning "kiss "in Italian). The candy was said to have been inspired by a love affair with her business partner. To hide their secret affair from her husband Spagnoli used the wrappings of the candy to write love notes. Baci kisses continue to be wrapped with poetic love notes, now in a signature silver foil with blue stars, and contain a romantic transparent love note in four languages. Poetic sayings such as "*con Baci non servono parole*" "*with kisses words are unnecessary"* were to become the language of romance and Perugina the chocolate of choice for generations of Italians. You can visit the Perugina Chocolate Factory and Museo Storico (historical museum) in San Sisto near Perugia. English speaking tours are available and my Umbrian friends, the Corneli family, were kind enough to arrange a tour of the factory when I last visited them. Admission is free and begins with a short video. But it's easy to get distracted by the scent of chocolate and you soon find yourself following an enthusiastic guide along an elevated walkway that looks down on the factory. Kids and adults were mesmerized by the process and Ethan, a 4 year old taste traveler in our group was heard to say "That's a lot of chocolate" as we watched chocolate being made with Willie Wonkonian precision that rivaled any Hollywood set. There were no "umpa lumpas" but it's still fascinating to see how the chocolates are processed, poured and molded into the most imaginative of shapes. From the late 1950's to the mid 1970's Italian TV commercials often featured Perugina chocolates during what was called *Carosello*, or carousel. At about 8:45pm Italian TV viewers looked forward to a 10 minute commercial segment that was more

129

like a mini variety show or cartoons than hard sell advertising. A whole generation of Italian children knew it was almost bedtime when *Carosello* came on theTV. Vintage Carosello commercials advertising Perugina chocolates are shown during tours of the Perugina Chocolate Factory. It is great fun to see what Italians were watching on TV back then. Take some time to let the Perugina experience imprint in your chocolate memory because photographs are not allowed at the Perugina Chocolate Factory. Your time spent there is best preserved in the chocolates you can buy at the factory store. Perugina chocolate is now part of Nestlé European.

Chocolate is never far from the hearts and minds of the Italians. They like chocolate, pure and simple. In fact Italians care so much about the purity of ingredients that the AIDI (Italy's Confectioners Association) has taken issue with the EU's permits for chocolate to contain certain percentages of vegetable oils, like palm oil, to substitute for the more expensive cocoa butter. Mario Piccialuti, Director of AIDI defiantly stating that for "Italians this is NOT pure chocolate but a chocolate-like substance and should be labeled accordingly." Italians also like their chocolate frothy hot, with sparkling wine or made into all manner of whimsical shapes like the cocoa dusted chocolate "rusty tools" made by the gifted chocolatier, Andrea Slitti. Slitti's signature "rusty tools "are solid chocolate (56% cocoa) dusted in cocoa powder to give a rusty effect. They also like their chocolate dusted on pastries like tiramisu, Italy's most famous dessert. Tiramisu is said to have originated in 17th century Siena. A confection similar to *tiramisu (tih-ruh-mee-SOO)* was first created for Cosimo de' Medici III, the Grand Duke of Tuscany. The duke so favored the creamy, pudding-like layered desert that he took the recipe back to Florence where it was called *zuppa del duca,* the "dukes soup". However my friends from the Veneto region of Italy tell me that the perfection of this dessert happened much later, in the 1970's, when a restaurant in Treviso began making the classic *tiramisu*; using finger shaped sponge cakes known as *savoiardi* (ladyfingers) soaked in espresso (sometimes Marsala wine) and layered with a mascarpone-zabaglione cream then dusted with bittersweet chocolate. One may have morphed into the other and the truth may be somewhere in between (the "dukes soup" may actually have become *zuppa inglese* which was similar to an English trifle) but no matter. *Tiramisu* was the first Italian dessert I sought out on my first trip to Italy. It was my goal to experience *tiramisu* whenever and where ever I could, in restaurants, in friend's homes, from the local *pasticcerria.* I did and the meaning of *tiramisu* ("pick me up") was never truer as I took bite after bite.

See and Savor More

Glandulotti, also known as *gianduia* (jon-du-ja) is a specialty of Torino in the Piedmont region of Northern Italy. It takes its name from *Gianduja* a popular character from *Commedia dell'arte*, a type of improvisational comedy developed in Italy in the 16th and 17th centuries.

In 2006, Italian writer and broadcaster Bruno Gambarotta wrote a comic gastro-thriller entitled *Il codice Gianduiotto*, the Gianduiotti Code, about the mysteries of the secret formula for *Gianduitto*. The novel, published by Morganti Editori is a parody of the bestselling novel, the <u>Da Vinci Code</u>.

Chefs from Piedmonte, Lombardia, Venice and Tuscany all claim to have invented *tiramisu*. Even the Romans who are outside the region of origin take credit for it as "all roads lead to Rome". Even though a classic *tiramisu* is made with a *zabaglione* custard (a very old recipe from the Veneto), food historians believe *tiramisu,* as we know it, to have been invented in the 1970's at a restaurant called *Le Beccherie*, in the town of Treviso in northern Italy. Culinarily, *tiramisu* is considered a *semifreddo* (a dessert served cold, but not frozen). Although now prepared in an infinite number of ways, a classic *tiramisu* is made with ladyfingers soaked in strong espresso coffee, with a mascarpone-zabaglione cream and bitter cocoa powder. As in all Italian food, the success of a good *tiramisu* depends on the quality of ingredients. The original shape of *tiramisu alle Beccherie* was round and in the traditional *tiramisu* there is no alcohol because it was served to "children and the elderly." Today Marsala wine or rum is often added to the mix. Most Italian cookbooks will have a recipe for *tiramisu.* I like a recipe from Lorenza De Medici that uses Vin Santo in place of Marsala wine. You can also line a custard glass or goblet with the savioardi (ladyfingers) rather than use a bowl and this makes a nice presentation. Be sure to use mascarpone cheese and strong Italian espresso coffee as there is no substitute for the flavor these ingredients bring to the classic *tiramisu*.

WINE

Chapter 17 Sideways Through Italy

I'm no wine expert. I'll leave the ratings and analyses, annotations and reviews to the Robert Parker, Jrs and Andrea Zimmers. My rating system is more in tune with the number of glasses I like to drink than the number of points on a scale of 50-100. I don't suppose to know everything there is about Italian wines. That I'll leave to Batali and Bastianich. But like most of us, I know what I like and over the last 10 years and 10,000 miles eating, traveling, cooking, shopping and drinking in Northern Italy, Tuscany and Umbria I've come to experience and learn some things about regional Italian wines. I've traveled *le strade dei vini e sapori*, the regional wine and food routes that criss cross Northern Italian, Tuscany and Umbria Italian to taste and tour artisan producers who handcraft their products with a heartfelt passion and respect for the land and its traditions. I've sat at the tables of my Italian family and friends for some memorable meals made even more so by the wine that was served. I've come to understand that Italians think of wine as a natural resource, a companion to food, a link to the ancient past and a tradition to be preserved. I've learned that the best wines in Italy are not always called "Super" nor are they the most expensive and that every time you drink a glass of wine in Italy you taste a part of history.

According to Alexis Lichine, wine authority and writer of the first encyclopedic guide to wine and spirits "the best way to learn about wine is the drinking". I could not agree with him more. Year

133

after year as I travel to Italy, my taste for wine becomes more refined because I AM TASTING MORE WINE. If you are interested in learning more about wine, you must study about wine, surround yourself with people and places that know about fine wine and taste more wine and there is no better place to do this than in Italy. The gift of the grape has been part of the cultural landscape of Italy since the time of the Etruscans. Vine cultivation and vinification have been part of the psyche of the Italian people for almost 3,000 years. Frescoes found in Etruscan tombs show people drinking and enjoying wine. Artifacts found at Monte Bibile, an Etruscan-Celtic site near Monterezio, south of Bologna, show evidences of wine and the growing of grapes. Excavations near the site have uncovered houses and warehouses with remains of wine amphora and by the 1st century BC vast agricultural estates of grapes and olives produced wine and oil for trade. Today vineyards still cover the hillsides and Italy is the largest producer and exporter of wines in the world.

Wine and food go hand in hand in Italy. *L'abbinamento*, "the match" is the word Italians use for the happy marriage of Italian food and wine. One completes the other and both enhance each other. Wine is an essential part of the culinary experience of eating Italian. What would a Chianina *bistecca* be without a Brunello or Vin Nobile, a plate of Tuscan salumi without a Chianti or the Sud-Tyrolean food from Italy's Trentino Alto Adige without a Teroldego? I hardly know where to stop the two are so deeply connected, connected by the geography of the region and by the history, culture, climate and the creativity of the Italian people. Italian wine is a pleasure to drink, full of character and authentic to the region in which it is produced. Is it little wonder that an

134

Italian meal would be incomplete without wine? In their book <u>Vino Italian</u>, Joseph Bastianich and David Lynch admit that getting to know Italian wine takes some doing saying that"from the top to the tip of the boot there are more than three hundred officially delimited wine zones (California, by contrast, has around eighty) and hundreds of different grape varieties". I don't remember every wine I've ever had in Italy although I do have a wine stained notebook that I turn to from time to time. What I do remember are snapshots of memories when an experience was transformed by a singular moment that tasted of wine. All the more reason for traveling "sideways" through Italy and if by chance you find yourself on a journey of self discovery as the characters did in the movie then so be it for it has been said in wine there is truth.

Here are some of the most memorable wines I've tasted eating and drinking at the tables of my Italian family and friends and at *trattorie, ristoranti, enoteche*, vineyards and farms throughout Northern Italy, Tuscany and Umbria. Almost every one of them resulted in a mini journey of discovery.

Chianti Classico

Elizabeth Barrett Browning after living in Italy was inspired to write "the sun with a golden mouth can blow blue bubbles of grapes down a vineyard row". The idyllic landscape of Tuscany she described attracts wine lovers from all over the world. Although not the largest or most productive wine growing region in Italy, it is the most recognized and for this reason a recommended starting point to discover Italian wine. The Chianti region of Tuscany was delimited as a wine territory in 1716 by decree of the Medici Grand Duke Cosimo III. Today the ancient area of production is referred to as Chianti Classico and has its own official DOCG appellation. That means wine labeled as Chianti Classico has a "controlled denomination of origin" with government regulations that guarantee the origin and quality of the wine including what grape varieties can be used in the making of the wine, where the grapes are grown and how and where the wine is produced. Government testers analyze color, aroma, flavor and sugar and examine and taste the wines prior to bottling before awarding the DOCG status. The wine must be sold in containers smaller than 5 liters and the bottles are often numbered with a "state mark" or colored strip placed over the capsule or cork to guarantee origin and quality. Chianti Classico wines will have a special emblem printed on the wine label, the Black Rooster (*Gallo Nero*) adopted by the Chianti Classico Wine Consortium that attests to the authenticity of production from vine to bottle. According to the Consortium this emblem symbolizes the territorial rivalries between Florence and Siena who fought over the region in the Middle Ages. In order to cease their endless fighting, it was decided that the boundary between the two Tuscan villages would be determined by a remarkable feat between knights on horseback. Each knight was to leave their respective village when the rooster crowed at dawn and wherever they met each other, that exact spot would be the border between the two republics. For this purpose, the citizens of Siena raised a white rooster which grew big and fat. The Florentines chose a black rooster and never fed him, so that on the fateful day he was so hungry that he started to crow even before sunrise. As a result, the Florentine knight was able to set out very early in the morning. This allowed him to ride a far

136

greater distance and claim a large territory for the city of Florence. As a result, almost all of the Chianti territory was united under the rule of the Florentine Republic due to a starved rooster.

Follow the way of the Black Rooster, *le strade del Gallo Nero*, by car, down SS222 through the ancient hill towns of Gaiole, Radda, Castellina and Greve in Chianti towards Montelpulciano. The first road trip I ever took through Italy and my first experience tasting the wines of Chianti was along SS222 (Strada Statale 222). On our way from Florence to Siena, we drove the winding *Via Chiantigiana* in my cousin Lidia's Fiat for about 150km one September with the vineyards of Chianti Classico lying on both sides and the Black Rooster leading me on to Greve. Greve is the chief town of the Chianti Classico wine zone and the home of Chianti's largest wine fair held every September. *Le Cantine di Greve* is a good if somewhat touristy place to get an overview of the wines of the region. You can also taste food products, cheese (they have a slick little machine that dispenses an antipasti plate) and olive oils typical of the region as well as tasting some great wines. You purchase a wine card that you insert into various tasting stations that dispense a prescribed amount of wine in your glass. A practical, high tech way of tasting wine in Tuscany and a one stop shop to buy wine. Convenient, yes, but this is no substitute for tasting wine at its source so be sure to schedule a visit to one of the many local vineyards in the area. You can do some advance planning by reading about the wines of Tuscany before your trip. A little pre-trip knowledge about Italian wines will bring a lot to the table and enrich your taste and travel experience. Hugh Johnson's <u>Tuscany and Its Wines</u> is an evocative book with photos and text that will

137

seriously tempt you to book your flight today. Oz Clarkes's <u>Wine Companion Tuscany</u> is a guidebook with a fold out map, lots of facts and suggested wine itineraries. <u>Vino Italiano, The Regional Wines of Italy,</u> by Joseph Bastianich and David Lynch is the bible of Italian wine with recipes by either Mario Batali or Lidia Bastianich that showcase regional foods paired with regional wines. There is a very good section on *La Storia*, the history of Italian wine, that gives a short but concise overview of Italian winemaking that should be required reading for all wine lovers.

The Noble Wines of Tuscany

Chianti and Chianti Classico are not the only wines made in Tuscany. Brunello di Montalcino and Vino Nobile di Montepulciano are destination wines that take you beyond the rolling hills of Chianti into the rugged *crete senesi* south of Siena to the imposing fortress hill towns of Montalcino and Montepulciano where wines were made for Popes and Kings. Montalcino and Montepulciano are the tasting sites for two formidable Italian wines with an international reputation that makes this region more than just a blimp on a wine lover's radar.

Brunello di Montalcino is one of the most expensive and revered wines of Italy. It is very concentrated both in color (intense ruby red maroon color), aroma (perfumed violets and aromatic woods) and flavor (vanilla and fruity jams). DOCG controlled, it must be barrel aged for a minimum of 36 months and one year after bottling before release. Some Brunellos have been cellared for 50 years. If you don't have time to wait for your Brunello to age look for a Rosso di Montalcino, a lighter, younger version that are marketed without the required length of aging. Brunello is at its best when paired with the rustic foods of Tuscany; red meat, wild game, mushrooms, aged cheeses. This wine needs decanting, pouring and swirling to appreciate its character.

Vying for your affection is another great regional Sangiovese wine, Vin Nobile di Montepulciano. The coronation of Vin Nobile dates to 1549 when Sante Lancerio, master of wines to Pope Paul III, called the Nobile of Montepulciano "il *vino perfettissimo da Signori*", the preferred wine of the nobility. The distinctive nature of this wine was admired by Thomas Jefferson and praised by Voltaire in Candide. You can decide if it lives up to its reputation while visiting the walled city of Montepulciano. Vin Nobile di Montepulciano is lighter than a Chianti Classico and on the softer side of Brunello and if the bold tannins of Tuscany need more tempering, try the lighter Rosso di Montepulciano. Don't confuse Montepulciano d'Abuzzo with either of the above. Montepulciano d'Abruzzo is made from the Montepulciano grape, an ancient grape variety from the Abruzzi region of central Italy. The main grape varietal of the wines of Tuscany including Chianti is Sangiovese. Indigenous to Tuscany and of ancient origin, translated it means Blood of Jove (Jupiter). A periodic transfusion of the blood of Jove may be of beneficial as medical experts tell us drinking red wine in moderation may be cardioprotective due to the antioxidants present in the skin and seeds of red grapes.

Not all of the wines I drink with my Italian family and friends can easily be found outside of Italy. Because of their star power these can. When I'm home I look for the Avignonesi wines of Montepulciano.

They are among my favorites including the Super Tuscan "Desiderio" but more about that later. Avignonesi is one of the most ancient wineries in the region with an interesting history. In 1309 Pope Clement V transferred the papal residence from Rome to Avignon France. In 1377 when Gregory XI returned the papacy to Rome some noble families of Avignon left France to follow him. One of the families adopted the Italianized version of the word Avignon to become the Avignonesi. No different than some Italians who left Italy during the early 1900's for America and eliminated rather than added a vowel or two from their family name.

When you are back in the States, keep these wines in mind. They are meant to impress although as with most nobility with a past you would be wise to check references. Many of the Italian white table restaurants in the States have Brunellos and Vin Nobiles on their wine lists. Ask the waiter or sommelier for their recommendation as to vintage and producer. Your friends will certainly be impressed when you order something other than a Chianti especially if you can pronounce Montepulciano (Mon-teh-pull-chee-AH-no).

Designer Tuscans

Not all Italian designers can be found along the fashionable Via Napoleone in Milan centro. Among the vines and marl soils of the Tuscan countryside there is another type of Italian designer. As well known and respected among the world of Italian wines as the fashion designers of Milano, these designer vintners have changed the style of Italian wine making using blends and barrels that would have been unheard of under the more traditional DOC(G) system. With names
140

like Sassicaia, Solaia, Tignanello and Ornellaia a new breed of Tuscan wines, the "Super Tuscans", were introduced to the world and like all great design have made a lasting impression. However the "haute couture" of Italian wine is not without a high price tag, typically in the three figure range and the popularity of these designer wines has resulted in some knock offs. Surprisingly most of the Super Tuscans I have tasted have been in the States and not in Italy. The iconic nature of the Super Tuscans had made them the "it" wines outside of Italy and Italian wine fashionistas were quick to buy and try what they could. These blends were innovative, new and seductive. Characteristics that made them especially appealing to wine lovers in the States. They came from some of Italy's oldest and most respected estate vineyards and winemakers including Piero Antinori whose family has been making wine for more than 600 years. Feeling constrained by the rules of Italian wine making regarding grapes, blending and barrels they sought to interpret the wines of their region in a new way and like most cutting edge designers they were received with mixed emotions. Because of the high price tag their appeal may be limited but they have created a new trend in premium wines that is recognized all over the world. In Italy Super Tuscans are not the only kids on the block and are part of the many not the few great wines you can taste. Italians typically drink their wines to accompany the food of the region and will choose their wines accordingly rather than based on marketing or hype. The Italian palate for both food and wine tends to be traditional but the Italian sense of style is intrigued by the artisan quality of a Super Tuscan wine. Gambero Rosso the Italian equivalent of the Wine Spectator and widely accepted as the authority on Italian wine, routinely awards Tre Bicchieri (three glasses) to many Super

141

Tuscan wines. So if you're looking for the "haute couture" of Italian wine, don't overlook the vineyards of Tuscany for a taste of vin-design. By the way the favorite color of Italian designer wines is *rosso,* red. Tuscany makes a small amount of white, trebbiano being the main grape varietal but the deep ruby red of the wines of Tuscany is the chosen color palate for the innovative designs of the Super Tuscans.

Wine Roads Less Traveled

If you're willing to look for the wine roads less traveled in Tuscany, you can find some truly memorable wines like those among the olive groves and vineyards of Tenuta di Capezzana, a 1600 acre estate farm near the village of Carmignano, northwest of Florence. Olive oil and wine making at Capezzana goes back to the year 804 with a history of families living on the property that included a Medici. Wine produced here is from vines grown in the ancient Medici Barco Reale or "royal property" mentioned in Cosimo de Medici's "*Decreto Motu Proprio*" in 1716. This decree set Italy's first laws establishing boundaries and production standards for quality wines. The historic cellars, Renaissance villa and adjacent farm are now owned by the Contini Bonacossi family.

After visiting the olive orchards and *frantoio* with Benedetta Contini Bonacossi, the principal winemaker at Capezzana, I toured the estate's wine making facility and underground wine cellars. The deep tradition and passion for wine making was palpable. All my senses were engaged in the experience as I was led on a vitners journey from the growing and harvesting of the grapes to the making and cellaring

142

of the wine. The rare character of these wines was born centuries ago but the warm and generous personality of the winemaker is reflected in every bottle of wine at Capezzana. I spent the rest of the afternoon experiencing the hospitality of the Contini Bonacossi family at the table in the dining room of their villa. Beatrice, Benedetta's sister, had a wonderful lunch prepared especially for us. Together with Beatrice's husband and nephew Leone, we ate a Tuscan meal fit for a Medici, tasting the historical Capezzana Carmignano and the younger, lighter Capezzana Barco Reale. Capezzana also makes other wines (Chiaie della Furba is their Super Tuscan Cabernet blend) and an exceptional Vin Santo dessert wine. The behind the scenes look at the *vinsanteria* to see the making of this amber colored "meditation" wine was one of the best experiences I have had seeing and savoring Italy. Besides preserving the historical and vinicultural traditions of Capezzana, the Contini Bonacossi family are curators of a large private collection of paintings, Tuscan Renaissance furniture, ceramics and statues acquired by Alessandro Contini Bonacossi (1878-1955). Exhibited in the Uffizi Gallery in Florence, the collection includes works attributed to Cimabue and Bernini, a large wooden panel by Giovanni del Biondo and paintings by Venetian artists including TIntoretto. Among the paintings is Sassetta's *Madonna della Neve* (Our Lady of the Snows) from the 1420's that depicts a miraculous August snowfall in 352 in Rome where the fallen snow precisely outlined the plans for a church that was to be built on the site that would become Santa Maria Maggiore, one of Rome's major basilicas. The Contini Bonacossi collection at the Uffizi in Florence is regarded as one of the most important known in Europe in this century. It is open to the public on a limited basis or

143

by special arrangement of the Contini Bonacossi family. The art of wine making is but one expression of the creativity of Capezzana. I have already mentioned their exceptional oil and culinary skills but there is another unexpected pleasure within sight of the villa. Among the vineyards and orchards of Capezzana, there is a studio where artist Leone Contini Bonacossi finds inspiration among the vines. Using natural materials he paints and constructs installations where seedlings sprout from trumpet cases and wine sediments (*feccia*) become a medium for multi-paneled polyptych paintings of continuous organic forms reminiscent of Renaissance altarpieces to be found in the cathedrals of nature. Leone frequently travels to New York to participate in exhibitions and has been an artist in residence with the Harlem Studio Fellowship Program NYC. His paintings are truly unique and exceptional as is everything you will experience at Capezzana.

My Cousins Wine

The first wines I drank in Italy were at my cousin's table. They were especially selected by my cousin Lidia's husband Roberto who wanted to celebrate our first trip to Italy. We were to meet a family we had only heard about in a place we had only read about. Yet Nonna's letters and visits had already introduced us and sight unseen we all felt a deep connection because of this. So when Michael and I arrived in Milano for the first time we were welcomed with open arms and a wonderful dinner. The meal was memorable and my first taste of Italy only wetted my appetite for more. The wine served at that meal was a Bonarda Oltrepo Pavese with a deep ruby purple color. It was bright and cheerful with an aroma of violets, a taste of black berries and easy to drink. It was a perfect introduction to *vino italiano* and it still remains a favorite on my wine list. My cousins from Lombardia are very high on the wines of Piedmonte. A Barola, Barbera, Barberesco, Nebbiolo or Lombardian Bonarda is more likely than not to be at the table when we're together. While my cousins from the Veneto favor Valpolicella and of course *prosecco*, the dry *vini spumante,* sparkling Italian wine, from Conegliano and Valdobbiadene in the hills north of Treviso. The name "*prosecco*" can only be applied to wine that is made from *prosecco* grapes grown in this region of Italy. My wine memories of *prosecco* center around two spectacular meals. One along the Brenta Canal in a town called Mira and the other along the Levante di Caorle, an old fishing port on the Adriatic near Venice now a popular seaside resort. On the Brenta we feasted on *scampi giganti alla griglia* (giant grilled shrimp) and other assorted fresh seafood. My cousin Roberto suggested we begin our meal with a glass of prosecco which we did. The crisp, bright taste reminiscent of citrus, herbs and melon with a mere 10.5% alcohol content make *prosecco* a perfect apertivo. Oftentimes in Italy, restaurants will serve a complimentary *prosecco* before a meal. In the Veneto *prosecco* is mixed with vodka and lemon gelato to make an after dinner drink called a *sgroppino* "little unknotter". This frothy fruit sparkler is a perfect *digestivo* to untie any knots in your stomach if you've eaten more than you should which I did at *Da Eugenio Ristorante La Ritrovata* in Caorle. Located near the beach, you can enjoy all manner of seafood in a rustic atmosphere where some of the old *casoni,* straw fisherman's huts, still stand. The menu is seven pages with mouthwatering pictures based entirely on fish; grilled, fried or raw. There were shellfish, crabs,

145

mussels, prawns, squid, clams, sole, sardines, bass and original local favorites like *Rigatoni alla Pescatora* and *Risotto di Mare*. And for dessert there is a *torta polenta,* (sweet polenta cake) typical of the region that is unbelievable. So what kind of wine did we drink with a seafood meal on the Adriatic. Actually I don't remember. My cousins kept ordering the food and wine and one melded into the other in a most agreeable way. It was a wonderful evening with lasting memories. I do remember the wine was white and the wine was good which means if you are taste traveling in Italy you do not need to order a bottle of premium wine at every meal. Italians typically order *il vino della casa (rosso o bianco)*, the wine of the house. It is the preferred wine of the restaurant, typical of the region and well priced In fact I don't think I've ever had a bad *vino della casa* in Italy. Unlike the US, the house wine is not the lesser wine offering on the menu but usually one of the best because it reflects the reputation of the restaurant and the owner only wants to offer his guests the finest he can.

It would be impossible to leave the Veneto without mentioning Venice's most fashionable wine cocktail, *il Bellini di Venezia*. A true Bellini is made with the nectar of white peaches and *prosecco*. Don't confuse *prosecco* with Asti Spumante from Piedmonte. The grapes used to make Asti, another Italian sparkling wine, result in a sweeter wine that is often served as a dessert wine. Do not use champagne when making a Bellini. Champagne will overpower the delicate peach flavor of this drink. The perfect peach puree needed to make a Bellini like they serve at Harry's Bar in Venice is difficult to find in the States. You can order it on line but it is expensive because it is fresh and comes to you frozen packed in dry ice. But you don't need to make a

146

special cocktail or have a special occasion to drink *prosecco*. Star caps on a popular imported brand and the easy to open corks with a string attached on the more traditional bottles encourage you to drink *prosecco* and to enjoy it often.

Another effervescent wine that my cousins introduced me to comes from the Piedmonte and is named after the "*brachetto*" grape grown around the town of Acqui Terme. Brachetto d'Acqui, has been described as a "delicious bottle of silky rose colored bubbles". I first tasted this wine at an afternoon reception in the Milanese apartment of Laura and Luccio and I have loved it ever since. The color of rose petals, it is soft and creamy with hints of wild strawberries, raspberries and roses. This frothy, semisweet lightly sparkling *(frizzante)* wine goes well with dark or bittersweet chocolate and is a wonderful dessert wine with fruit tarts. People love this wine. It is romantic and fun with a low (5.5%) alcohol content that allows you to spend time at the end of a meal or in your *terme* or hot tub and if the evening lingers on pairs well with French toast.

Over the years I've come to taste and enjoy the wines of Piedmonte and Lombardia and find that I tend to seek them out more often than not when I'm back in the States. From the aged Barolo's and Barbaresco's to the "foggy" Nebbiolo (*nebbia* is Italian for fog), whose grapes grow in the mists of fog that roll into the Langhe region of Piedmonte during the fall harvest, I am under the influence of the fruits, florals, spices and rustic flavors these wines seem to capture. And when I'm looking for something a little less complex and a little softer, I look to a Barbera di Alba or Barbera d'Asti.

147

Umbrian Wine

Umbria is one of my favorite regions in Italy and Orvieto one of my favorite Umbrian cities. Two of my friends from Italy grew up here and played on the steps of the Orvieto Duomo. The drive from Tuscany into Umbria past Lake Trasimeno is one of the most picturesque in all of Italy. The town itself sits on the top of a cliff of volcanic tufa in an impressive setting said to be "among the most dramatic in Europe". An ancient city of the Etruscans, with a network of secret underground tunnels, makes Orvieto an intriguing place to visit. The Orvieto Duomo (cathedral) striped in white travertine and green basalt make it a top tourist attraction for those traveling in Umbria and the special nature of the soil makes for some very delicious wine. Most taste travelers know about the white wines of Orvieto. Vinosus, located off the Pizza dell' Duomo, is a wonderfully evocative *enoteca* to sample Umbrian wines and plates of salumi and formaggi typical of the region. The outside terrace across from the cathedral is prime real estate to see and savor Italy. Orvieto Classico, a recognized Italian white wine that once graced the tables of Renaissance popes is among the many wines of the region.

As for me and my Italian friends we prefer a Montefalco Sagrantino. The town of Montefalco, south of Perugia, is less well known than the hilltowns of Tuscany and the wine of the region a little less known in the States and slightly askew in Italy. Vino Italiano writes that "the dense, dark, sappy reds made from the sagrantino (grape) are like nothing else in Italy". My high regard for this wine begins with its introduction. I spent an afternoon with my Umbrian friends, Luca and

Luigi learning about all the wonderful nuances of Umbrian wines over a bottle of Sagrantino and a plate of Umbrian salumi. It was not only an introduction into the world of Italian food and wine but an introduction into Italian culture and living. I may have said this before but it bears saying again, this was "*la dolce vita*" squared. My 'Italian education" was now complete as I basked in the glow of the Umbrian autumn sun gazing into a glass of perfection. The faint aroma of violets and blackberries and the dark garnet nuances swirling in my glass led me into the spicy, warm, full bodied flavor of a wine that some have called the best expression of true Italian wine making. I know that says a lot but believe me you can have an out of body experience drinking this wine in Montefalco.

The Sagrantino grape varietal grows only around the hilltop town of Montefalco and there is very little Sagrantino produced. According to Vino Italiano only about 400 acres of Sagrantino vines are in existence. So if you are fortunate enough to travel to Umbria, open a bottle of Sagrantino and enjoy a very special wine that I first learned about from two very special friends.

Teroldego – The Gold of Tirol
I first tasted this wine in March 2007 on a trip to the Trentino Alto Adige region of Northern Italy. After many years traveling in Italy, my Italian cousins decided that it was about time for me to venture into the Sudtirol. They wanted me to see the Dolomites, visit the Ice Man, eat some Italian/German food and taste Tyrolean Gold. The urban legend surrounding the wine, Teroldego, says that its name is the German dialect for gold of Tirol. Wine texts say that this wine takes

149

its name from the traditional method of cultivation in which the vines are trained on a system of "tirelle" or wire harnesses. I'm going with the urban legend because after I tasted this wine I knew I had struck gold and found another Italian treasure. The king of the Trentino wines, Teroldego Rotaliano has been produced since Roman times. In the glass, the ruby red garnet color of the wine leads you into an extremely aromatic, heady aroma of spices, wild flowers and juicy red fruit. It is low in tannins, very easy to drink and food friendly. Wine critics describe this wine as having an absolute sense of balance when paired with game, meats or cheese. My wine memories of Teroldego include a family dinner at the restaurant of the Hotel Alpino in the Val di Fiemme. The meal was spectacular and the wine exceptional and as with all good wines a classic symbol of regional oenology. This wine is hard to find outside of Italy and can vary in quality. I like Zeni Teroldego Rotaliano.

Dolce Vino

A sweet ending to an Italian meal often includes a sweet wine. If you're traveling in Northern Italy and Tuscany you will most likely meet up with a sparkling lightly sweet Moscato d'Asti or the deep, amber sherry-like Vin Santo. A Tuscan treasure, Vin Santo is an amber colored Italian dessert wine traditionally served with *biscotti di Prato* or *cantucci* from Siena. Vin Santo has a unique taste and texture that is meditative. After all, the name Vin Santo means "wine of the saints". Tasting Vin Santo in Tuscany is an experience not to be missed. Although there are other regions of Italy that produce Vin Santo (the Valle dei Laghi in Trentino and the region around the northern tip of Lago di Garda), Tuscan Vin Santo is considered to be the best. Many Italian dessert wines like Tuscan *Vin Santo* and the rare, sweet, delicate Cinque Terre *Sciacchetra* from Liguria are considered to be *passito* wines, late harvest wines made from grapes that are dried, either on mats or by hanging, until they shrivel into raisins. The flavors, aromas and textures of these wines are sweet and intense and favored by Italians from North to South (Sicily and Sardinia are great producers of sweet *passiti* wines). The *passiti* wines of Emilia Romagna are among my favorites. When I'm in Ferrara I always make time for dinner at La Romantica Ristorante and finish my meal with a glass of *Albana di Romagna Passito.* It can only be described as luscious. A wine that so impressed Galla Placida, daughter of the Eastern Roman Emperor Theodosius II, that when offered a terracotta jug of the sweet wine from Albana, she remarked, "You should not drink this wine in such a humble container. Rather it should be drunk in gold to render homage to its smoothness." I knew Galla Placida appreciated earthly delights when I visited her tomb in Ravenna. Looking at the vaulted deep midnight blue ceiling of the tiny mausoleum shimmering in gold covered with stars and flowers, she must have wanted to surround herself with the beauty and goodness of nature even in death. The "most pius and eternal Empress" was carried off and held hostage by the Visigoth Alaric during the sack of Rome in 410. She was later returned and continued to reign until her death in 450 where she now rests if not actually than metaphorically (she is thought to be buried elsewhere) under a starry mosaic sky.

Have I left any wines out of my taste and travel wine list. Of course I have. With more than 1 million vineyards in Italy, I'm sure I missed quite a few. But remember when I started to travel sideways in I was no wine expert. But I know what I like and eating, traveling, cooking, shopping and drinking in Northern Italy, Tuscany and Umbria over the last 10 years has given me an opportunity to learn about Italian wine through food, family and friends. I can't think of a better way to further my Italian education about wine and about life.

See and Savor More

Here are a few terms that are important to know when seeing and savoring wines in Italy. ***Vino da Tavola* means** of wine of the table; a table wine labeled with the color of the wine, the trademark and the name of the producer. ***Indicazione Geografica Tipia (IGT)* means** that the wine is typical for a certain area. It means that the grapes have been grown in the area and that the vinification took place in the same area. The IGT areas are larger than the DOC/DOCG areas established under Italian law and the IGT designation is less restrictive. ***Denominazione di Origine Controllata (DOC)* means** that the wine has "controlled denomination of origin". There are government regulations about what grape varieties can be used, where they are grown and how and where the wine is produced. These wines are tasted and evaluated before they are allowed to be released. ***Denominazione di Origine Controllata e Garantita (DOCG)* means** further restrictions on top of the DOC ones. Wines must be sold in containers less than 5 liters and bottles are often numbered with a "state mark" guaranteeing origin and quality.

Before traveling to Italy create your own Italian wine experience at home by reading about the wines of Italy. Choose a region or a wine that interests you and learn more about it by way of a *degustazioni* (tasting). Many wine shops have scheduled tastings or begin to buy and try your selections at home or at your favorite Italian *ristorante*. Wine doesn't exist as an island all to itself so while you're enjoying *una bottiglia di vino* pair it with some regional Italian food. In Italy, wine is part of a tradition and culture so remember to eat and drink because as so well put in Vino Italiano "regional Italian wines are best showcased accompanying the regional food products that grow (or are made) alongside them".

Since 1986, the Gambero Rosso guide to Italian wines has grown into the authoritative guide to *vino italiano*. Its trademark "uno, due, and tre bicchieri" (one, two, and three glasses) rating system for wines has become Italy's gold standard for evaluating Italian vine. The guide is now printed in English, German and Italian with 912 pages and reviews about 14,000 wines produced in Italy each year.

After Piedmonte and the Veneto, Tuscany produces the third highest volume of DOCG quality wines. Tuscany is Italy's third most planted region (behind Sicily and Apulia) but it is eighth in production volume. This is partly because the soil of Tuscany is poor and producers emphasize lower yields and higher quality in their wine.

A favorite drink of my Italian cousins is the Venetian *Sgroppino*. To make a *sgroppino* whisk all ingredients in a small bowl or pitcher and pour into chilled flutes.

1-1/2 cups lemon gelato (can use lemon sorbet)
3/4 cups *prosecco*
¼ cup vodka

A *Sgroppino* at *Da Eugenia Ristorante La Ritrovata in Caorle*

Another favorite wine of mine is Colli Piacentini Mont'Arquato Duca di Ferro Gutturnio* Riserva. The Italian wines from the hills of Piacenza have been appreciated by popes and kings and those who would be including Napoleon, Michelangelo and me. Because it is little known outside of Italy and often overshadowed by the wines of Tuscany, this wine may not be as familiar as a Chianti, Brunello or Super Tuscan but well worth your consideration.

* gutturnio comes from the Latin word "gutturnium",a Roman silver goblet that was used to serve wine in ancient times

154

Chapter 18 The Italian Happy Hour

Around 6 or 7 o'clock, as stores and offices close, Italians find their way to the many cafes and bars throughout Italy to *prendanno un apertivo*, take an apertivo, a pre-dinner drink designed to stimulate the appetite with bittersweet flavors and aromatic herbs. Unlike the American cocktail hour where there are as many permutations of the classic Martini as there are configurations of Rubik's cube, the Italian aperitivo is meant to open your taste buds rather than anesthetize them. In Italy apertivi are usually accompanied by complimentary appetizers. These small bites, served as a buffet, often include a selection of olives, various chips and nuts, tiny meatballs, cured meats, cheeses, pizette, marinated vegetables, foccacia and traditional snacks of the region. Yes I did say complimentary and yes it is OK to help yourself and go back for more. You can nibble and nip on *stuzzichini* at the apertivo bars of Milano or *cicchetti* on an Italian pub crawl through Venice. The custom of apertivo is a perfect opportunity to taste a variety of regional foods in a casual atmosphere and experience the Italian lifestyle.

One of my favorite "small bites" of Italy is *Olive all'Ascolana*, stuffed olives ascolana style. A regional specialty from Ascoli Piceno in Marche, you can sometimes find them in apertivo bars and on antipasti menus in other parts of Italy. I have had them in Milano on several occasions. The olives of Ascolana are famous for their size and mild flavor. Found in the food markets of Imperial Rome, they were cultivated since medieval times by the Olivetan Benedictines who recognized their potential when brought to the table. Ascolana olives are big, fat, meaty olives that are packed in a brine of water and sea salt and are perfect for stuffing. The olives must be stoned before stuffing, a laborious task to say the least although Italian cooks have devised a special kitchen tool for hand pitting these olives. My cousins either buy the olives already pitted or buy the appetizer already made. If you would like to try to make it, the recipe will follow. Filling the olives is a bit of a challenge. You can use a pastry bag or slit the olive lengthwise creating a seam for the filling that will self seal when you coat the olives with the breading mixture and refrigerate them for a few minutes before frying.

Apertivo foods are meant to be a prelude to a meal with flavors and textures designed to stimulate your appetite. There are a wide variety of apertivo bars in Italy. Some cater to tourists with expensive drinks and elaborate buffets. I favor the neighborhood bars where savory "small bites" are served right at the bar and accompany the traditional apertivo drinks, a glass of a simple white wine, bubbly *prosecco* or apertivo liquors known as bitters. Bitters are the bottled extracts of aromatic herbs and roots blended with spirits in alchemic proportions like those used to make the classic Italian *apertivo,* Campari. The refined history of Campari begins in Milano in the late 1860's when Campari was introduced at a cafe in the Galleria Vittorio Emanuele. Campari is made from more than 60 natural ingredients including herbs, spices, fruit peels and the scented bark of a tree grown in the Bahamas! The formula has remained a secret for almost 150 years and according to Gruppo Campari there is only one person in the world who knows the entire formula for the original family recipe. Campari soda was first launched in its signature flask shaped bottle in

156

1932. The bottle was designed by futurist artist Fortunato Depero who produced hundreds of posters, ad designs, sketches and package configurations for Campari. The company's innovative idea to commission artists to create posters to market the brand resulted in some of advertising's most memorable art posters. The most well known poster is Cappiello's 'Folletto' (1921), displaying a dancing clown in an orange peel spiral holding a Campari bottle high above his head. Campari introduced the idea of "bar advertising" and the illustrative advertising work of Campari's Mad Men has influenced commercial art and Madison Avenue Ad agencies up to the present. You can still visit the iconic Cafe Zucca Galleria in the shadow of Milan's Duomo where Gaspare Campari first introduced Italians to the drink known then as "bitter Campari". The elegant Art Nouveau style of Cafe Zucca was the post opera watering hole of Giuseppe Verdi and Arturo Toscanini after their performances at La Scala and it still retains the historical ambiance of a bye gone era. In 1904, Campari's first production plant was opened in Sesto San Giovanni, now a suburb of Milano northeast of the city. The Sestonians claim that their town is the birthplace of Campari and have been known to say, "*Campari era nato a Sesto*", "Campari was born in Sesto". My Italian cousins live in Sesto San Giovanni and I have enjoyed many an Italian Happy Hour sipping a Campari Orange when I am staying there.

Another classic Italian apertivo made with Campari is the Negroni, named after Count Camillo Negroni of Florence who always asked his favorite bartender to mix him this drink. Made with ½ to 1 oz of Campari, ½ to 1 oz of sweet vermouth, ½ to 1 oz of gin, it can be

157

shaken or stired. Strained into a chilled cocktail glass and garnished with orange and lemon peel it comes as close to an Italian Martini as you can get. To most Americans, vermouth is nothing more than a splash in a martini shaker but to Italians it is an ancient and illustrious spirit used to make some of Italy's most classic apertivi. Said to have been invented by the Greek physician Hippocrates, vermouth is a wine, fortified with spirits, flavored with herbs and spices and then aged in wood. There are 2 types of vermouth, the dry white vermouths traditionally associated with France and the reddish (*rosso*), sweeter versions associated with Italy.The *rosso* vermouth's of Cinzano and Martini and Rossi are known worldwide. Cinzano, made in Torino from aromatic plants from the Italian Alps combines 35 ingredients including marjoram, thyme and musk and yarrow, in a recipe that remains a secret to this day. Martini and Rossi, also located in Torino, has been producing its famous Rosso vermouth since 1863. But there are other vermouths in Italy including Antica Formula Carpano Vermouth, also made in Torino in 1786 by Antonio Benedetto Carpano. He has been credited for the original development of vermouth by mixing the local wine with herbs and then sweetening it by adding spirit. His new drink proved so popular and met with such enthusiasm that his shop had to stay open 24 hours a day to satisfy demand and soon competitors began to produce this aromatic fortified wine.

Everyone can enjoy the Italian Happy Hour as non-alcoholic arpertivi are equally inviting. Many Italians enjoy San Pelligrino Bitter (San bitter). My cousin Lidia likes Crodino, a non-alcoholic orange flavored bitter apertivo the color of Conan O'Brien's hair. Crodino comes from Crodo, an area in northern Piedmonte and is usually served with a slice of lemon. My friend Luca introduced me to Chinotto (ki-notto), Coca Cola's Italian cousin, similar in taste but not as sweet as a cola. Chinotto takes its name from the fruit of the myrtle-leaved orange tree (*chinotto* in Italian), one of the ingredients in Campari and there are some similarities in flavor. These sodas are insider drinks but if you want to taste travel in Italy and drink like an Italian, consider trying one for a taste of Italy beyond wine.

This section is written for my brother who happens to like beer (*birra* in Italian). It's not all about wine and bitters during the Italian Happy Hour. You can order a beer apertivo, proforably Gorman.

See and Savor More

The Mad Men (AMC's popular TV drama) of Campari included artists Cappiello, Hohenstein, Dudovich, Metlicovitz, Mauzan, Sacchetti, Laskoff, Nizzoli, Sinopico, Depero and Munari whose vintage Italian poster art is highly collectable today. Under the direction of Davide Campari, commissioned artists created advertising posters with sophisticated images that continued to build the brand name throughout the 1900's and make Campari recognizable and unique.

"Intern, get me a Campari" said by Bill Murray's character in the quirkly comedy The LIfe Acquatic with Steve Zissou , introduced Campari to American film audiences who were intriqued by the Italian bitter.

159

Campari *"era nato a Sesto"* – the Campari plant in Sesto San Giovanni

Olive All'Ascolana

as described to me by Italian friends from Ascoli Piceno, a town in the Marche region of Northern Italy

Ingredients

- 20 jumbo Italian olives from Ascoli (pitted) pached in a brine of sea salt and water

- 1/2 pound Italian fennel salami, crumbled and finely chopped

- 2 T unsalted butter

160

- ½ c dry white wine

- 1 T parsley

- 1 T minced garlic

- 1 c grated Grana Padano or Parmiggiano Reggiano cheese

- pinch of freshly grated nutmeg

- 2 eggs

- 1/2 cup flour

- 1/2 cup bread fine crumbs

- 2 cups olive oil for frying

Directions

Heat oil to 375 degrees F. Saute sausage in.butter until pink is gone than sprinkle with wine and allow wine to evaporate from pan. Remove from heat, retaining pan drippings. Let cool then stir in 2 heaping tablespoons of bread crumbs, parsley, garlic, cheese, nutmeg and 1 egg lightly beaten to make a stuffing, adding more breadcrumbs if needed. This is a typical recipe used in Italy for stuffing vegetables like peppers. Fill each olive with a small amount of stuffing being carefull not to overstuff. Roll each olive in a paste made of flour, egg and remaining breadcrumbs. Place in refrigerator to set for about 5 minutes. Remove from refrigerator and gently place olives in hot but not smoking oil. Fry 1-2 minutes until olives arel golden brown. Serve warm as an aperitivo.

Chapter 19 Wine of the Saints

D.H. Lawrence, the English author, poet, playwright and literary critic referred to Tuscany as "the perfect center of man's universe", high praise for a region only a little larger than the state of Massachusetts. Lawrence first traveled to Italy in 1912 and wrote of his travels reflecting on the meaning of life. In his writings about Tuscany, Lawrence mused about "a country so perfectly constructed where half the produce of five acres of land will support ten human mouths, yet still has so much room for the wild flowers". Lawrence's musings and meditative state must surely have been induced by a glass of Vin Santo, an amber colored sweet wine with a unique taste and velvety texture that is meant for sipping at the end of a meal. Vin Santo is a sweet wine made from grapes that are left on the vine late to condense and develop their sugar content resulting in a *vino dolce*; a smooth, intensely flavored wine with a high alcohol content, usually about 16 to 18 percent.

Vin Santo is Tuscany in a glass and reflects Tuscan life at its best, life that is to be savored with a holy devotion to the grapes of the vine. Because of its name Vin Santo, "wine of the saints", the wine was thought to have orginated as a sacramental wine. However there are other accounts that link the name to historical references that are less ecclesiastical. In particular to a certain incident in the 15th century when a visiting Greek prelate upon drinking it exclaimed "This is the wine of Xanthos"! which was mistaken for the word "santos", meaning saints ergo naming the wine Vin Santo. There are other reports that the name was derived from the accounts of a 14th century Franciscan friar from Siena who used it to cure the plague or was it a Carmelite monk who always carried a flask to ease the suffering of the of the sick. All I know is that Vin Santo has cured my overworked, overwrought psyche on more than one occassion and I continue to find it the end of a proper Tuscan meal.

Although I have enjoyed many a glass of Vin Santo both in Italy and at home I always look forward to tasting the Vin Santo from Tenuta di Capezzana. The Vin Santo from Capezzana is highly sought after and considered to be among the best of its class. Selected white grapes are held in baskets then strung together on cane stands where they are dried for several months then fermented and matured for over 4 years in *caratelli*, small chestnut barrels. The yield is very low, from ¼ to 1/5 of tho original weight of the grapes. At the time of my visit to Capezzana, the Vin Santo had already been bottled and sold but we were able to walk through the cellars and *vinsantaie,* a large ventilated room with many windows where the grapes are hung to dry. The windows in the room are opened and closed to control the flow of air. Here the grapes are subjected to seasonal temperature changes which create a unique taste and texture to the wine. At Capezzana the windows of the *vinsantaie* are opened and closed daily according to the winds and weather.There are other producers in Tuscany that make a notable Vin Santo including Avignonesi Vin Santo di Montepulciano.

Vin Santo is traditionally served with *biscotti di Prato* or *cantucci* from Siena. The cookies are dipped in Vin Santo to soften, the adult version of Oreos and milk. Tuscans have been drowning their
163

cantucci in Vin Santo since the time of the Renaissance. Tuscan bakers refined the recipe for the unleavened biscuts used by Roman travelers and served them with the local sweet wine. A marriage of form and function, the dry, crunchy texture and narrow shape of the *cantucc*i were perfect for dipping and soaking up the flavors of the wine. Vino Italiano, comments that the best Vin Santo are desserts in themselves saying "with these you can forget the biscotti". It is true that the intoxicating aroma of Vin Santo with its deep amber color and nutty caramel flavor is a perfect ending to a satisfying meal but I believe that you can't forget the biscotti. Italians are very fond of pairing a sweet wine with a "dry" dessert and *cantucci e vin santo* are the perfect match. The Tuscan town of Siena is well known for the making of *cantucci.* You will find many *pasticceria* and artisan food shops as you explore the narrow medieval streets and alleys of Siena. Two shops that are not to be missed are *Pasticceria Nannini*, Siena's oldest pasticceria on Via Banchi di Sopra 22-24 and *Antica Drogheria Manganelli,* Via di Città 71-73 who has been making Sienese *dolce* since 1879. And if you are in Prato, NW of Florence, be sure to stop by the award-winning *biscottificio* Antonio Mattei, Via Ricasoli 20-22 which has been selling Prato's famous cantucci and Vin Santo since 1858. I'm somewhat of a cantucci purist so please don't take offense if I say that most of the *cantucci* I have tasted outside of Italy is mass produced and poorly made. I know that there are many small batch artisan producers in the States who value the traditional making of *cantucci* and you should seek them out. However there are many producers who use Italian sounding names to market an Amercanized version of cantucci creating a false impression of the true nature of biscotti cantucci. Biscotti cantucci are what they are, a hard almond
164

twice baked (*biscotti*) cookie (the name *cantucci* means "little stones," the "little stones" being the almonds). Many bakery products in Italy were twice baked as a method of preservation. So don't expect a soft, chewy chocolate chip cookie to dunk in a glass of milk. Instead pour yourself a glass of the wine of the saints and meditate about the history and traditional of a a cookie that was a staple of the Roman legions and a wine that has a place of honour at the Tuscan table.

There are other foods that pair well with this dessert wine such as plain cakes, nuts and cheese. The dryer version of Vin Santo is a perfect accompaniment to Gorgonzola and other aged cheeses and if you want to try something really unique look for Vin Santo wine jelly. Zazzeri from Pienza condenses the intense flavor and aroma of Vin Santo in a jar that can be used as a condiment for roasted meats and poultry, a glaze on baked hams or fruit tarts or on muffins or French toast for a stimulating breakfast. No cork screw needed.

Chapter 20 Eric's Wine

Colli Senesi south of Chianti Classico in the Siena hills is a sub region in the Chianti wine zone that produces some very good well priced wines. If the patriarch of the family is the mature Chianti Classico than the wines of the Colli Senesi might be described as part of the extended Chianti family that incudes seven sub regions. Colli Senesi still retains the character of the Sangiovese, Chianti's prinicipal grape varietal but because of the location (about 1 mile outside of the Chianto Classico zone) you have a different denomination and another world of Chianti wines to explore as you travel through the Sienese hills. With a lower alcohol content than the "Classico" type, Chianti Colli Senesi is generous in aroma and flavor making it a very appealing wine with a dedicated following.

One of the dedicated followers of vino Colli Senesi is Eric who has traveled to Italy pre and post partum. What I mean by that is before and after he and his wife Rosiel had children. Eric and Rosiel first traveled through Tuscany with a backpack. Now they travel with an entourage of luggage that includes carseats, strollers and *due bambini*. Their love of Italy and the Italian lifestyle will not be denied and so they find a way to return even if that means paying extra for luggage. One of their favorite places to visit in Tuscany is Siena. Described by many as the perfect medieval city, the art, culture, history, food and wine of Tuscany are concentrated in the narrow streets and alleyways of a city "where every stone has remained the same" since medieval times. The distinctive Duomo (cathedral) of Siena with its black and white striped *campanile* (bell tower) and black

and white interior pillars dates from 1313 and the town s
del Campo), shaped like a shell, is divided to represent
contrada or wards of the 17 city states that govern Siena. Each
contrada has its own distinct identity, its own seat of government, its
own constitution, church, fountain, anthem, motto, insignia, patron
saint and geographical boundaries which were established in 1729,
when the number of *contrade* was also fixed by decree at 17.
Historically *contrade* were organized garrisons used to supply troops
to defend Siena from Florence. Today the *contrade* are neighborhood
organizations where civic pride and tradition govern holiday
celebrations and festivals. Each *contrada* is represented by an animal.
As you walk the medieval streets of Siena look for the various
contrade animal symbols; *Aquila*, the eagle, *Drago* the dragon,
Tartuca the tortoise, *Oca* the goose, *Lupa* the she-wolf, *Chiocciola*
the snail and *Bruco* the caterpillar are some of the animal totems
displayed on buildings or secretly hidden in scrollwork or decorations
throughout the city.   *Restaurant in Siena*

Eric was spending a few quiet days at a Tuscan farmhouse in San
Casciano in Val di Pesa when the urge to travel to Siena took hold.
He wanted to stop at his favorite *enoteca* to buy a few bottles of
Chianti Colli Senesi and eat at one of his favorite restaurants, *Da
Mugolone* on Via dei Pellegrini 8/12. *Ristorante Mugolone* is part of a
regional network (*Ventrina Toscana a Tavola*) of 630 restaurants,
trattorias and taverns throughout Tuscany who are committed to
"introducing the customer to the traditional taste of Tuscan food". The
mission of *Ventrina Toscana a Tavola* is to showcase the remarkable
cusine of Tuscany and *Da Mugolone* does this very well. *Da*

167

Mugolone serves a wonderful meat lasagna and fresh pasta with truffles and a *timballo* (pasta bound with eggs and cheese baked in a mold with a savory sauce) that every taste traveler I know raves about. Trying to find an Italian restaurant in the States like *Da Mugolone* is like trying to find a needle in a haystack. They are few and far between. Eric knew this so he was looking forward to a great meal and some great wine. With wife and kids in tow, he drove the 40 km into Siena picked up the wine, made his way past the crowds of tourists to Via dei Pellegrini 8/12 only to find the restuarant was closed. It was Thursday. To us that may seem strange. Most restaurants in the States are open weekdays but in Italy the scheduled hours of operation for eating establishments are subject to, what? I'm not sure. Remember you are in a country that takes the whole month of August off. So be sure to check and keep track of the days that your favorite resturants, shops, museums and galleries are open. They could be closed on Thursday, or Monday or Sunday and can vary from city to city. Also remember that Italians typically take time for a midday break. So many shops will be closed for two or three hours in the afternoon. Eric had forgotten about the Thursday closure and he was also going to forget another important thing about traveling with kids.

When traveling with kids in Italy be prepared for the Italian meltdown. In a country that engages your senses on such a grand scale everything becomes magnified. Kids get hungrier, more tired and can only handle so much. Much less than what they can handle at home. Parents become more frustrated and often get distracted. Much more than when they are at home. That's what happened to Eric when he

168

was getting ready to leave for the airport for the trip back home. After packaging the three extra suitcases, two strollers, wooden toy sword and PreNatal outlet purchases there was no room for the Colli Senesi. Somewhat distracted he shoved the wine in his carry on thinking he would re-pack at the airport. Well he forgot and as airport security informed him that they would be confiscating his three bottles of Chianti Colli Senesi wine, 4 year old Ethan came running down the airport concourse frantically announcing to anyone who would listen "they took my Dad's vino"! Eric left Italy that year *senza vino* (without wine) but with wonderful memories of traveling as a family in Italy.

See and Savor More

Chianti Colli Senesi wine pairs well with typical Tuscan pasta dishes such as *pici* a type of big spaghetti, whose diameter is never under 3mm [0.118inches]), *pappardelle* (wider tagliolini-like pasta), *salume, salami and salsiccia* and roasted red meats and aged cheese.

The 17 Siense Contrade are

- Aquila (Eagle), Casato di Sotto
- Bruco (Caterpillar), Via del Comune 48
- Chiocciola (Snail), Via S. Marco 37
- Civetta (Owl), Piazzetta del Castellare
- Drago (Dragon), Piazza Matteotti 19
- Giraffa (Giraffe), Via delle Vergine 18
- Istrice (Hedgehog), Via Camollia 87
- Leocorno (Unicorn), Via di Follonica 15
- Lupa (She-Wolf), Via Vallerozzi 71/73

- Nicchio (Shell), Via dei Pispini 68
- Oca (Goose), Vicolo del Tiratoio 13
- Onda (Wave), Via G. Duprè 111
- Pantera (Panther), Via S. Quirico
- Selva (Forest), Piazzetta della Selva
- Tartuca (Tortoise), Via T. Pendola 21/25
- Torre (Tower), Via Salicotto 76
- Valdimontone (Ram), Via di Valdimontone 6

The insigna for the *Nobile Contrada dell Lupa.*

Art and Design

Chapter 21 Walk Into a Postcard

It has often been said that Italy is an open air museum where you can find yourself surrounded by masterpieces of art and architecture around every corner. This happens so frequently that I often feel as if I am walking into a postcard every time I am traveling in Italy. From the moment I exit the tube (subway) at the Duomo stop in downtown Milan I am overwhelmed by some of the most magnificent architecture in the entire world, the spires of Milan's Duomo and the glass vaulted Galleria Vittorio Emanuele. Then I cross the piazza to Milan's historic library, *Pinacoteca Ambrosiana* where ancient manuscripts and paintings including Leonardo's *Codex Atlanticus* and Caravaggio's Basket of Fruit are on display. You feel as if you are walking into a postcard when you travel through the windswept landscape of Tuscany's Crete Senesi or walk the Bellagio promenade along Lake Como. The natural beauty of Italy has been many an artist's muse and Italian design a benchmark of artistic excellence all over the world. In fact, there are so many great cities of art and architecture in Italy that UNESCO, the United Nations Educational, Scientific and Cultural Organization, has designated Italy a World Heritage site with 44 properties considered to be of significant natural or cultural merit that deserve the protection of our world community. Some are well known like the city of Florence, Venice and its Lagoon and the historic center of Rome and properties of the Holy See. Others are hidden treasures like the mosaics of Ravenna or the Palladian villas of the Veneto.

171

When I first started to visit Italy the last thing on my mind was UNESCO. I was more interested in the vineyards of Tuscany, the fashions of Milano and the food of Emilia Romagna. Over the last 10 years my trips to Italy have been an on going journey to discover the Italy of my family and friends. Now I travel to Italy on business as well with my company, Cositutti, to bring artisan Italian food and unique handcrafted items to CosituttiMarketPlace.com. But somewhere along the way I realized that I had visited 19 UNESCO World Heritage sites in Italy. Something I now know to be very special. Established in 1972, UNESCO encourages the identification and preservation of cultural and natural heritage sites around the world considered to be of significant value to humanity. Places with outstanding natural or cultural merit that deserve our protection. The World Heritage list includes 878 sites in 185 countries from Afghanistan to Zimbabwe. The US is home to 20 sites including the Statue of Liberty, the Pueblos of Taos, Grand Canyon National Park, Smoky Mountain National Park, Yellowstone National Park, the Frank Lloyd Wright Buildings and Independence Hall (for a complete list go to http://whc.unesco.org/en/statesparties/it). Twenty seven places around the globe were recently added to the list including the Monarch Butterfly Biosphere northwest of Mexico City. I now make it a priority to visit or re-visit at least one or two of the UNESCO sites every time I travel to Italy. There are certainly more to add to my list. I appreciated these sites in the past for their historical significance and remarkable beauty. I now appreciate them as our legacy and a source of inspiration for future generations. Unfortunately World Heritage status is no guarantee of protection. Tourist related activities and time all take a toll on the preservation of World Heritage sites. The

172

Galapagos Islands, in fact, was placed on UNESCO's lesser known list, the List of World Heritage in danger.

So when traveling, travel responsibly and travel with a desire to know. See and savor Italy with an eye to the past and future. Learn about the art, architecture, food, wine, landscape and cultural heritage of a region. The more you know about the sites you are seeing the more meaningful they become and the more respect you will have for their legacy. Reading books or looking at photo journals is a good starting point to make your trip more interesting. Books and pictures help create a mood and background that will heighten your travel experience. Knowing about the Medici family when traveling to Florence makes seeing the Church of San Lorenzo and the Medici Chapels more meaningful and reading about the River Arno makes crossing the Ponte Vecchio feel like a walk through the Renaissance. Don't overlook cookbooks and lifestyle magazines like Food and Wine and Cucina Italiana. They are particularly useful because they often showcase regional foods with pictures and background information . Travel with a desire to give yourself up to the experience and allow enough time to appreciate what you're doing. After all you wouldn't think of making a reservation in a fine restaurant with the intention of eating your meal in 15 minutes. Allow enough time to enjoy all aspects of your travels and be realistic about the time it takes to accomplish your travel goals.

Half of all the UNESCO World Heritage sites are in Italy and can easily be part of any taste and travel tour. They are preserved and protected in hundreds of archaeological sites and over 3,000

173

museums scattered throughout the country and in the cultural traditions of the Italian people. Many are part of the culinary heritage of the regional food of Italy through association. The natural beauty of these sites and the artistry of man have combined to create a legacy for the world.

THE 19 UNESCO World Heritage sites I have visited and in Italy are

- Milan-Church of Santa Maria delle Grazie with "The Last Supper" by Leonardo da Vinci
- Capriate di S. Gervasio-Crespi d'Adda
- Venice and its Lagoon
- City of Vicenza and the Palladian Villas of the Veneto
- Padua-Botanical Garden
- City of Verona
- Ferrara- The City of the Renaissance and the Po Delta
- Ravenna and the Mosaics and Early Christian Monuments
- Florence-Historic Centre
- Pisa-Piazza del Duomo
- San Gimignano-Historic Centre
- Pienza-Historic Center
- Siena-Historic Centre
- Val d'Orcia
- Assisi -The Basilica of San Francesco and Other Franciscan Sites
- Rome-Historic Centre of Rome, the Properties of the Holy See
- Mantua – The Historic Center
- Sabbioneta
- The Dolomites

See and Savor More

Other UNESCO World Heritage Sites located in Italy are

- The historic Center of Naples
- Cilento and Vallo di Diano National Park with the Archeological sites of Paestum and Velia, and the Certosa di Padula
- Portovenere, Cinque Terre and the Islands
- Rock Drawings in Valcamonica near Brescia
- Sacri Monti of Piedmont and Lombardy
- Castel del Monte
- Costiera Amalfitana
- The *trulli* of Alberobello
- Etruscan Necropolises of Cerveteri and Tarquinia
- Villa Romana del Casale
- Villa Adriana (Tivoli)
- Su Nuraxi di Barumini
- 18th century Royal Palace at Caserta
- Historic Centre of Urbino
- Residences of the Royal House of Savoy
- Cathedral Torre Civica and Piazza Grande in Modena
- Archaeological Area and the Patriarchal Basilica of Aquileia
- Archeological sites of Pompei, Herculaneum and Torre Annunziata
- Archaeological Area of Agrigento
- I Sassi di Materna and the Aeolian Islands
- Late Baroque Towns of the Val di Noto (South-eastern Sicily)
- Syracuse and Pantalic
- Le Strade Nuove, Genoa
- Rhaetian Railway in the Albula-Bernina Landscapes (joint listing with Switzerland)

175

Chapter 22 Byzantine Chic

Before Byzantine icons were an inspiration for haute couture, the art and architecture of Byzantium played a unique role in the art and history of Italy. The great Byzantine Empire was a fusion of Greek, Roman, European and Islamic elements that resulted in a style that influenced Italian architecture and the building of some of Italy's greatest churches. The art of the Byzantine originated in the ancient Greek town of Byzantium. In 330 AD, Emperor Constantine moved the capitol of the Roman Empire from the west to Byzantium on the Black Sea. While the empire of the west languished, the Byzantium Empire of the east flourished, lasting another thousand years. Byzantium was renamed Constantinople, a city where the art and culture of Rome were mixed with the mosaics and iconography of the Byzantine. During the late middle ages, the long standing relationship between Venice and her eastern trading partner Constantinople resulted in Venice exporting the exotic character of the East to the city on the Lagoon. Venetians still enjoy the flavors and styles of Byzantium as they look out the eastern inspired ogee windows of their waterfront palazzi.

Seeing and savoring this side of Italy was important to me because I am Byzantine. That is to say that part of my cultural heritage includes ancestors who followed the Eastern Roman traditions of the Catholic Church. My Italian cousins knew this so on my first trip to Italy we drove from Milano toward the Adriatic Sea to the town of Ravenna and the ancient city of Classe to visit the Basilica di Sant'Apollinare. Classe was an important commercial and military port for the Roman fleet (classis) during the 6th century and today is evocative of a time and place that has faded into history. The basilica at Classe stands in an open field south of the city as an austerne moument to early Christianity. Basilica architecture is actually very minimalistic and in a sense has two meanings. Originally a basilica was a large roofed hall with an interior colonnade and clerestory windows to allow light to enter. It was used in Rome as a public space for transacting business and matters of state. The basilica style of architecture was adopted by the early Christians as a place of worship and eccelsiastical basilicas came to refer to large and important churches that were given special ceremonial rites by the Pope. The ornate basilicas of the Renaissance and St. Peters in Rome are embellished basilicas with inspiration taken from their distant architectural cousin. However the simple and somewhat austern outward appearance of the Basilica di Sant'Apollinare belies an interior space of radiant beauty that is reflected in the Byzantine mosaics that have been described as some of the finest in the world. Originally the nave walls, floor and clerestory were covered in mosaics but these have mostly disappeared. Yet what remains is breathtaking. The aspe mosaic of Sant'Appollinare depicts the saint standing with 12 lambs in a field of flowers and pine trees against a green background with glittering golden skies with the cross of the Transfiguration above. The open fields with pine trees and flowers that surround Sant'Appollinare must have inspired early Christian artisans as they recreated the natural beauty of the landscape in the mosaics of Sant'Appollinare.

Visiting Ravenna is like looking into a jewel box and finding a hidden treasure. Behind somewhat somber exteriors are mosaics of such

177

quality that Ravenna has been designated a UNESCO World Heritage Site because of the "outstanding universal value and remarkable significance" of the mosaics. The art and architecture of Ravenna create an atmosphere of an ancient time and place that will leave you in awe. The Mausoleum of Galla Placidia described as "the earliest and best preserved of all mosaic monuments and at the same time one of the most artistically perfect" is located in Ravenna as is the Basilica of San Vitale. Both are glittering examples of the symbolic world of Early Christian culture and Byzantine mosaic art. The luminous effects of the mosaics spread over the walls and vaults of the interiors create jewel like surfaces of ethereal beauty.

Entering the tiny mausoleum of Galla Placidia is a Laura Croft experience. You almost feel as if you are tomb raider who has no right to see the wonders that lie within. Yet upon leaving you know that what you experienced was profound and possibily life changing. Even if you miss the hidden iconological message of life and rebirth you still will be moved by the simple yet dramatic beauty of Byzantine mosaic art. The mausoleum, shaped like a Latin cross, contains some of the oldest mosaics found in Ravenna, dating to the mid 5th century. The deep blue vaulted ceiling covered with stars, shimmering in gold is spectacular in design and architecture befitting a Roman princess, Visigoth Queen and later Empress (Augusta) of the Roman Empire. There are mosaics with festoons of foliage and flowers, animals and birds. Brillant white mosaic doves drink from a bowl of sapphire blue spring water. Light streaming through alabaster windows creates an almost other worldly effect with the mosaic symbolism of the celestial harmony of heaven and earth all around.

Beside the Mausoleum of Galla Placidia is the octagonal Basilica of San Vitale dating from the 6th century with more intricate and detailed mosaics. The basilica contains a pair of mosaic panels representing Emperor Justinian and Empress Theodora attended by their court. The colored glass and gold leaf of the mosaic of a bejeweled Theodora adorned with mother of pearl and dazzling mosaic gems is meant to impress. The theology and politics of the rule of the Byzantine Empire are woven into visual symbolism and language of mosaic art. Altogether there are eight Early Christian monuments in Ravenna that are inscribed on the World Heritage List and several other sites that are definitely worth seeing including Dante's Tomb. All are easily accessible and most within walking distance. An overnight stay in Ravenna is most delightful and an ideal launching point to see and savor Venice.

The Byzantine influence in Venice is almost everywhere. Architectural elements used in the construction of the Basilica of San Marco and the 12th century Cathedral of Santa Maria Assunta on the island of Torcello are distinctly eastern. Most apparent are the mosaics. Many of the mosaicists who worked on the Venetian cathedral of San Marco came from Byzantium. With more than 8,000 square meters of interior surface covered with gold mosaics, the opulent design and Byzantine mosaics have given the Basilica of San Marco the name, *Chiesa d'Oro*, church of gold.

See and Savor More

The Basilica of Sant'Apollinare in Classe owes its survival from Allied bombing during World War II to the intervention Vladimir Peniakoff, an Anglo-Belgian-Russian Colonel who commanded a small group of hand picked men serving behind enemy lines in Italy during the War. In his book "Popski's Private Army," he tells how he was able to postpone an attack by his gunners on Sant'Apollinare in Classe for 24 hours while he sent a party to visit the bell tower where Germans were believed to be posted. The rumor proved untrue and the basilica and its 6th century mosaics were saved.

Today Byzantine inspired designs can be found in everything from jewelry to note cards. The Austrian magazine "Diva" featured an amazing Byzantine icon-inspired photo shoot with clothes by Jean Paul Gaultier, Chanel, Christian Lacroix and Givenchy.

Mosaic "sky" from the mausoleum of Galla Placidia in Ravenna

Chapter 23 500 Rooms of Renaissance Glory

My first trip to Mantova was somewhat of an afterthought. I was in
Ferrara and found that I had an extra day before I needed to get back
to Milano to meet my cousins. The city of Mantova (Mantua in the
local dialect) met several criteria for a taste and travel destination and
was an easy drive to Milano on S482. Located at the bend of the
Mincio River, about two hours from Milan, Mantova is surrounded by
three man-made lakes. It is a beautiful and historic city with
restaurants that open onto a series of piazze that join together at the
town center.The restaurants of Mantova are known for their wonderful
food including *tortelli di zucca*, tortelli filled with pumpkin or squash,
ground amaretti cookies, *mostarda* and grana cheese. On my last trip
to Mantova I ate at *Trattoria alla Nuova Marasca* (no relation to me)!
But with the same last name as mine, I had to try it. Located off
Piazza Leon Battista Alberti behind the Basilica di' San Andrea, the
trattoria is family run with local cooking and a great place for couples
and families with kids. It even has a small play area near the outdoor
patio. The restaurant logo is three bright red cherries. The Italian word
marasca is often associated with cherries, specifically a type of cherry
grown in Northern Italy and Croatia. The Marasca cherry is used to
make the orginal Maraschino cherries (today Maraschino cherries are
most often artificially colored and flavoured Royal Anne cherries) and
Maraschino liqueur, a bitter sweet clear liqueur made from the
crushed cherries and cherry pits.

However the typical Mantuan liqueur is *il nocino*, a digestivo made
from green walnuts steeped in distilled spirits. According to tradition,

the walnuts are gathered during the Midsummer night (June 23-24), a time when fairies and witches gather the fruits of the earth to make elixirs for a long life. _Nocino_ is made from cut green walnuts, cloves and cinnamon, sometimes lemon peel, a handful of coffee beans and coriander, although ingredients can vary according to the local customs. At about 40% alcohol by volume and 80 proof, _Nocino_ is not for the faint of heart. Meant to be sipped, it is very much appreciated by the Mantuans who enjoy a small glass at cafes over looking one of the many piazze in the city.

The "urban squares" of Italy never fail to amaze me. Every piazza is a combination of the art, architecture, sites, sounds and smells that make a town or village in Italy what it is. They are the living rooms of Italy where the townspeople come to meet, greet and leisurely past time contemplating their corner of the world and their place in it. Some urban planners have even gone so far as to say that certain public squares evoke a "psychogeographical" reaction. This has certainly been the case for me. Piazza del Campo in Siena, Piazza San Marco in Venice, Piazza Navonna in Rome, Piazza Duomo in Milan are just a few of the many piazze in Italy that hold a special place in the hearts and minds of anyone who has been there. So when I was in Mantova I planned to visit the renown Piazza Sordello, site of the Ducal Palace of the Gonzaga family. The Gonzagas ruled Mantova for over 300 years and their reign resulted in a vast complex of buildings, a "city within a city", with palaces, courtyards, gardens and over 500 rooms of Renaissance glory. Now a museum facing Piazza Sordello, Palazzo Ducale represents one of the richest and most refined of the Renaissance courts. The 34,000 square meters of space house unbelievable works of art, the most famous being the frescoes in the *Camera degli Sposi* (wedding chamber). The portrait scenes in the chamber, also known as the *Camera Picta* or painted room, were done by Andrea Mantegna and took ten years to complete. They depict Ludovico Gonzaga, his family and friends all within a sensory overload of figures, walled cities, towers and landscapes that cover almost every surface of the room. There are scenes of courtiers, family, friends and friends of friends with Roman Emperors thrown in for good measure. The famous Gonzaga Court Scene is a snapshot of the elegant lifestyle of the early Renaissance but looks more like a political ad campaign focusing on the candidate's family values. In the painting Ludovico, portrayed as a paternalistic ruler, discusses a letter with one of his aids while surrounded by his wife and children and various family members including the family dog, Rubino. Apparently the Gonzagas were found of dogs as there is another famous scene of an outdoor meeting with Ludovico and his children that includes a small curly-coated dog known as a Lagotto Romangnolo (once a duck retriever in the marshes of Northern Italy now used to hunt truffles) and another that includes an impressive painting of groomsmen with a horse and hunting dogs.

But the most excellent fresco of all is the dramatic ceiling fresco painted as a doomed oculus in the *Camera degli Sposi*. Opening on to a painted blue clouded sky, assorted characters are part of a *trompe l'oeil* scene looking down into the room with curiosity and amusement while winged *putti* (cherubs) playfully cling to a balustrade, on the brink of falling into the room. The oculus remains a classic illusionist painting and a masterpiece of perspective. Take someone you love to

183

see the 15th century frescoes in the Ducal Palace's *Camera degli Sposi* in Mantova. It was mentioned on Forbe's 10 Things to Do Before You Die list. I would prefer to include it on my Seeing and Savoring Italy list. It sounds more positive.

See and Savor More

When the Ducal Palace in Mantova was sacked by the Hapsburgs in 1630, eighty carriages were needed to carry the two thousand works of art contained in its five hundred rooms

The mystical making of *nocino* uses ingredients that are measured in amounts of 3, 7 and 21; numbers often associated with magical concoctions. There are several recipes for making homemade *nocino* from various sources. Here is one

- 21 green walnuts, cleaned and quartered (wear gloves- walnuts stain)
- 2 cinnamon sticks
- 3 vanilla beans
- zest of an orange or lemon
- 1 1/2 to 2 1/2 cup sugar(depending on how sweet you like liqueur to be)
- 7 juniper berries
- 3 whole cloves
- 1 quart vodka

Clean and quarter the green walnuts. Put the quartered walnuts, sugar, orange zest, cloves, cinnamon sticks, juniper berries, whole vanilla beans and vodka into a jar or glass crock and place in warm and shady place for 7 weeks; shake every 2-3 days. It will become very dark brown. After 7 weeks, remove the walnuts and other ingredients and strain the liqueur through layers of cheesecloth or filter paper. Leave for at least 6 months, strain again and bottle.

Ceiling oculus in the *Camera degli Sposi* at the Palazzo Ducale in Mantova

Chapter 24 The Duomo

There are a few defining sights in Italy that are indelible in my mind because of a fond memory or special meaning they have taken on in my travels. You will probably find this to be so too. In your travels there will be that unforgettable site, that unique experience, that one moment in time where you will feel changed by your travels that creates a memory that will stay with you forever. For me it is the sight of the Milan Duomo. This is probably because of several reasons. The Duomo of Milan was the first major site I saw in Italy with my Italian cousins. We walked up the steps from the tube at the Duomo Metro station and before me was this massive spired cathedral rising out of the concrete earth of the piazza like it had materialized from thin air. It was unexpected and impressive and in a way was to represent what Italy would become for me.

An Italian cathedral *(cattedrale)* *duomo* from the Latin word "domus", means house, as in the "house of God", or *domus Dei*. It's difficult to describe the influence or impact of the duomo to someone who is not from Italy. The Italian view of the Duomo is far different from the view most Americans have of a cathedral or church. For Italians the Duomo is more than a religious space. It is a symbol of their city, a representation of their history and cultural traditions. The personal connection of the Italian people with the duomos of Italy can best be described by Ernesto Brivio in his book about the Duomo of Milan. He writes "entering here (the duomo) is reliving the atmosphere of past times, when men, highly skilled and courageous, of great professionalism and united by the same faith dedicated themselves to great undertakings". To Italians that is something heroic and they want to preserve the ideals and efforts of those who have gone before them.

The immense size and grandeur of the duomos of Italy is testament to their importance. The act of building a duomo in itself is a monumental task. The Duomo of Milan, described as one of the greatest churches in the world (second only to St. Peter's Basilica in Rome), took more than 500 years to complete. It is 515 ft long, 302 ft wide and 148 ft in height. There are 5 naves divided by 40 pillars with a capacity of 40,000. The Candolglia Marble used to build the Milan Duomo was transported from quarries in the lower Val d'Ossola in Northern Italy by barges and then loaded onto oxen drawn carts. A further system of canals, hoists and rollers moved the massive blocks of marble until they reached the *Cassina*, an area behind the Duomo where the workshops of the architects, engineers, sculptors, carpenters and master masons were found. An organization, the *Veneranda Fabbrica del Duomo di Milano* was created in 1387 to oversee the work and is still in existenance today. It is now responsible for the maintenance and conservation of the Duomo.

As you emerge from the Metro at Milan's Duomo station you are dwarfed by the scale of one largest Gothic cathedrals in the world. There are 3,400 statues both inside and outside the Duomo and 135 spires. To experience the sheer size of the Milan Duomo, visit the rarified air of the roof terraces of the cathedral. It is a fairyland of pinnacles, spires and flying buttresses, described by Mark Twain as "a delusion of frostwork that might vanish with a breath". You can go

187

to the *salita* (roof) *con ascensore* (by lift) or *a piedi* (by stairs) for a spectacular view of Milano (on a clear day you can see the Alps). I recommend that you take a walk on the terraces of the Duomo to view the roof statuary. There are 1800 statues up on the roof, "a silent population of prophets, saints, virgins, martyrs and bishops". I did this with my cousin Lidia and it was truly spectacular. Perched on the top of the highest cathedral spire a gilded statue of the Madonna overlooks the city. Dating back to 1774, the statue is called the *Madonnina,* or the little Madonna, despite being 4 meters tall.

As are many sacred spaces in Italy, the duomos of Italy are also repositories of some of the world greatest art. The art and architecture of the Duomo of Florence, *Santa Maria del Fiore*, reads like a Who's Who of Renaissance art. Brunelleschi, Giottto, Ghiberti, Donatello, Vasari, Pisano, Uccello and Castagno all worked on the cathedral. Siena's Duomo, the *Cathedral di Santa Maria*, is a black and white marble treasury of Gothic art from the 13th and 14th centuries with an octagonal Gothic pulpit designed by Nicola Pisano. The marble, mosaics, bronze statues and spectacular Rose Window of Orvieto's Duomo are a course in art history and the ceiling fresco of the Assumption by Correggio in the 12th-century Romanesque cathedral of Parma is considered a masterpiece of Renaissance fresco art.

The concept of a church/museum makes visiting the duomos of Italy somewhat of a paradox. The devout are seen kneeling in prayer or attending Mass while others are seen taking pictures (sometimes prohibited) or listening to audio guided tours on headsets and MP3 players. The fine line between sacred and profane is always present when traveling in Italy. Many of the monuments, buildings and art works are associated with deeply held religious beliefs that should be respected. Viewing the two side by side is possible and for some a purely secular approach to religious art and architecture will be the main focus. However the art of the Duomo is in a sacred space so be prepared to follow instructions regarding dress codes (no shorts or sleeveless tops) and use of photographic equipment which will be posted at the entry way of the church.

The art and architecture of Italy's duomos is not necessarily on view for all to see. Some is hidden and unexpected and goes back to a pre-Christian era literally hidden below the surface of the city. The 135 spires of the Milan Duomo overshadow a little known paleo-Christian archeological site located under the cathedral with baptismal pools (circa 378) used by the early Christians of Milano. Through a staircase on the left of the main door you descend into the excavated remains of a brick wall around the perimeter of a Baptistery and a Roman road. Walking along a raised platform you will see a large octagonal fontal pool where the catechumens were baptized. The pool is impressive because of its size (6.10 m in diameter) with concealed pipes that provided a channel of "holy water" sprouting from several jets. A description of the space talks about the pool being clad in Greek marble and the original flooring and walls being made of black and white marble in geometric designs. It must have been an awe inspiring event to be led to this place on the eve of Easter and to be immersed in the water to receive the sacrament that cleanses you of your sins and binds you to all of Christendom. You may need to ask for directions at the information booth of the Duomo to find the

189

staircase that leads to Baptistery of *St. Giovanni alle Fonti.* There is a second archeological site of the remains of the Baptistery of *St. Stefano alle Fonti* that can be reached from the outside of the Duomo. It has been said that St. Ambrose (*Sant' Ambroggio*), patron saint of Milano, was baptized here.

There are of course many other particularities of the Duomo of Milano. An architectural monument to faith, art and history that took centuries to build will undoubtedly take some time to reveal itself to you. I once complained to my cousin Ornella about all the unfinished work I had to do, she looked at me, smiled and said "It is your Duomo", meaning it (my work) will never be finished! It is an ongoing process; for some people a life's journey. In fact, in Italy, the expression *"fabbrica del Duomo"* means a long, complex task that may be even impossible to complete. I have been visiting the Duomo of Milano for the last 11 years and each time I visit, I look up at the spires of this Gothic Cathedral and again realize the wisdom of the Italian people who approach each day with a purpose yet with the pleasure of *"la dolce vita"*. Traveling in Italy and staying with my Italian family and friends has led me to believe that Italians seem to know how to balance work and relaxation. They travel through the work day with a mid day break, surrounding themselves with beauty and art in their homes and businesses, eating fresh and vibrant food that connects them to their cultural traditions. Understanding that not everything has to be finished right now removes the intensity from a situation, diffuses stress and oftentimes allows for a better outcome or resolution. And whether by design, default or fortuitous placement in the universe, the Italians seem to get it. So when I am in Italy I try to taste, travel and

190

think like an Italian hoping that something will rub off on me and create a patina that reflects the faith, art and history of who I am.

See and Savor More

Various studies including one published in the Journal of Applied and Environmental Microbiology report that the pinkish-white crystalline Candolglia marble found in the Milan Cathedral has a characteristic pearly luminescence that is now in danger due to surface erosion, micro fractures, detachments, biological growths (fungus) and air pollution resulting in a series of lengthly restoration projects.

When visiting the Milan Duomo look up at the ceiling for a small red light bulb in the dome. It is said to mark the spot where one of the nails from Christ's Crucifixion has been placed. One of two recovered in the Holy Land by Saint Helena, mother of Emperor Constantine, the Holy Nail is part of a horse's bit used by Constantine who is said to have melted the holy nail into a bridle for his favorite horse. The relic is removed from the cathedral tabernacle once a year by the Archbishop of Milan. The Archbishop descends from the top of the cathedral in a basket decorated with angels and clouds to bring down the holy nail (*nivola*) for veneration. The *Festa della Nivola* is held every September on the Saturday before September 14, the Feast of the Exaltation of the Cross.

Chapter 25   The Beautiful and Famous Daughter of Rome

One of the pleasures about traveling in Italy is having the opportunity to experience some of the world's greatest art and design while tasting some of the world's best food and this is never truer than when traveling in Florence. According to statistics produced by UNESCO, 60% of the world's most important works of art are in Italy and approximately half of those are in Florence. The city of Florence has been listed by Travel and Leisure Magazine readers as one of the Best Cities in the World for the collective experience of travelers who judged it based on the sights, culture and arts, restaurants and food, people, shopping and value. Seeing and savoring Florence can be a Renaissance dream.

Around 1200 Florence became a leading economic city in Tuscany and never looked back. In the 15th century, the powerful and influential Medici created a dynasty that would define the history and culture of the city for the next two and a half centuries. Their passion for the arts, literature and learning created an intellectual and economic rebirth with larger than life personalities. Brunelleschi, Michelangelo, Leonardo da Vinci, Donatello, Masaccio and Fra Angelico were all commissioned by the Medici to create works of Renaissance art that still inspire and influence us today. This means that the sensory experience of visiting Florence is huge. The sights, sounds, monuments, churches, cathedrals, museums and markets can be overwhelming. The *enoteche, osterie, ristorante, trattorie*, bars and *gelaterie* offer a dizzying array of food choices. Florence is a cosmopolitan city, a worldwide destination for both business and pleasure and together with Rome an entry point for most first time travelers to Italy. So there is a lot to taste and see. You will need time to get to know Florence and you may not be able to do that in one trip, nor should you. It took me four trips to Florence before I began to understand, experience and appreciate the true beauty of this remarkable city on the Arno River. There are many wonderful books written about Florence and you might consider reading a few before your trip. They will help you sort through all the tourist babble and hone in on a few significant sites that appeal to you rather than your tour guide. There will be a first time you travel to Florence; most tours of Italy include Florence on their itineraries. On my first trip to Italy my cousin Lidia told me you cannot see all of Florence at one time, so you must choose to see what you can then you will return and see more and little by little you will discover the beauty of Florence. After all Dante called Florence "the beautiful and famous daughter of Rome" and as you know Rome wasn't built in a day.

I almost feel a magnetized drawn to visit Florence again and again. Like many of the sites in Italy Florence seems to need a longer look, another glance. The Duomo of Florence is one place I have visited many times but never get tired of seeing. It is located in the San Giovanni District of Florence which has the highest concentration of art per square meter on the planet. Here you will find museums, statues, churches, historical buildings and towers. The Duomo or Cathedral of Santa Maria del Fiore is the result of years of work that spanned over six centuries. *Fiore* is the Italian word for flower. The cathedral's name refers to the lily (which is actually an iris) on Florence's coat of arms but the white, pink and green Tuscan marble

193

of the cathedral's façade reminds me of a field of flowers. Santa Maria del Fiore is the fourth largest church in Europe in company with St. Peter's in Rome and the great Duomo of Milan. The Baptistery is thought to date back to the 4th century and is where Dante was baptized. The north and east bronze doors of the Baptistery were designed by Lorenzo Ghiberti after a famous competition with Brunelleschi and Donatello. The *campanile* (bell tower) of the cathedral was designed by Giotto and stands 85 meters (277.9 feet) high. You can climb the 414 steps to the top of the tower for a spectacular but dizzying view of Florence and the surrounding hills. The orange-tiled dome of the cathedral, rising over the rooftops of Florence is the classic symbol of the city. Constructed by Brunelleschi, it was built without scaffolding using an innovative, and at the time, highly debated method of construction.

You can get a panoramic view of Florence, the Duomo and Dome from Piazza Michelangelo, on the south bank of the Arno River. If you are driving, consider parking outside of Florence at Piazza Michelangelo. You can park here for free and take a city bus (#12 or13) into the main center of Florence where parking is prohibited and driving is best left to the Italians. For me it was a great place to park the car and leave the driving to "us", in this case the city of Florence's Department of Public Transportation. The bus trip into the city allows you to see a side of Florence that most tourists never see and get up close and personal with everyday Italians. On one bus trip we were sitting with a group of Florentine high school students and like high school students everywhere they had lots of energy, talking and laughing with great enthusiasm. So when the bus got stuck in the

194

typical traffic of Florence centro, they decided to take matters in their own hands and began to climb out the bus windows. The bus driver protested and like high school students everywhere some listened, some didn't. I never had any intention of climbing out the window of the bus so when the bus finally started to move, I moved up to the front and got off at the first stop. Another reason I like to park at P. Michelangelo is for the spectacular view of the Arno River, the Ponte Vecchio, the Duomo and the city of Florence. Travelers and Florentines alike will travel the distance from city centro to the piazza for the view or to park and watch the sunset that baths the city in a sepia colored living Renaissance painting. The *pizzale,* dedicated to Michelangelo, includes a copy of David in the middle of the space where people meet and greet. An urban hike from Porta Romana to P. Michelangelo would make a great experience although it does take some time and energy. The route includes circular boulevards that lead up into the hills that overlook Florence and was designed by architect Giuseppe Poggi between 1865 and 1871, during the period in which Florence was the capital city of the kingdom of Italy.

For many people Michelangelo's David defines Florence and his image can be seen all over the city. In the autumn of 1504 the Florentines gathered in Piazza Signoria to witness the arrival of the original David. It was an event of great importance. After four days traveling around the city, transported with the care and attention inside a wooden cage running on greased beams, Michelangelo's David finally reached its destination and was immediately celebrated as one of the greatest masterpieces of the Renaissance. David was so successful that Michelangelo was immediately called back to

Rome by the Pope himself for whom he would then paint the famous Sistine Chapel. David celebrated his 500th anniversary in 2004. There is a copy standing in place of the original which can be viewed at the Academia Gallery.

The art and architecture in Florence evokes the atmosphere of the Renaissance. Crossing the Ponte Vecchio, the oldest of Florence's six bridges, you can almost hear the footsteps of the Medici on the elevated walkway that separated them from the rest of the world. On the other side of the Arno, the Oltrarno, you can visit one of the city's largest palaces with museums that are second only to the Uffizi and get a feeling for how the rich and famous entertained and dined during the Renaissance. The 35,000 sq foot *Palazzo Pitti* (Pitti Palace), on the grounds of the Boboli Gardens, was often a venue for the elaborate dinners of the Medici Grand Dukes and the site of lavish and renowned banquets including one given by Grand Duke Ferdinando I who flooded the courtyard with water and filled it with a parade of sailing ships. The palace and gardens are spectacular, a mixture of Renaissance art and architecture with an eccentric touch of the owner's personal whimsy. Be sure to look for the statue of Nano Morgante, Cosimo Medici's favorite dwarf, riding a turtle. He is naked with a potbelly and is said to be an allegory of business and wisdom. The Medici were living large from the 13th to the 17th century. This powerful Florentine family produced three popes (Leo X, Clement VII, and Leo XI), numerous rulers of Florence (notably Lorenzo the Magnificent, patron of some of the most famous works of Renaissance art) and later members of the French and English royalty. They ate, drank and made merry and some would say led

196

Italy into the Renaissance. Through banking and commerce they achieved great wealth and political influence throughout Europe. So I was a little surprised when I first saw the unassuming Church of San Lorenzo, the official church of the Medici where six of the Medici dukes are buried as well as other family members. The monochromatic gray and white interior and austere facade of San Lorenzo seemed out of character. But once inside the understated elegance of the Medici Chapels with Michelangelo's famous sculptures of Dusk and Dawn, Night and Day reflected the commanding presence of the grand dukes who are are buried there. The less is more approach may not necessarily have been by design but rather due to a lack of funds. Work on the church was abruptly cancelled by Michelangelo's financially-strapped patrons before any real progress had been made so the minimalistic basilica lacks a facade to this day.

Seeing Florence is only part of one of the best experiences you will have In Italy. Another would be savoring the food of the city. Like the art of the Renaissance the Medici defined the taste of the Renaissance and influenced the culinary style of all European cooking. The kitchens of the Medici were in a constant state of experimentation and innovation. Caterina de' Medici was especially known for her love of good food and entertainment. Her interest in the culinary arts influenced the course of French cooking when she became the wife of Henry II of France and her party planning skills were spun into elaborate court banquets and entertainments known as "magnificence's". With her retinue of chefs, pastry makers and gardeners, she brought many Tuscan cooking customs with her to

197

France. She decorated her tables with flowers and introduced the use of silverware and forks which had long been at the tables of Florence but were almost never found on French tables. She introduced olive oil, Chianti wines, artichokes, spinach and white beans to French cooks. It has been said that is was a "Florentine who reformed the antique French cooking of medieval tradition" that gave rise to the science of cooking and the art of eating well. Dinner with the Medici would be served in many courses and include roasted meats of game or fowl like capon, pigeon or peacock. Pine nuts and raisins were common in Italian Renaissance cooking and were used in both sweet and savory dishes. Tarts, custards and puddings made with cherries sweetened with wine were popular. There would be no tomatoes, peppers, kidney beans, turkey or potatoes. These ingredients native to the Americas were not yet known in Europe. *Cibreo*, a local Florentine dish is said to have been a favorite of Caterina de' Medici. Traditionally made with various parts of the chicken including the crest or comb, *Cibreo* dates from the Renaissance and was originally served at the beginning of important banquets. The word *cibreo* comes from the Latin "*cibus regis*" meaning "king's food". Caterina is said to have loved this dish so much that she almost died of indigestion from eating too much.

Today you don't need a royal invitation to experience a taste of the Renaissance. The flavors once enjoyed at the tables of the Dukes of Tuscany are available at almost every *osteria, trattoria* and *ristorante* in Florence and throughout Tuscany. Walk through the streets of Florence and stop along the way for a glass of wine and a *panino* at a street side café' (*I Fratelli* is very popular) or search the web for the many reviews and ratings of places to eat in Florence and choose one or two that appeal to you. Look for *trattorie* that are less expensive sisters of well known Florentine restaurants like *Trattoria Cibreino* (near Santa Croce) similar to the fashionable *Cibreo*, where you can find traditional Florentine dishes with a twist and *Vineria alle Murate* the less expensive sister of *Alle Murate*, next door. Just remember the cuisine of the Medici is alive and well and ready to taste all over Florence but as in any large city variations in quality and service abound. So do your research and if you are willing to go off the tourist radar, motor out to the 'burbs" and spend time in country. Explore the walled medieval village of Artimino, visiting two of the famous Medici villas in the area. You can eat at *Da Delfina*, a guidebook recommended restaurant near the *Villa dell'Artimino*. If you don't have a car, take a 15 minute train ride from Santa Maria Novella station in Florence to the town of Signa and a cab from there to *Da Delfina*. Or if you are driving, continue farther afield to the towns and villages outside of Florence and stop in a local *trattoria* for a typical meal of the region. Most all are good and allow you to see and savor the famous and beautiful daughter of Rome.

See and Savor More

Florence has more than one million works of Renaissance art throughout the city including the paintings and sculptures found in the famous museums of Florence; the *Galleria degli Uffizi, Bargello, Accademia, Museo dell'Opera del Duomo* (directly behind the Cathedral) and Pitti Palace.

The Medici have always been represented with balls. Although no one would dispute that this family was testosterone driven, the red balls on the gold shield in the family crest are said to have several meanings. Some say that the balls represent dents in the battle shield of one of Charlemagne's knights from whom, legend claims, the family were descended. Another story claims that the round balls are medicinal pills representing the family's origins as doctors (*medici*) or apothecaries although this has been disputed as well. Many believe that this story was made up by the French who were not happy with Caterina, their Tuscan imported Queen who was not of noble blood. A more plausible explanation may be that the balls are actually coins inspired by the *Arte del Cambio*, the Guild of Moneychangers, a bankers' association to which the Medici belonged.

The Medici coat of arms can be found throughout Florence on buildings and manuscripts, ledgers and wine jars as a symbol of the power and patronage of the Medici. It can also be found with the keys of St. Peter and the papal tiara as part of the coat of arms of Pope Leo XI (1605-1605) who was born Alessandro Ottaviano de' Medici.

The Medici ruled Florence for most of the period from 1434-1737. It is interesting to note that during that time the number of red balls on the Medici family crest changed. According to the Florence Art Guide there were originally eleven balls on a golden field. During the rule of Cosimo the Elder there were eight; while his son Piero the Gouty reduced them to seven. The Medici crest of Lorenzo the Magnificent has six and at the tomb of Cosimo I in the Medici Chapels there are five. The Medici family crest was also altered over time with a stamp of the lilies of France added to one of the Medici balls. This distinction was received from King Louis XI in exchange for diplomatic services and upon receipt the ball became blue.

The Medici Crest

Chapter 26   Atonement for Your Sins

Religion was often a reason or rhyme for the creation of Renaissance art. God's power, perfection and politics were intriguing subject matter for artists with patrons ready to pay for impressive works of art. Fresco art in particular lended itself to such broad majestic themes. Done on plaster walls or ceilings, the artist could paint expansive scenes or cycles that unfolded like visual pages from a book. Signorelli's massive frescoes of the *Last Judgment* (1499–1503) in the Orvieto Cathedral, Michelangelo's ceiling frescoes in the Sistine Chapel and Lorenzetti's allegorical frescoes of Good and Bad Government in Siena's Palazzo Pubblico all made an unmistakable statement about the consequences of evil and the rewards of time well spent. So it's not surprising that one of the most important masterpieces of Western art was painted as a fresco cycle with inspiring scenes from the life of Christ and his mother Mary. What is surprising is that this most celebrated work of art, by the Italian Renaissance master Giotto, is located in a chapel on the estate grounds of a money lenders son who in atonement for his father's sins commissioned the fresco.

Reginaldo Scrovegni was a wealthy moneylender from the city of Padua. He was portrayed in the Seventh Circle of Hell in Dante's Divine Comedy, where usurers are to be found swatting away fire, like animals swat bugs, with purses around their necks emblazoned with their family coat of arm, their punishment to be served.

So I went on alone and even farther (43)

Along the seventh circle's outer margin,

To where the melancholy people sat.

When I had set my eyes upon the faces (52)

Of some on who the painful fire falls,

I recognized no one; but I did notice

That from the neck of each a purse was hung (55)

That had a special color or an emblem,

And their eyes seemed to feast upon these pouches.

Then, as I let my eyes move further on, (61)

I saw another purse that was blood red,

And it displayed a goose more white than butter.

And one who had an azure, pregnant sow

From Dante's Inferno (Mandelbaum Translation)

In the above excerpt from Dante's Inferno, the emblem with the azure
pregnant sow referred to the coat of arms of the Scrovegni family. It's
no wonder that Enrico Scrovegni, Reginaldo's son felt compelled to
build a private chapel next to the family palazzo in penitence for his
father's sins. He must have been frightened out of his mind after
reading of his impending doom and hoped not only to atone for the
sins of his father but his own as it was suggested that Enrico was also
involved in usurious practices. So Enrico commissioned Giotto to
design a chapel with a series of frescoes on the site of a Roman
arena that was on the grounds of his family estate. The vaulted chapel

203

is a work of breathtaking beauty with a ceiling that resembles a starry blue sky. There are generational scenes of Jesus, his mother Mary and her parents Joachim and Anna that unfold like a family album and a particularly sweet scene of the nativity of Jesus and the adoration of the Magi that you might expect on the front of a Christmas card. The walls of the chapel contain 37 panels in three tiers with scenes of the Annunciation, Allegories of the Vices and Virtues and a compelling scene of the Final Judgment. Rather than a fire and brimstone rendition, the Final Judgment scene is a gentler reminder of the consequences of sin. One that might be part of a children's catechism in which their elders stand in judgment with Christ while the saints and angels gather in support of their good deeds and mitigate the bad. Viewing the frescoes begins with a short minute video on the history, design and restoration of the chapel. You must arrive at least five minutes before the time (*ore*) printed on your ticket (*il biglietto*) to pass through an environmentally controlled chamber. The area is sealed to allow for cleansing the air before a group is admitted into the chapel. There you are allowed fifteen minutes to view the frescoes. Although some have complained about the monitored viewing of the Scrovegni frescoes calling it "an unpleasant experience", I did not find it to be so. I would rather have the experience of seeing a preserved historical site in its indigenous state than having a facsimile where sightseers indulge their Disneyesque needs in a contrived computer generated avatar. Such experiences have their place but for those of us who what to get up close and personal with what's left of the endangered species of the art and architecture of our planet the desire to save and conserve an artifact, painting or monument in its truest form is important and the inconvenience is accepted.

The Scrovegni Chapel in Padua is considered to be one of the Great
Fresco Cycles of the Renaissance. It has been over 700 years since
the *Cappella degli Scrovegni* was consecrated yet the frescoes found
here remain timeless. Giotto's achievements in Italian art and
architecture are substantial. He designed the Campanile (bell tower)
of the Florence Cathedral and in 1296 a series of frescoes called the
St. Francis cycle in the Upper Church of San Francesco in Assisi. The
St. Francis frescoes are part of what has been called the "stubborn
mystery of Giotto", meaning that attributing authorship of the frescoes
is troublesome for some who feel that Giotto may not have had a
hand in creating them. An Italian art restorer Bruno Zanardi, who
cleaned the frescoes between 1978 and 1982 believes that Giotto did
not paint the 1296 St. Francis Legend. Zanardi contends that the
style, color and form of these frescoes don't fit the Giotto profile.
Zanardi and others attribute the St. Francis series to a school of
Roman artists rather than the Florentine Giotto. Among some, it has
even been heard that Florence was not the birthplace of the
Renaissance but rather it was Rome. Rome in atonement for the
artistic shortcomings of Florence. *Non possibile.* Yet I would not speak
such heresy. The power, privilege and patrons of the art of
Renaissance Rome are not to be taken lightly. I will leave it to Dante
to define the creative soul of the Renaissance and their place in the
Divine Comedy.

Chapter 27 The Chimneys of Portogruaro

The architectural elements of Italian design read like a Who's Who of the architecture of the Western world. Together with Greece, Italy set the standard for what was to follow in the art and design of living in the material world. The great arches and domes, vaulted ceilings, arcades, masonry, marble and brickwork of Italy continue to be a reference point and model for architectural study. Students look to Italy as an open air classroom that far exceeds the pictures and pages of their textbooks. Tourists have a must see list of the great buildings and monuments of Italy one camera click at a time and architecturally inspired travelers linger at every piazza trying to absorb as much of the visual culture as they can. With all the extraordinary architectural treasures to be found in Italy it's easy to overlook the unique architecture found in the towns and villages that are off the tourist radar. Florence, Siena, San Gimignano, Venice and Rome have become world famous for their domes and facades, carvings, arches and towers but the chimneys of Portogruaro in the Veneto create a rooftop landscape that would make the magical world of Mary Poppins a reality.

Once protected by the Venetian Republic, Portogruaro continues to retain the charm of a favored child. The canals, medieval arcades and stone bridges of Portogruaro remind you of a miniature version of Venice. The noble houses and palaces in the historical center of the city have double entrances, one from the street side and one from the water. You know you are in the *terre dei Doge* because the ancient influence of the Venetian empire is still felt in the local gastronomy, wine and architecture of the region. My Italian cousins live in the Commune of Fossalto di Portogruaro in the Veneto. When I visited them last September I mentioned that the chimneys in Portogruaro were different. Almost every building in town had a unique chimney creating a fantasmagorical skyline. Yes, fantasmagorical as in fantastic, amazing, magical. But when my cousins explained the reason behind the unusual chimney design it wasn't as much of a Tim Burton experience as I imagined. In fact it was more like a Louis Sullivan-Frank Lloyd Wright collaboration with an Italian twist. That is to say it was more of "form follows function" with an Italian sense of style. According to my cousin Mirna, chimneys played an important role in Portogruaran society because of the *stufa a legna*, wood burning stove. Principally used in cooking, the *stufa* was the center of the household *il focolare e il cuore della casa*, the hearth and the heart of the house. To this day my cousins in Portogruaro have a *stufa* in their kitchen. One of the most traditional foods cooked on the stufas of the Veneto is *Baccala' alla vicentina* made with unsalted dried cod, butter, flour, olive oil, milk, onion, anchovies and grated Parmigiano served with soft polenta. In Italy, unsalted dried cod is known as stockfish, *stoccafisso* in Italian. It is used to make this dish although it seems that in Italian the word *bacala* means any dish made with dried cod in general. My cousin Mirna made this dish for me on a recent visit to Portogruaro. It was warm and creamy; Italian comfort food. *Baccala' alla vicentina* is native to this region where legend has it that in the late 1800's a *trattoria* operated by a certain Mrs. Gluseppina Terribile in Bianco, nicknamed "Siora Vitoria" first served the dish that shortly became the culinary attraction of the area. It was said that exclamations of satisfaction met in every dining room,

207

from courtyard to courtyard and people traveled from near and far to taste the delicate, creamy *bacala* studded sauce simmering in the wood fired stoves of the Veneto.

Now I suppose many other parts of Italy cooked and heated their homes with woodburning stoves and ventilated the stoves with chimneys but for the people of Portogruaro ordinary boring chimneys would not do. They got creative with their chimneys, very creative. Every building in town with a *stufa* is topped off with a trumpet shaped cap, crown, helmet or miniature pavilion. The chimneys of Portogruaro seem to have no purposeful form other than to express the pleasure of design. The chimneys in nearby Venice are also different in style and number and were said to reflect the wealth and prestige of the landowner much like the towers of San Gimignano rising above the Tuscan hills like medieval skyscrapers. In the 1500's there were more than 10,000 chimneys in Venice.The noble families of Venice afforded themselves the luxury of multiple fireplaces ergo multiple chimneys. So like the towers of San Gimignano, the chimneys of Venice may be more a demonstration of conspicuous consumption than utilitarian design. But the funnel shaped chimney pots of La Serenessima and the whimsical chimneys of Portogruaro are not all for show. The large funnel shaped chimney pots improved the drawing power of the wood burning *stufa* and trapped cinders to control the risk of fires. The added charm and unmistakable flare of this overlooked architectural element only make visiting this region of Italy all the more appealing.

Visiting Portogruaro reminded me that after 10 years and 10,000 miles taste traveling in Italy, Italy offers more. For those willing to take the road to Venice less traveled you can do no better than to stop in Portogruaro. Here you will find a city with Venetian arches and arcades, canals, a leaning Roman tower and noble houses that overlook the historic watermills on the Lemene River. All within the watchful eye of the "gru", a type of crane that is the town's symbol and from which the city gets its name "port of the gru". You can easily spend a day or two wandering and relaxing in Portogruaro with a side trip to the Adriatic beaches and Venice. And when you're there don't forget to look up at the rooftops and chimneys and think about all the *stufa* happily cooking below.

See and Savor More

Chimneys of Portogruaro

Chapter 28 Ancient Farmacia

In Italy, between art and beauty there is fragrance; essences originally derived from the ethos of healing with ingredients from nature that are meant to create a sense of *benessere* (well being). A weary taste traveler could greatly benefit from knowing about the ancient workshops and *antica farmacia* (pharmacies) where these products are still made. One of the oldest is the Officina Profumo Farmaceutica di Santa Maria Novella in Florence. A fragrant universe filled with terra cotta jars and gilded urns that was already well known in Dante's time. It was established in the 13th century by the Dominican friars of Florence who began to cultivate and prepare medicinal plants and herbs used for the treatment of the sick. Many of the products and lotions available for purchase today are based on the ancient recipes used by the friars.

A five minute walk from the Santa Maria Novella train station, the Officina Profumo Farmaceutica di Santa Maria Novella is miles away from the frantic pace of modern day Florence. Behind the unassuming entrance on Via della Scala 16, Florence becomes Firenze and you are transported to the time of Caterina di Medici whose renowned perfumes are still being made according to formulas from the 1500's. The elixirs, essences, distillations and powders have remained world famous over the centuries and inhaling their aromas is like breathing in Renaissance Italy. Santa Maria Novella products and preparations are truly unique. Soaps are made by hand, molded with antique soap making equipment and aged like a fine chesse. Potpourris are made with flowers and herbs grown in the Florentine hills then seasoned in old terra cotta jars for several months. When you enter the sales salon, the former Chapel of St. Nicholas, at SMN Farmaceutica you are given *la Nota dell'essenze,* the list of essences. *Pomate, spiriti, balsami, acque, liquori e altre preparazion* are listed on a parchment like scroll in both Italian and English. Every pomade, spirit, balm, water and other preparation a Medici could possibly want. I too wanted these perfumes and medieval elixirs displayed on the apothecary shelves amid antique ceramic jars and the copper and bronze *apparati* of the friar chemist. Everytime I travel to Florence I live the life of a Medici princess and buy soaps, scented wax tablets and powders made from the ground rhizome of the Florentine iris and *carta d'Armenia*, little strips of paper that smolder and freshen the air. I bring Italy home with potpourri from the Florentine hills and the most exquisite handmade terracotta pomegranate infuser that has been immersed in a vat of pomegranate oil essence to create a fragrant "objet d' art. I also make sure to buy a bottle of Alkermes, formulated by the friar-chemist Fra Cosimo to offset weary and lazy spirits and to flavor the savoiardi (ladyfingers) when making a zuppa Inglese or English trifle. There are calming waters for tired or puffy eyes and an antihysteria water which I'm pleased to say I haven't needed yet. You can buy a refreshing tonic for red eyes that was already available for sale in the second half of the fourteenth century and aromatic vinegar, *Aceto dei Sette Ladri*, still produced following the old formulary said to be very useful in the case of fainting spells. There are cleansing milks, tonics, creams, shampoos and hair conditioners for men and women and light fragrances especially for children. There is even an insect repellant that you will find very useful traveling in summer and early fall when the Italian mosquito (*zanzara)* can be very persistent. One of the first alcohol based perfumes, *Aqua della Regina*, was created here for Caterina de'Medici, an essence that she took with her to Paris when she became the queen of France where it was named, *Eau de la Reine*. The pharmacy still produces a fragrance similar to the "water of the queen" called Eau de Cologne Classica.

Although the Renaissance frescoes and imposing salons of SMN Farmacia may seem more like a museum than a working pharmacy don't let the ornate interior and gilded furnishings deter you from shopping till you drop. There is much to see and enjoy and the sales staff are very helpful. Everything was put into perspective one afternoon when I was looking at the list of essences and checking it twice. Gazing up at the frescoed vaulted ceiling of the main sales salon (the *antica spezieria* - old spice shop), I noticed an unusual fluorescent design. It was in the shape of a red car like the one from the Disney cartoon movie of the same name. A helium balloon from one of SMN's little customers had floated to the top of the vaulted ceiling and lodged itself amid the gilded stucco ornamentation happily floating, an alien creature from another time and place, a metaphor for SMN and the future. The company now has shops in London and Paris and can be bought at high end stores in the States but the centuries old formulas of the Dominican friars of Florence still are kept in trust at the Officina Profumo-Farmaceutica di Santa Maria Novella where the atmosphere of the Renaissance still lingers.

Adjacent to the *farmacia*, there is a monastery complex, cloisters and the Basilica of Santa Maria Novella, from which the *farmacia*, nearby piazza and railway station take their name. Although often

212

overshadowed by the Florence's Duomo of Santa Maria del Fiore with Brunelleschi's famous orange tiled dome, the Basilica of Santa Maria Novella is one of the most beautiful churches in Italy. The basilica was the first great basilica in Florence and the piazza that fronts the church was once the site of chariot races held every June to celebrate the feast of John the Baptist, patron saint of Florence. The course was marked by two obelisks around which the chariots were to turn. The obelisks were made of marble from the Versilian quarries favored by Michelangelo. They marked the internal limits of the course of the race and can still be seen today. The inlaid black and white marble facade of the church creates a very graphic background for a round window crowned by a pediment. The pediment contains the Dominican solar emblem and is flanked on both sides by enormous S-curved volutes or scrolls giving it a particular harmony of design. Santa Maria Novella with its chapels and adjoining Green Cloister (the name is taken from the pigment used in the frescoes) should not be missed and can easily be visited on your way to the Farmaceutica of Santa Maria Novella.

There are other monastic apothecaries and herbalists in Italy that still make natural products that follow ancient recipes for health and well being. One of the most evocative is the monastic pharmacy at Santuario La Verna in the Tuscan Apennines where St. Francis of Assisi lived a life of spiritual contemplation and penitence. Another is the Benedictine Abbey of Monte Oliveta Maggiore in the Crete Senesi south of Siena. The abbey still produces honey and distilled herbal spirits made according to various ancient recipes. And then there is the Certosa di Pavia (Charterhouse of Pavia) a Carthusian monastery near Milan, a huge complex of art and architecture that is amazing. A hallway with a botanical collection of preserved healing plants leads to the monastic pharmacy where you can buy honey, chocolate and the famous Chartreuse liqueur.

In Italy plant derived products have always been associated with beauty and health and the idyllic Tuscan landscape continues to be an inspiration and source for many companies who want to take the simple and natural ingredients from the countryside combined with traditional methods of production and make these products commercially available throughout the world. The Italian company L'Erbario Toscano recreates the scents and properties of the aromatic plants and wild field flowers from the hillsides of Tuscany. Founded over 40 years ago with the inspiration that "nature is the essence", L'Erbario Toscano products are now sold in numerous boutiques in Italy, the United States, the United Kingdom, Japan, Hong Kong, Aruba, Denmark, Norway, Venezuela, Dubai, Australia, New Zealand and Vietnam. I fell in love with L'Erbario Toscano on my first trip to Italy. By car from Milano through Chianti on our way to Siena stopping to visit Monteriggioni where my cousin's husband Roberto was born, we found a unique shop in Volterra that sold L'Erbario Toscano products. For me they represent the rustic beauty of Tuscany and a time when I was a novice taste traveler just learning about the art and beauty of Italy and wanting more. Remember seeing and savoring Italy is about engaging all your senses in the experience of travel. Don't miss out on the scents of Italy. They are a great way to "bring Italy home" and remind you of your trip.

See and Savor More

Aceto dei Sette Ladri, or Seven Thieves' Vinegar is named for a band of seven thieves who would strip the bodies of the dead during the plague. They protected themselves from infection by rubbing this preparation on themselves. I guess you could call this the original hand sanitizer.

The pulpit at the Basilica of Santa Maria Novella was the site of the first attack on the beliefs of Galileo that eventually lead to his indictment by the Church.

The enormous s-curved scrolls on the façade of the Basilica of Santa Maria Novella were the first ever used in architecture. The volute scrolls were later copied by other architects when building churches throughout Italy.

L'Erbario Toscano products

215

Chapter 29 The Pope Slept Here

Pienza is known around the world for being one of Tuscany's Renaissance treasures and the home of a Pope with a vision to transform his birthplace into the "ideal" Renaissance city. Located in the breathtakingly beautiful Val d'Orcia (a UNESCO World Heritage Site), overlooking Monte Amiata, the medieval town of Corsignano was to be Italy's 15th century version of Renovation Nation. Reconstructed and renamed Pienza under the Piccolomini Pope Pius II, a new cathedral, town hall and palazzo were built. I spent an afternoon in Pienza and visited the Palazzo Piccolomini (the pope's summer residence) with a *signorina* who spoke an Italian version of Spanglish. Slightly difficult to understand but well intended.

The elegant open courtyard, the halls of period furniture and memorabilia and the gardens that overlook the valley below were well worth the cost of admission. *Il biglietto d'ingresso interno* was 7EU and for that price I got to see where the Pope slept.

I also got to see priceless masterpieces, tapestries, weaponry and paintings and a *scagliola* table representing a map of the Sienese States. There was a chair that was used to carry the Pope in his travels and a medieval baby's high chair. But my favorite was the More or Less Clock, a huge medieval clock that is called more or less because it only works in 15 minute increments (instead of seconds). Now I understand the Italian sense of time! However what engaged me the most was the furniture in the palazzo. Like walking through a decorator show house you got a sense of the style of the family who lived here and what types of things they liked to come home to. It turns out that the Pope was not so different from us at least in his dining room. Among the tables and chairs, along the side wall of the dining room, I recognized a familiar piece of furniture found in the homes of my Italian family and friends since I was a little girl, *la credenza*, Sometimes refered to as a "sideboard", *la credenza* played a prominent role at family dinners and gatherings. The credenza became popular in the second half of the 19th century as a stage or platform for serving meals at the dining room table. The style and construction would have varied depending on whether you were wealthly or of more moderate means. Some credenzas were elaborate pieces of furniture with marquetry and inland wood. Many had glass display cabinents for china and silver and drawers for cutlery. Our Italian family's credenza was simpler, with a classic Milanese design. Made of walnut with recessed handles, it was elegantly understated. I can remember many a happy meal served from the family credenza on a Sunday afternoon with Hunter's Chicken, polenta and *contorni* of sauted mushrooms and steamed and sauted fresh green beans served with grated Parmigiano Reggiano cheese.

Today credenzas have stepped out of the dining room into the conference room and almost any other room in the house. Re-purposed credenzas can be found in the bedroom, bathroom or baby's room to become a bookcase, a storage cabinet, a computer home office desk or an entertainment center for your Flat panel TV. Today credenzas are often referred to as "hospitality buffets" working in hotels and restaurants as serving stages for continental breakfasts and cocktail hor'dourves. Traditional woods like walnut, oak or pine

217

have been replaced with more unusal materials like white lacquer or Brazilian teak. I have seen hybrid credenzas made from Plexiglas, wooden shelving and metal legs and IKEA inspired contemporary credenzas that are part of everyone's interior design on a dime. In past times, because of their ornate and elaborte design, credenzas were referred to as "highbrow" furniture. Often a part a matching dining room set that would be the showpiece of the home, having a credenza became a furniture status symbol for American families.

But the history of *la credenza* is one of practicality and pragmatism that begins with the tasting of food. In 16th century Italy "*credenza*" was the act of tasting food and drinks by a servant for a lord or another important person (pope or cardinal) before it was served. By tasting it they made sure the food was not poisoned. The word *la credenza* (Italian for belief or confidence) passed from the room where the act took place to the name of the long tables on which food was served. The word further morphed into the English language as "credence"'meaning credibility or trust. While traveling in Italy I've had a chance to taste some remarkable food from the credenzas of some wonderful *ristorante* and *trattorie* and from the homes of my Italian family and friends. I've seen credenzas in museums, private gallerys and in the design studios and shops of Italian artisans. Every year I become more interested in and more excited by this uniquely Italian piece of furniture that has been adopted by the whole world. Now everytime I see a credenza I think about the wonderful times I've had at the tables of Italy. Like the spectacular *fattoria* credenza in Treviso groaning with the weight of *l'arrosto di pavone* (roasted peacock) and goose from the family farm. Or the credenza in my friend Alice's

218

country house in the Bolognese hills where the buffet breakfast served at the Lodole Country House in Monzuno is the finest I've had in Italy with an assortment of meats, cheeses, tarts, cereals and honey that are *fantastici*! Or the Tuscan credenza in the dining room of Tenuta di Capezzana near the town of Carmignano, northwest of Florence, where I spent a delightful September afternoon experiencing the warm hospitality of the Contini Bonacossi family in the dining room of their Medici villa. I won't soon forget the credenza in the kitchens of Castello Gropparello with my friend Rita learning the fine art of *cucina Piacentina*, Emilian Romagnan cooking from the hills of Piacenza. Our efforts filled the credenza with platters of *faraona* (Guinea fowl), stuffed vegetables, *maltagliata* pasta and a Piacenza tart filled with plum jam. At the other end of the credenza, standing at attention were bottles of Gutturnio wine ready to be poured. Pius's city is known for the quality of its pecorino cheese and the credenzas of Azienda Zazzeri in Pienza are filled with wheels of pecorino where soft Sauvis, semi-matured Fucus and wine infused Vinaceus are displayed with great attention. The aromas and intoxicating flavors make history palpable as you walk into a culinary garden of eden where cheese is as tempting as Eve's apple. One of my favorite shops in Pienza, the owner works directly with a consortium of small farms, ranches and quality manufacturers in Tuscany who believe in preserving and protecting the culinary traditions of the region.

But as impressive as the credenza at Palazzo Piccolomini is, its purpose was no different than the credenzas found in homes and restaurants throughout the world. It was meant to serve. The Italian credenza reflects the warm and gracious hospitality of the Italian

219

people and their desire to introduce you to their country and traditions. Seeing and savoring a country can be no better than this.

So what type of credenza do I have in my home; a simple Southern style mahogany hunt board (another name and adaptation of the Italian credenza). Someone else acquired the family credenza much to my dismay and I have been on a quest to replace it ever since but can find nothing quite like it. This year I plan to start building a Tuscan farmhouse in the cornfields of Indiana so I will be looking in earnest for that perfect Italian credenza that is sure to play a prominent role in my family gatherings.

See and Savor More

Scagliola comes from the Italian word meaning "chips" and refers to a technique using ground gypsum and glue colored with marble or granite dust to imitate the look of ornamental marble. In the United States *scagliola* was popular in the 19th and 20th centuries. Important US buildings featuring *scagliola* include the Allen County Courthouse in Fort Wayne, IN, the old El Paso County Courthouse in Colorado Springs, CO, the Kansas State Capitol in Topeka, KS and St. Louis Union Station in St. Louis, MO. *Scagliola* decoration is also featured in the Rialto Square Theatre, Joliet, IL, Cathedral of St. Helena in Helena, MT, Milwaukee Public Library Central Library in Milwaukee, WI and the French Lick Resort Casino in French Lick, IN.

Travel

Chapter 30 Traveling Outside the Box

I'm always trying to think of a way to describe to my friends what it was like when I return from a trip to Italy. Invariably they end up with a wide eyed stare and their mouths open in disbelief. At first I'm not sure if this is good or bad but as my journey continues and I talk about my experiences the most frequent comment I end up getting is AMAZING. I always get to spend time with people who are passionate about Italian food and culture and I'm fortunate to spend time with them eating and cooking some fabulous food. I've traveled to small towns and villages and some hidden places that are typically off the tourist radar for most Americans. And my Italian family and friends make sure that I see Italy through their eyes to experience the heart and soul of the Italian people. So I guess that in some ways you can describe my travels in Italy as somewhat unconventional, what I call "traveling outside of the box". And what I've learned is that there is a different way of traveling in Italy, a way that is more than just a "show and tell" tour and results in some unique and memorable travel adventures.

People often ask me how to plan a taste and travel trip. Begin by looking for sites that pair food with the history and culture of a region, an evocative site where you can imagine the history of the food being prepared and eaten. For example if one of your favorite Italian foods is pasta with Bolognese sauce, plan on visiting Emilia Romagna to eat *tagliatelli alla Bolognese* under the porticos of Bologna. Incorporate

221

the experience of eating into the experience of traveling. Let food become more than a necessity. Let it become part of the experience and not just an afterthought. Most travelers don't think of pairing food and travel in quite this way. We eat on the run at home and end up doing the same thing when we travel. We don't think about making our travel experience more meaning through the food we eat. Yet unique and exceptional experiences are everyway when taste traveling in Italy. There should be no excuse to come back from a trip to Italy without boasting about the most wonderful food you ate, wine you drank and what you saw. But what often happens is that our impatient nature translates into the most expedient meal or worse yet a meal that is contrived simulation of an authentic Italian experience right off the tour bus.

So begin to re-think your travels in Italy. You don't have to settle for a show and tell tour or a neatly boxed set. You can design your own play list that allows you to see and savor Italy in a way that makes sense to you. To begin you will need a **travel goal** that will be the driving force behind your trip. Choose it wisely. Defining the focus of your trip including specific choices about where you want to go, what you want to see and where you want to stay can go a long way in making your trip all you hoped it would be. Seeing and savoring Italy is not just for the gourmet traveler. If you're interested in art, history, horse trekking, hiking, biking, adventure travel, shopping or fashion you can combine any of these activities into your taste and travel itinerary. In fact I have arranged many tours that include a few days at a cooking school in Emilia Romagna with a visit to an outlet mall and driving a Ferrari in Maranello. An attainable travel goal can sometimes be difficult to define. You may not be able to do everything you want at one time but that's perfectly all right. Traveling in Italy is not meant to be a once in a lifetime experience. A well defined travel goal is just one in a series of reasons that you will have to return to Italy again and again.

Be realistic about your travel goals but **add a dream**. You cannot possibly travel through the Tuscany of Leonardo, the Florence of the Medici or the canals of Venice without being drawn into the magic of Italy. Choose a secondary travel goal that may be a little out of reach but may also be attainable and build it into your schedule. You're in Italy among the finest art in the Western world, eating the most glorious food, surrounded by monuments of great historical significance, dodging Vespas and being transformed by the beauty and romance of a landscape that will touch your very soul. View this goal as icing on the cake; as something that heightens your travel experience.

Once you've decided on the overall goal of your trip you can begin to plan how to **spend your time to the best advantage**. You can't manage the passage of time but you can manage your choices and decisions about how to spend your time while on your trip. It takes time to taste and travel. I know I've said this before but you wouldn't think of making a reservation in a fine restaurant with the intention of eating your meal in 15 minutes.

Allow enough time to enjoy all aspects of your travels and **be realistic about the time** it takes to accomplish your travel goals. A long weekend spent in Rome visiting and touring the Vatican and seeing a few other sites can easily be done but a drive through Chianti tasting wine along the way needs more time. Having a set itinerary with some wiggle room is important to allow for the unexpected occurrences that always seem to come up when traveling.

Also consider the time of the year. The months of September and October are considered by many to be the best time to travel in Italy because of the beautiful weather and seasonal festivals centering on food and wine. The colors of the season and the abundance of the harvest make this a popular time of the year to see and savor Italy. High seasons for the Italian traveler are the Christmas holidays, February school break (for ski resorts) Easter and the whole month of August. August 15th is *ferragosto*, this is when most of Italy celebrates summer with vacations and practically everything is closed. This is the time when my Italian family leaves their apartment in Milano and travels to the mountains or seashore. Cooling off in the blue waters of the Mediterranean Sea or eating *troppi gelati* on the shores of Lake Garda is how many Northern Italians escape the heat of the cities and enjoy Italy during the summer months. But don't discount the summer season for traveling in Italy. For many American families this is the time for their annual summer vacation. But remember this is a popular time for Italians to travel to these destinations as well so expect more crowds. Also many accommodations in Italy do not have air conditioning or screens on windows. Mosquitoes can sometimes be a problem so when traveling from June on make sure to bring an insect repellent.

In my mind there is no bad time to travel to Italy. Every season has its appeal. One year I traveled to Milano in February, probably one of the least popular months to travel to Italy but one of the best times to travel because of low airfares and had a wonderful five day trip shopping, visiting museums and eating in and around Milano.

Next think about **who you will be traveling with**. Companions in travel can be a joy or a pain. The best traveling companions are like minded about most of their travel goals so try to get a consensus about what each member in your group thinks is important and settle on an underlying collective goal for the trip. You want everyone to feel the trip was both their own as well as part of a total group experience. Common consensus needs room for individuality. A certain level of diversity among travelers is important because everyone's background and knowledge can enrich the total group experience (think about planning the guest list for a dinner party). However if everyone doesn't agree on a collective travel goal problems are sure to arise and problems take time to solve and cause unnecessary stress. You want to have a convivial relationship with your traveling companions. Remember you will be living, eating, learning, playing, and traveling together for X number of days. Disagreements are bound to occur but if you have a common goal you are more likely to get back on track and not waste valuable time. Plan to spend time together as a group and time alone. Collective memories shared between friends and family makes lasting memories but even if you're traveling as a couple or with your best friends everyone needs time by themselves to discover the Italy that is truly meaningful for them. To find that one place, that special wine, that inspiring work of art, that

225

landscape or moment that makes Italy magical and creates a unique memory. Don't make the mistake of gobbling up everyone's time. Everyone needs some breathing room. And don't allow anyone in the group to say "I'm just along for the ride". This is seldom true. Most people have definite opinions about what they want to do on a trip. It is better to have these known during the planning stages to avoid misunderstandings later on.

I like to **travel in small groups** of 6-12 people (once again think about the planning a dinner party) because they are most effective at decision making and tend to be the most convivial. You will want to arrange a meeting with your travel companions well in advance of your trip to decide on a common set of travel goals.

Don't try to do too much. This taste and travel book focuses on Northern Italy, Tuscany and Umbria; three regions of Italy that are closely connected by train and car travel. You can choose to spend your entire taste and travel trip in one of these regions and still return for more. There are a wide variety of cooking styles within these regions from the familiar pastas of Emilia Romagna eaten in a medieval castle to the adventurous dishes of Tuscany like *cinghiale* (wild boar) and *lepre* (hare) eaten at a country inn. Or you may want to do a vertical taste and travel trip that cuts across regional boundaries. Eating *Ragu' alla Bolognese* in Bologna one day and then traveling outside of Florence the next day to experience a *Bistecca alla fiorentina*, the famous Tuscan grilled T-bone steak. Choose one or two adjacent regions that interest you and then plan to return to see more.

What about the cost? **Taste traveling in Italy need not be expensive**. I have known people to spend more money on travel in the States than on a well thought out trip to Italy. Of course it depends on what you want to do and how you are willing and able to travel but in general you will find this type of trip very economical because you are traveling like an Italian not a tourist. Do your research in advance and comparison shop airlines for flight reservations. Internet sites like Trip Advisor and Venere have reviews that share information on accommodations, restaurants and things to see and do. But buyer beware. Some sites may look promising however savvy travelers know there is no substitute for references and recommendations. So do your homework. Even if you book your reservation on line and receive a printed confirmation you should always call the hotel or booking agency in person for a verbal confirmation and then call again two weeks before your trip for a final confirmation. Reservations have been known to get lost or mixed up and you don't want any surprises. Also there may be service fees attached to your booking; they are usually nominal but you should inquirewhen making your reservation.

Consider renting a GPS. A taste and travel trip means that there will be times you may be off the tourist radar visiting hidden and little known country inns and Etruscan ruins, looking for that perfect bowl of *ribollita*. A few years ago taking a trip off the beaten path in Italy would have been much more difficult. Today with the help of a GPS and some basic Italian grammar you can taste and travel the *Strada dei Vini e dei Sapori* (the Food and Wine Trails) of Northern Italy, Tuscany and Umbria with confidence. Recently I've started using a GPS and now would not drive or travel in Italy without it. That

227

doesn't mean that my well worn Michelin Travel Atlas has become obsolete. On the contrary, one complements and validates the other and together I am able to find my remotest of friends living in the hills around Radda. It also saves a lot of time and frustration asking directions (turn at the 2nd traffic light) especially if you don't speak Italian. By the way the Italian word for traffic light is *il semaforo*. Believe me, knowing it will come in handy.

Start reading about Italy. A taste and travel trip begins with a desire to enjoy traveling in Italy on all levels and pre–departure information shouldn't be limited to operational activities only. It's important to get travel tips on what type of clothes to bring along and how to exchange your money but it's also is important to have a general knowledge of the history, geography and people you will encounter on your trip. Learning a little about the history of places you will visit will help you sort through all the tourist babble. A little pre-trip knowledge goes a long way in helping understand on-the-spot descriptions of what you are seeing. Travel books, maps, your atlas, Italian lifestyle stories and Italian cookbooks all have information that will enrich your traveling experience and make such a difference once you've arrived in Italy. And remember, any references you take must be selected carefully. You don't want to be walking around Florence lugging a thick or outdated travel guide. Some travel guides are meant to be taken along on the trip and others are for reading at home or for reference. I carry a folder with my notes about what I want to see and do, pertinent travel information, my accommodations, MapQuest directions and restaurants I've researched before the trip and I often make copies of pages in guidebooks rather than carry the whole book

Traveling outside of the box literally means traveling out of a suitcase. That means that everything you need should be easily at hand and ready to go. The last thing you want is to be overburdened with too much luggage and with today's airline regulations the number of suitcases you check or take on board is an important consideration. Push the easy button when traveling so you can focus on the experience and not worry about wrinkled clothes and shoes that match every outfit. Begin by choosing your luggage and other travel accessories carefully. Make sure they are of good quality and durable. Your luggage will be your home away from home. It must be light weight and expandable. It must have wheels and be easily identifiable (brightly colored luggage tags). Spending a little more money on a well designed suitcase is money well spent, especially when traveling with kids. You don't want the handle to fall off when you're trying to make that connection between Zurich and Milano and you don't want the zipper to break when you're trying to stuff that Prada bag in your suitcase. Include a backpack (I like TUMI) or a nice roomy tote (I like Mandarina Duck). I'm not a big fan of the carry-on so either of these serves as a carry-on for me and should include only those things you can't live without during your flight like medicine, contact lens solution, glasses, toiletries (check current TSA and airline regulations). Include a few things you don't want going with the checked bag (should your airline loose it), then add a few extra conveniences, electronics, your favorite book or magazines. Some travelers like to carry their important documents in a boarding neck pouch while others use a money belt. There are also travel shirts or jackets with hidden pockets that are very popular. Pack an expandable tote that you can check if necessary for all the things you

229

will want to bring home. Remember packing in general is like writing a good term paper. You start with an outline, you write and then you edit and edit and edit. Ask yourself if you really need that book light, portable CD player, down travel pillow or laptop. And finally don't be a pack animal, pack light, light, light .There is little trunk space in Italian rental cars and you don't want to be trudging around carrying or pulling heavy, overstuffed luggage. Consider products that make travel easier like disposable underwear! Now don't laugh, disposable underwear is ideal for saving time and space when traveling. I personally have not used this product but it is on my favorite's list because many of my fellow male travelers like the convenience of disposable underwear because they can "just wear and toss" leaving more room in their suitcase for more important items to bring back home. Disposable underwear is not paper but 100% biodegradable cotton that is both comfortable and durable. If you choose to wash and wear pick up a tube of Biosuds shampoo for your clothes. You can wash almost any item with a small amount of this laundry detergent in the sink of your hotel alla Rick Steves. A 100 ml tube cost about $3.50 and last for several trips.

A word about clothing in general. Traveling is easier when you have clothes that are easier to travel with. Look for clothing brands that are geared for travel with fabrics, styles and finishes that are easy to pack, wear and care for. Quick drying stain and wrinkle resistant fabrics, zippered pockets for security, fabrics with sunscreen and odorless insect repellant are all readily available. What about wearing blue jeans? Jeans seem to be the universal uniform all over the world, also in Italy. Italians are very concerned about *la bella figura* that is to say they believe it is very important to present a good image, being well dressed and well groomed. Some of the most fashionable jeans are worn in Italy and Italian denim trends are followed around the world. So if you do like to wear jeans and want to wear them on your trip wear them with a sense of style and remember if you buy jeans in Italy Versace jeans run 2 sizes smaller as do most Italian clothes. *La bella figura* is cut very close!

See and Savor More

The first taste travelers in Italy were probably Christian pilgrims of the 13th and 14th centuries who traveled along the major medieval pilgrim routes that led to Rome. Stopping along the way they were offered bite size pieces of local cheese. For centuries, pilgrims from across Europe would trek across the Alps on their way to Rome. The *Via Francigena* (Pilgrims' Way) is a historical itinerary that can be followed today, although less penitential. Now there are shopping malls and restaurants but it is still an extraordinary experience.

On the Via Francigena (Chaucer's Wife of Bath)

231

Chapter 31 Driving a Taste and Travel Trip

Contrary to popular opinion, driving in Italy is not an extreme sport. Italy has an excellent network of motorways (Autostrade) although most Americans can sometimes find driving in Italy intimidating. They would rather be lulled into the complacency of a motorbus tour or buy a pass on the Eurostar. Both have their place and for some may be the best way to travel but don't be overly concerned about driving in Italy.

However there are a few things to consider before you take the keys to your Italian rental car. Arrange to rent a car before you go to Italy because then all terms for rental and pick up will be in place before you leave home and you will understand what you will be driving before you arrive in Italy. Rent a small car. There is a reason Italians drive small cars and it isn't just because of the price of fuel. Think of where you will be driving and more importantly where you will be parking. For all practical purposes there is no parking in Italy. Your choice of car is pivotal to a pleasurable driving experience in Italy. I have driven a Fiat, Lancia, Peugeot, Opal, PT Cruiser and Jaguar in Italy. You want to have enough trunk space but you want the car to be small enough to negotiate the narrow streets of the towns and villages you want to visit, make a quick exit off the autostrada, get out of a roundabout and get on or off the *tangenziale*/bypass (beltway around the city). My car preference for driving in Italy, the Lancia.

Understand how Italian's drive. Italian's are confident drivers who feel they know what needs to be done in order to get from one place to another. They may follow too close (but then again they have a different system of measurement than we do), they are opportunistic and want to fill in the space between each car length (but then again their country is smaller than ours) and they drive faster than we do ((I call the left lane, the passing lane on the Autostrada, the Ferrari lane). But they are not foolhardy and contrary to popular opinion they do obey travel signals. They are very courteous drivers and when driving on the Autostrada, using the passing lane only to pass.

Have a well planned driving itinerary and thoroughly familiarize yourself with it before you go. Don't be too ambitious and don't get too far off the beaten path if you haven't driven in Italy before. Pick a route, follow it and know where you're going. There are good touring books to consult and having a good road atlas and regional road maps should be part of your car kit. Study the maps before you arrive in Italy. You don't want to be driving on the Autostrada out of Milano at 130km (about 80 mph) trying to figure out where to exit for Como when you're really on your way to Parma or start looking in the map index for Florence and can't find it because you forgot that in Italian Florence is Firenze. I've used the Michelin Tourist and Motoring Atlas and the Touring Club Italiano (TCI) regional maps and road atlas - Atlante Stradale d'Italia. The TCI sets are an investment, $75.00 the last time I looked for 3 volume boxed set (Nord, Centro and Sud) or about $27.00 individually. You may want to consider the part of Italy you will be driving and then add a volume every year as you explore more of the country. However this is money well spent if you are serious about driving in Italy. Also various map sites such as MapQuest can be very helpful for calculating driving times and distance as well as Autostrade.it web site for up to date driving conditions in Italy.

Driving a car in Italy means parking a car in Italy and parking in Italy may qualify as an extreme sport. There is very little parking space available in Italy. In the small towns and villages most of the parking is on narrow streets with very little space. My Umbrian friends often park on the sidewalk but I don't recommend this. There are designated No Traffic Zones, especially in the city center. Remember medieval cities were not designed for modern car traffic. In some cities there are zones (ZTL) that limit traffic and cars that pass through without a permit can be fined. If you're visiting for the day, you may want to park outside the city and walk in or take a local bus. Look for parking lots on the outskirts of town and obey metered parking signs. Look for signs that say *parcheggio pubblico*, public parking. Pay attention to signs posted that say *sosta vietata* or *divieto parcheggio* - both mean NO PARKING. Do not park where you see these signs or anywhere there is a line through the word *parcheggio.* I have gotten a parking ticket in Italy and it is no fun. *Parcheggio privati* means private parking and Italians are very protective of their parking space as you might expect, so don't even think about it. A favorite for free parking lot in Firenze (Florence) is at Piazza Michaelangelo just outside the city. Park on the side of the piazza farthest from the view then take bus 12 or 13 into the city.

Italian road signs are notorious for being confusing. Many signs that look visually the same in the States take on a slightly different meaning when driving in Italy. The yield sign is one example. You

234

often see this sign when entering a roundabout. It means that you need to wait for all the other drivers to pass before you go but you need to keep going. Wait but keep going? Anotherwords don't stop yet yield. It is confusing. Also there are often a lot of signs posted at roundabouts. Signs that give directions and distances and signs that advertise local attractions and accommodations, all are stacked up like so many pieces of a jigsaw puzzle. If you find that you cannot read them fast enough just keep going in the proverbial Chevy Chase circle (remember European Vacation). Italian drivers don't like this but it is better than getting in an accident or getting off at the wrong exit. A stop sign is the same universal symbol, a red octagon with the word STOP but when I asked my cousin Lidia why she did not stop at a stop sign she said "the sign just means - pay close attention"! Never assume an Italian driver will indeed stop at a stop sign. However there is a substantial fine for going through a red light.

I've gotten better at driving in Italy but in the beginning there is a rite of passage every novice American driver must first go through. I was initiated into this rite by my cousins during my first Italian road trip from Milano in Lombardia to Montalcino in Toscana. I will never forget it. It started and ended with a gas pump. First of all I had to learn the secret language of pumping gas in Italy. Gasoline (*gasolio)* in Italian actually refers to diesel fuel. Many cars in Italy use diesel because of fuel economy. What we call gasoline in the States is called "*benzina*" in Italy. *Benzina* can be leaded or unleaded. Gasoline without lead is referred to as "*senza piombo or benzina verde*". Don't assume that when you ask the gas station attendant to fill it up (*il pieno per favore*) he/she will know what type of gasoline your car takes. If you use the

235

wrong gas your car can stop; not right away but down the road some. Nowhere is it more important to know a little Italian than at the gas pump. The self serve pump can be especially challenging. There is an Italian legend about an old witch named Befana, at times benevolent at times a little scary. Every time I would try to pump gas the Italian self service benzina pumps started to take on the appearance of a Befana. It became a contest between me and the pump. Benzina - Befana the two became one as I struggled to choose the right type of gas at the uncooperative pump, scowling at me, mocking me to decide on the correct change or credit card. It became a struggle of wits that in the beginning had me relying on attendant only gas stations but those were sometimes few and far between or closed when I ran out of gas. After a few road trips things got better. The Befana gas pump became friendlier and that was good because even as the years went by, even with my maps and GPS, I still get lost driving in Italy.

There is an old saying about driving in Italy. You will get lost when driving in Italy. Don't panic! Everybody does it, *italiani ed americani* alike. I was lost in Siena for two hours even after traveling and staying in this town several times. My Italian cousins generally get lost at least three or four times on our road trips. My Umbrian friends get lost traveling in their own town. What you must do is be able to ask for directions. My friends and I were lost and then "found in Siena" by two Italian boys (*i ragazzi*) who noticed we were *molti occupati.* Basically this means "beside ourselves" "ready to panic" and *i nervi a pezzi,* "nervous in pieces". Fortunately we were able to speak to them in Italian and describe where we wanted to go and they offered to take

236

us there at no charge - *molto gentili*. So if you decide to drive in Italy you should familiarize yourself with some basic Italian phrases especially the phrase "*Sono perso*" I am LOST!

Driving in Italy allows you to travel outside of the box for an insider's view of the country. Here is where you will find that one memorable experience that will make your trip unique and unforgettable. If you can, travel with some friends who have driven in Italy before. They can guide you along and build up your driving confidence. Drive on the autostrade and avoid driving in the larger cities with one rounabout after another or the medieval hill towns where the streets are narrow alleyways that are best left to the locals. There is nothing like driving in Italy and here are my top five reasons to give it a try.

The Top 5 Reasons for Driving in Italy

5. You can see the country at your own pace

4. You can explore hidden and little known places in Italy

3. You can get up close and personal with Ferraris

2. You can eat at an Autogrill

1. You can wear a teeshirt that says "I Drove Italy and Survived"

See and Savor More

It's important to know your roads when driving in Italy. The Autostrade are the superhighway toll roads that connect Italy from north to south, east to west. Italy's Autostrade have a speed limit of 130 km/h (81 mph) for cars and 80 km/h (50 mph) for trucks. Signage for toll booth lanes are marked blue for *Carte* (credit card), yellow for Telepass (*riservata clienti*) and white for attended cash or automatic self service payment. Autostrade are marked by signs with an "A" followed by the autostrada number on a green background, other roads are marked with road numbers on a blue background. *Strade statali* or state roads are labeled "SS" on the map. They are the more scenic roads that twist and turn through towns and villages that parallel the autostrada. The speed limit on this type of road is 90-110 km. Just as in the States, sometimes it's better to travel a superhighway and sometimes it's better to drive the road less traveled. Know your Autostrada. They are the main highways that link one region of Italy to another. For example, the main highways that link Milano to the rest of Italy are

A 1 Autostrada del Sole (Highway of the Sun) links Milan to Bologna, Firenze (Florence), Rome, Naples

A 4 Autostrada links Milan to Turin, Brescia, Bergamo, Verona and Venice

A 8 Autostrada dei Laghi (Highway of the Lakes) links Milan to Lake Como, Maggiore and Switzerland

A 7 Autostrada links Milan to Genoa

Chapter 32 Via Solferino

Sesto San Giovanni, or Sesto as it's commonly called, is about six miles from Milano. Sesto means sixth and according to my cousin, it took the Romans a distance of six stone markers to get from Milano to Sesto San Giovanni and that is how Sesto got its name. The city has many of the amenities of Milano but on a smaller scale and makes an attractive place to stay when visiting Milan and touring the Lombardy region. Sesto San Giovanni is the home of my Italian family and Milano my departure point for my travels in Italy. The art, architecture, location, fashion and food of Milano make it a perfect entry point for seeing and savoring Italy. At first glance Milan can be a little intimidating. It doesn't have the historical familiarity of Rome or the landscape setting of the Tuscan hill towns and for this reason many tourists tend to avoid spending time there. But that would be a pity because Milano has a style all its own, a style worth taking the time to see and get to know.

Although Milano is a large, cosmopolitan city with a population well over 1 million, the city center is well defined by the Gothic spires of the Duomo, Milan's great Cathedral. Milan's transportation system of trams, buses, trolleys and the three lines of the Metro (subway), referred to as "the tube", make it easy to get almost anywhere in the city. Look for a sign that says *vendita biglietti* to purchase your ticket (*il biglietti*) at a news stand or magazine shop. You cannot buy or pay for your transportation tickets on board. There are also exact money ticket machines in the subway stations for those of you who know enough Italian to be comfortable using them. Arriving at Pizza Duomo you can easily walk to many of the main sites of the city beginning with the area around the Duomo. This area of Milano, known as the Duomo District, contains some of the most important and historical sites in the city including Milan's Duomo, Galleria Vittorio Emanuale, the Palazzo Reale (Royal Palace) and the central tourist office. The IAT (*Informazioni eAssistenza Turistica*) is located at Piazza Duomo 19/A, near the Carlo Erba Pharmacy and is currently open Mon-Sat 8:45am-1pm and 2-6pm, Sun and on holidays 9am-1pm and 2-5pm. It's important to pinpoint the central tourist office in each city on your travel itinerary because here you will find a wealth of information to help you plan your trip once in country. Around P. Duomo are many other interesting sites including La Scala Opera (*Teatro alla Scala)* and the Ambrosiana art gallery (*Pinacoteca Ambrosiana*) with 30,000 manuscripts including early editions of Dante's Divine Comedy and paintings by Leonardo, Botticelli and Caravaggio. From here, you'll most likely walk down the nearby, always crowded Corso Vittorio Emanuele to visit the Galleria. Milan's Galleria Vittorio Emanuele is a 4 story arcade enclosed by a glass and iron arched roof that is absolutely stunning. It is Milan's jewel box with elegant shops, restaurants, bars and cafe's lining both sides of the arcade. You can visit the iconic Cafe Zucca where in the late 1860's Gaspari Campari first introduced Italians to a drink known then as "bitter Campari" while watching the fashionable Milanese who are fortunate to be able to call this their city "mall". The arched glass roof of the Galleria will keep you gazing upwards but be sure to look down. The floors are decorated with mosaics of the signs of the zodiac including a famous one of Taurus the Bull. There is a tradition among the Milanese of spinning three times on the heel of one foot on the well worn bulls' genitals for

240

good luck. My cousins insisted that I try it and that good luck will follow and I think it did!

But Milano is more than chic cafes and couture fashion. Edith Wharton described Milan as a "juxtaposition of different centuries and styles". You can attend a performance at the modern *Teatro degli Arcimboldi* where I saw a *La Scala* production of *Le Presbytere* with music by Queen and Mozart and costumes by Versace and the next day visit the Church of Santa Maria della Gracia where *il Cenacolo*, Leonardo's Last Supper is simply displayed on the refectory wall of the Dominican friary. You can shop till you drop at La Rinascente Duomo, Milan's most elegant department store and walk to *Castello Sforzesco*, once a Visconti palace now a series of museums, whose foreboding exterior belies the interior beauty of the Renaissance. Milano is a city of contrasts and for those in the know you can spend a few days happily discovering the different centuries and styles of one of Italy's most fascinating cities.

Sesto San Giovanni makes an ideal location from which to explore Milano and all points beyond. It is connected to the regional cities of the North and South by air, rail, bus lines and the Milan's Metro. I fly into Milan Malpensa airport (MXP) (31 miles NW of Milano) after a stopover in Zurich and take the Malpensa Express train from the airport to arrive at Cardorna Station in downtown Milano, near Duomo Square, in about 40 minutes. A one way ticket is 9 Eu. Then I take the "tube" into Sesto, another 20 minute subway ride. In Sesto San Giovanni you can experience the true Italian lifestyle, staying in an Italian community that is very typical of modern urban Italian life. The

241

ristoranti, negozi, and *alberghi* (the restaurants, shops and hotels) are a microcosm of Milan and Sesto, like Milano, is a mixture of traditional and modern Italy. With a population of about 76,000, Sesto is perfectly sized to allow you to feel as comfortable as if you were in your own town. Everything is conveniently located by walking. This is Italy and walking is the preferred mode of transportation but you can easily take the tube, a taxi or even drive through town, GPS in hand. Sesto is relatively easy to navigate. Although the streets are typically Italian (somewhat narrow) the town is modern in design with residential areas. It would be like staying in the suburbs of a major metropolitan city with a short commute into town. The Autostrada enters and exits into the various parts of the city so Sesto is a good starting point for a driving vacation to other parts of Italy. But remember, Sesto San Giovanni is an Italian town and few Americans live here so it would be helpful to know some basic Italian. And if you try to speak Italian the Sestonians will be pleased to help you. They are friendly and appreciate your efforts to communicate with them in their language. As there are not many tourists, it would be a good idea to let them know you are an American (*sono americano(a)* - I am American) so they will know what to expect when you speak. You will not be disappointed staying in Sesto San Giovanni for the convenience to Milano by way of the subway, for accommodations and services that are less expensive than Milano and for Italian food at reasonable prices served in family style restaurants. Save your money *per andare fare la spesa a Milano* (to go shopping in Milan) although savvy travelers know that the shops in Sesto and nearby Monza are where most Italians shop.

Because you are staying off the tourist radar, Sesto is a wonderful starting point to begin to discover your inner Italian. You can walk down the street to the cinema, stop at the corner espresso bar in the morning for a *cornetto* or enjoy a late afternoon apertivo at a street side cafe.The first production plant for the famous Italian apertivo Campari was opened in Sesto San Giovanni in 1904 so be sure and stop for a Negroni or a Campari and soda at one of the bars or cafes off Via Solferino. Via Solferino is a street that I am very familiar with. When I visit my cousins in Sesto San Giovanni, I stay at the Hotel Nuovo Rondo on Via Solferino No. 5. It is a 3 star hotel conveniently located near restaurants, cafes and pubs. You can walk to the bookstore down the street, to the bakery and to the neighborhood shops. You can buy flowers in the piazza, cheese around the corner and walk to the neighborhood park to watch the locals play bocce and basketball. You can catch the subway across the street to visit Milano. There are 16 rooms in the hotel. The accommodations are clean, comfortable and Carmelo, the proprietor is "molto gentile". Via Solferino is a slice of Italian life that allows me to fantasize about what it would be like if I lived in Italy. Not in the Italy that is under the Tuscan sun but the urban working class Italy that is similar to where I live today, alike yet different. I sit on the bench in front of the hotel and watch the Italian view of the world go by. I listen to the sounds of Vespas and bicycles, babies in prams and teenagers laughing and teasing and speaking Italian much faster than I can keep up with. I think that I have come to realize that for me taste traveling in Italy is more than just eating good food and drinking memorable wine in a country that is an open air museum. It's about acquiring a taste for living, something I have come to learn Italians do very well. I haven't

243

quite developed my lifestyle palate to the extent that I am able to discern the difference between the bitter and sweet flavors of life, keeping them in balance. One often overpowers the other and leaves a bad taste in my mouth. So I keep coming back to Italy year after year to Via Solferino 5 where I meet my cousin Lidia on the street in front of the hotel where she says to me in her proudly perfect English, "I have been waiting for you" and my journey continues and begins again.

See and Savor More

The Hotel Nuovo Rondo on Via Solferina 5 is a typical Italian hotel where most Italians would stay while traveling. It is not a tour bus hotel. Real Italians check in and out. Because of its location near the red line subway station (Sesto Rondo' M) it is a convenient way to get into the center of Milan, spend the day shopping or site seeing and then return for a good night's sleep. The hotel faces a pedestrian walkway with shops and restaurants close by. If you have been studying Italian it is a perfect place for urban immersion on a small scale as everyone is helpful and accommodating. You will experience Italy staying here and get up close and personal with the Italian people.

L'albergo Nuovo Rondo in Sesto San Giovanni

244

Chapter 33 Como and Bellagio

My first visit to the Italian Lake Region of Lombardy was before
Clooney discovered Como. It was on a road trip with my Milanese
cousin Lidia and her husband Roberto. Roberto loves to fish and he
wanted to take us to Bellagio, a lake side town with a ristorante bar
that specializes in fresh caught lake fish. He said that the fish
prepared here was "molto buono". Surrounded by snowy alpine
peaks and lush palm trees, Lake Como is one of the deepest lakes in
Europe and Bellagio one of the most beautiful places in Italy. A driving
trip around Lake Como, Garda and Maggiore is listed by Frommer's
as one of the 25 most unforgettable driving itineraries in Italy. The
elegant villas with mountains that seem to rise out of the lake and the
romance and beauty of *Lago di Como* have made it one of the most
popular destinations in the world. Along the shores of Lake Como rock
stars and celebrities mingle with travelers and everyday Italians
walking along the the waterfront thinking that the sweet life of Italy can
be no sweeter than here.

Lago di Como has been desirable real estate since Roman times.
Today international celebrities like Richard Branson, Sting, Richard
Gere and Michael Schumacher have become captivated by Como's
charm and George Clooney has a 25-room villa in the village of
Laglio, on the western shores of the lake. The Villa d' Este at
Cernobbio, built in 1568 (now the Villa D'Este Hotel), was rated the
number two luxury hotel on the planet and the fashionable shops
along the lakeside promenade of Bellagio can fulfill almost any
shopinista's dream. But don't shy away from the high profile status

of this region of Italy, even the budget conscious taste traveler can eat well along the shores of Lake Como and savvy shoppers can find affordable luxuries on the Bellagio promenade.

Roberto's choice for lakeside dining is *Ristorante Bar Mella*, an unpretentious gastronomic delight that is within anyone's budget. A short walk along the lake, pass the gardens of Villa Melzi, *Ristorante Bar Mella* is located in San Giovanni, one mile from the center of Bellagio. San Giovanni is a small fishermen's village with cobblestone streets and beautiful views. Fisherman's boats still moor at the city's port and the half-fisherman half-owner of *Ristorante Bar Mella* makes sure that the fresh catch of the day will be brought to the table. This restaurant is a favorite of my Milanese cousins and every time we come to visit we all travel to Bellagio to eat there. Roberto loves to fish and this restaurant specializes in fresh caught fish from the lake. From the time you enter the restaurant you can see there is a special connection between the lake and the restaurant. The owner is a professional fisherman who is trying to keep Como's fishing tradition alive. There is a beautiful view of the lake from the dining room. The staff is most hospitable and will be happy to explain the variety of dishes served. Two of my favorites are rice with perch and *Missoltino*. To prepare a *Missoltino* a local fish known as *agone* is washed, salted and dried in the open air, then packed into containers and pressed for about four months. Then they are grilled until warm and served with minced parsley, vinegar and oil and roasted polenta. The long and difficult preparation to make a Missoltino is well worth it. I spent one memorable afternoon with my cousins, eating through most of the menu and drinking spumante. Then we walked down to the lake to see the fishing boats and were introduced to an Italian Spinone. The Italian Spinone, also known as the Italian Griffon, is one of the most endearing dogs I have ever met. He was running along the lake by the fishing boats and he looked like he could be an experienced fisherman as well. The AKC describes the Spinone as "robust, sociable and docile with a wiry, dense coat and thick skin that enable him to negotiate underbrush and endure cold water that would severely punish any dog not so naturally armored". Thought to be a cross between an Italian Setter and the White Mastiff or French Griffon, the Spinone has a bearded face and a sweet expression. The Spinone I saw had a coat of white with orange-brown markings and as most Italians along the lake was having great fun enjoying the day. It's easy to attribute human characteristics to a dog that looks like he could come up to you and carry on a conversation. His dangling ears and almost human like eyes reminded me of a story book dog who becomes your child's best friend. We watched as the Spinone kept running along the shore and into the water as the nearby fishermen threw sticks for him to catch.

Bellagio has a distinct feeling of the Mediterranean. Its location on a hilly peninsula overlooking the deep blue waters of Lake Como make it one of the most romantic places in Italy. Simply put, Bellagio is stunning. It so impressed the American writer Henry Wardsworth Longfellow that he wrote a poem about the beauty of Bellagio asking if it was a dream that would vanish into air. The lakeside promenade lined with flowering trees and palms in the distance, the pastel colored buildings with their tropical gardens, the elegant villas along the shore have made Bellagio one of Italy's top holiday destinations and an

247

international favorite. If the celebrity status of Bellagio becomes intrusive, drive the winding roads around the lake shore to visit the other lake side villages or take SS342 to Bergamo and Lake Garda to visit the lakeside resort of Sirmione where gelateria line the streets and a medieval fortress (*Rocca Scaligera*) allows you to channel your inner Shrek.

See and Savor More

There are 28 species of freshwater fish living in Lake Como. One of the most popular is *Lavarello*, a type of whitefish usually served fried with a squeeze of lemon. You can bring the flavors of Como home with this recipe that comes close to how this fish is served along the Lake with rice, similar to a *risotto.*

Ingredients for this recipe (Serves 5-6)

- ☐ 3 ½ tbsp butter
- ☐ 2 cups Arborio rice
- ☐ 1 small onion, finely chopped
- ☐ ½ cup dry white wine
- ☐ salt and black pepper for seasoning
- ☐ ½ cup grated Parmigiano Reggiano cheese
- ☐ 4 cups broth (chicken or vegetable stock)
- ☐ 4 lake perch fillets (per person) about 18 in total
- ☐ flour or bread crumbs for coating
- ☐ butter and olive oil for frying

In a heavy saucepan, sauté the onion in the butter until it is tender. When the onion has become transparent add the rice and stir well. Let it cook for a couple of minutes. Then, before the rice gets limp, add the wine to the pot. Mix the rice until the liquid has evaporated, and then add the broth, a small amount at a time, stirring it constantly to allow even absorption of the liquid. When the rice is just about tender, add the salt, pepper and cheese and allow to melt To cook the fish, batter the fillets in the flour or bread crumbs and then cook in a hot skillet of butter and olive oil turning once until each side is golden brown. Spoon the rice onto each dish and top with a few fish fillets.

The town of Como produces 80% of Europe's silk and has been doing so since the 14th century when silk worms were first imported. The lake area is known for its silk production and the shops in Bellagio carry the finest. Look for the many boutiques that line the waterfront promenade and picturesque alleyways and streets of Bellagio to buy a silk scarf or tie. The boutiques are exquisite and not for the faint of wallet but well worth your consideration. I always buy ties for my male friends when I am in Bellagio. Even though most men do not wear ties very often when they do they should be made of Italian silk.

Chapter 34 A Country House in the Bolognese Hills

Wanted . . . a charming bed and breakfast among the windswept hills south of Bologna with a most gracious host who makes her guests feel as if she has been waiting for them to arrive and welcome them home.

Finding a place like the one described above is what dreaming of Italy is all about. For me that dream was realized in a country house in the Bolognese hills that I could enjoy with my eyes wide open. Each year as I travel in Italy with my Italian family and friends, I realize that place matters. Not just the places you visit in the guide books but the places of the heart where the Who and Where of travel is just as important as what you see. So on my way from Milano to Tuscany on the A1 Autostrada, passing through Bologna I drive a little further south to the town of Monzuno to spend the night at one of my all time favorite places to stay in Italy, the Lodole Country House.

Alice, (pronounced Al-ee-che in Italian) the owner, is a true Renaissance woman. A master of the art of hospitality she deftly combines traditional Italian charm with contemporary Italian design to create a sanctuary of rest and relaxation in the Bolognese hills. I met Alice midway through my taste travels in Italy when I was looking to experience a bed and breakfast in the countryside near Bologna. My good fortune led to me Lodole. Alice and Daniele bought the property when it was little more than a vision and a ruin and transformed it into a destination where they have realized their dream of creating an informal yet exclusive country house with a peaceful, relaxed

250

atmosphere. Located among the endless hills and valleys of the northern foot of the Bolognese Appennines, Lodole Country House is named after the lodole, a small falcon like bird (*lodolaio* in Italian) who inhabits the windswept hills of the region. The atmosphere and accommodations at this Italian Bed and Breakfast are exceptional. The decor is a modern interpretation of provincial Italian country with a decor that is antique chic. You get a sense of the timeless beauty of artisan Italian furniture and design but all fresh, new and updated. No musty rooms full of old furniture or outdated plumbing. The beds are comfortable, the showers invigorating, the rooms restful and there is a wonderful well kept pool on a hill that has a panoramic view of the countryside. At night our taste travelers sat on a loggia that overlooked the course of the *Il Molino del Pero* Golf Club and listened to music wafting over the hills from the clubhouse. Each room is named after a celestial manifestation; *Alba, Sole, Cielo, Stelle, Tramonto* and *Luna* (Dawn, Sun, Sky, Star, Dusk and Moon). I have always stayed in *la camera Tramanto*, a double room at the top of the stairs and have been most comfortable, sleeping well and waking up to a breakfast that is never lacking. The assortment of meats, cheeses, tarts, cereals and honey was *fantastici*. Alice also makes a mean cappuccino, flavorful and frothy. It is one of the best I have had in Italy and her semolina breakfast cake is phenomenal.

At the Lodole Country House everything is done with great care and attention including planning activities in and around Lodole. You can enjoy golf (one of Italy's most challenging courses is down the road), go mountain biking, horseback riding, visit archeological sites and museums, sample local Emilian farm products or just sit by the stunning pool overlooking the valley below. One afternoon Alice and I were discussing a trip to the Luigi Fontini Celtic Etruscan museum in nearby Monterenzio when she invited me to her house across the pavement from where we were staying. Yes, she is a hands on host, never far from the wants and needs of her guests. From the outside the house is the quintessional rustic Italian farmhouse I have been coveting for years. Each stone and tile incorporates centuries of tradition and the timeless character of Italy. From the inside it was like walking into the pages of the Italian version of House Beautiful. The kitchen was contemporary Italian and exquisite, the living space had a massive mid century modern Eames style fireplace that was the center of the room together with a frosted retractable section of floor that opened to a eight person whirlpool facing a wall with a flat panel TV. There was a room with a sauna and a second floor with a surrounding iron balcony. The modern art on the walls was exceptional especially a stylized map of the world with countries whose leaders were women highlighted in dots of red. But perhaps the most unique and impressive work of art hidden behind the closed doors of this *casa colonnica* was a glossy red sculpture of a woman's body hanging on a crucifix suspended from the wall on the balcony. It was large and a definite focal point in the room. In some ways it represents all the strong and persistent women I have met in Italy like Alice. The traditions of Italy are reinvented and given new life by the entrepreneurial spirit and love of Italy they all share.

One year when I was in Italy in March I noticed bouquets of tiny yellow mimosa and banners in every city with the words *festa delle donne* (festival of women). It was March 8th, Women's Day, and Italy was celebrating women and their achievements. The Italians have always valued women and their role in society. Italy is like a great caldron of sensuality and emotion. History and art are sprinkled in for good measure and the outcome allows creativity to flourish and for women it allows their special talents to emerge. If the number of yellow flowered mimosa I have seen in Italy during March is any indication of the esteem Italy has for its women than I think they are greatly appreciated. I feel very fortunate to have a number of Italian women as my friends and business associates including Alice, Rita, Fiorella, Nora, Beatrice, Benedetta, Lidia, Mirna, Ornella, Marika, Adele, Pinota, Chiara, Michela, Stellina, Daniela and many others who without their generous hospitality and willingness to help me learn about the authentic Italy this book could not have been written and my taste and travel journeys incomplete at best.

On my next trip to Emilia Romagna, I plan to grab 6 of my best friends (there are 6 double rooms at Lodole), play a little golf, visit the watermills along the Savena and Idice Rivers and travel to *Rocchetta Mattei* at *Riola di Vergato*, a Neo-Gothic Moorish style castle that dates to the late nineteenth century. It is suppose to be a little unusual and funky being designed by the man who invented electro-homeopathy. It is built on a rocky plateau near Bologna and was badly damaged during WWII. For the engineers in my family, they might be interested to know that due to the 250-EC-B 12 Litronic Flat Top Crane and special foundation anchors, the difficult conditions that presented in the renovation of the castle were overcome. The thermal springs of Poretta are also nearby and after having visited several *termes* (Italian hot springs) over the last several years they have

253

become a focal point of my travels. Food, wine, the artistic beauty of the Italian countryside and a relaxing spa spring what could be better? The springs at Porretta have been enjoyed since Roman times and legend has it that they were discovered thanks to a tired old ox who was seen drinking the waters and immediately became energetic again.

Travels to Bologna often just focus on the *tagliatelli* but there is much more going on in the Bolognese hills than bubbling pots of *ragu'*. So take the time and make the effort to discover this hidden and little know part of Italy. The Italians know about it and now so do you.

See and Savor More

The loggia at the Lodole Country House overlooking the Bolognese Hills is a perfect place to see and savor Italy over a cup of cappuccino and a slice of Alice's Semolina Breakfast Cake.

Loggia at the Lodole Country House

Recipe and Ingredients for Lodole CountryHouse Semolina Breakfast Cake

1 litre of milk
4 hg of sugar
1 hg of semolina
5 eggs
1 hg of almonds
1 glass of bitter almond liqueur

Let the milk boiling with the sugar; when the milk boil add the semolina and mix together for 5 minutes; make the mixture cold and meanwhile mince the almonds. When the mixture is cold add the eggs, the almonds and the liqueur and mix all together. Take a baking-tin and do the caramel. When the caramel is ready put inside the baking-tin the mixture and cook inside the oven for 1 hour at 170°. When you take the cake outside the oven, upside down it on a plate and let cool. (hg = hectogram =100 grams)

The *Lodolaio* also known as the *Falco subbuteo* are capable of some impressive aerial acrobatics flying very fast at speeds up to 100 mph.

Lodolaio

On *Feasta della Donna* men bring yellow Mimosa to the women in their lives. Restaurants have special *Festa della Donna* meals and there are often small local festivals or concerts. The Mimosa, symbol of *Festa della Donna*, blooms for a short time during this part of March,

Electro-homeopathy is a method of healing in which the bio-energy of plants is extracted for therapeutic value. Developed in the 19th century by Count Cesare Mattei whose critics wrote that "his theory in spite of its utter idiocy has attracted a considerable following and earned a large fortune for its chief promoter". (EJ Kempf, 'European Medicine: a Resume of Medical Progress During the Eighteenth and Nineteenth Centuries', *Medical Library and Historical Journal*, 1906 March; 4(1): 86–100.) Mattei separated and purified his preparations in a "secret chamber" of his castle in Rochetta Mattei near Bologna. There is a legend that the secrets of his studies are written on the castle walls and disappeared because of other paintings that followed his death in 1896.

Chapter 35 Ponte degli Alpini

What does a glass of grappa have to do with the heroism and history of a World War and a grandfather's walk across a bridge? The Italian involvement in WWII is historically documented in academic textbooks, war novels, TV documentaries and Hollywood films but I didn't know how it impacted our Italian family until I began to travel to Italy and learn about the images of the war that still lived on in our family archives. Beginning with my cousin Lidia's account of how her parents sent her to Monza to escape the bombings in Milan. That day, we visited Monza only thinking about Formula One racing to relive the sobriety of her experiences hiding from the Allied bombs. Or our visit to Bassano del Grappa in Vicenza to taste grappa from Nardini, one of Italy's most traditional distilleries located on the same bridge that our family's grandfather crossed during WWI.

We drove to Bassano del Grappa after we left Padua with my cousin Lidia and her husband Roberto. Bassano has been described as an "authentic Italian river town" with a historical center split in half by the Brenta River. There is a covered wooden bridge designed in 1569 by the famous Italian architect Andrea Palladio that crosses the Brenta. The bridge, *Ponte degli Alpini* (Bridge of the Alpini), is what Lidia wanted us to see. The grappa is what Roberto wanted us to taste. Although Bassano del Grappa gets its name from Monte Grappa (*grappa* means crag in ancient pre-Latin), the town is famous for the Italian liqueur known as grappa (from *grappolo* meaning clusters of grapes). There are grappa shops on either side of the bridge as well as several machine gun bullet holes on the buildings next to the bridge from WWII. During WWI Bassano was a pivotal point in the war with Austro-Hungary and the site of heavy fighting. Over 12,000 Italian and 10,000 Austrian soldiers lost their lives on Monte Grappa. Our grandfather crossed this bridge, during WWI as a young interpreter with the Italian Army. During WWII, Italian resistance soldiers organized raids on the German army from Monte Grappa. In retaliation, German soldiers brutally killed or publically hung any towns' people and civilians suspected of assisting the partisans. The bridge was destroyed by the retreating Germans at the end of war and rebuilt by Italy's special mountain soldiers (*degli Alpini*) who renamed the bridge *Ponte degli Alpini*, the Bridge of the Alpini, in honor of their fallen comrades. There is a museum located on the eastern side of bridge, the *Museo degli Alpini,* that has a collection of war memorabilia with many photos, uniforms and original artifacts and several small museums and war memorials in the area that commemorate the dead. Bassano like many Italian towns I have seen that were affected by the war has moved beyond the tragedy of the experience. Today it is a vibrant, evocative town with small squares, arcades, frescoed houses and Renaissance palaces. Known for the making of grappa and the rare white asparagus, it is a mandatory see and savor site in Northern Italy. The town is charming, the grappa is hot and the river and bridge showcase another part of Italy that most Americans have never seen. My cousin Roberto liked grappa, as do most red blooded Italian males, and was eager to teach us the finer points of Italy's infamous liqueur. My interest in grappa was purely academic, the Italian version of firewater being way too strong for me. But I was eager to learn and besides I love the design of those grappa spirit glasses.

In Italy grappa is considered a national treasure whose production is protected and regulated by national and EU laws just like Parmigiano Reggiano cheese and Chianti Classico wine. As early as 1600 the production of grappa was codified with rules for the concentration of alcohol through distillation, although it is thought that the making of a grappa-like distillate goes back to the time of the Crusaders if not earlier. Back then it was prescribed as a cure for various diseases and even today many Italians believe that grappa is a general purifying agent for what ails you. For many Americans grappa is considered to be a colorless, flavorless and very strong spirit without the subtlety of wine or the aromatic interest of other Italian liqueurs. Vanilla, tobacco, chamomile, dried fig, caramel, hazelnut, dried plum, chocolate, coffee, ripe banana and cinnamon would not be terms that we would generally use to describe grappa. Yet a pleasing hint of the above flavors and others including raspberry, raisin, honey and date are part of the lexicon of the fine grappas of Italy. You see grappa can be very agreeable. Made from the pomace or skins of the grape left over from winemaking after pressing, the type of grapes and the skill used in distillation will affect the quality and taste of the grappa. The pomace from Sangiovese, Canaiolo Nero and Malvasia grapes produces a grappa with a pleasing sweet hint of dried plum, hazelnut and licorice. The pomace from the wine of the Trebbiano grape, *Vino di uva Trebbiano*, produces a grappa with flavors of vanilla, caramel and chocolate. All this happens at *grapperia* like Nonino whose grappa is made from the Picolit grape said to produce a grappa with floral aromas of peach and apricot. Or at other the traditional *grapperie* like Poli and Nardini where generational families produce artisan grappa with a refined flavor that captures the spirit of Italy.

259

Tasting grappa is not for the faint of heart. The alcohol content of grappa can range from 40-80% by volume. While grappaphile Roberto was able to savor his tasting in Bassano, a novice grappa taster like myself started to see double shortly after my first sip. I was told that another way to "taste" grappa is by rubbing a few drops on the back of your hand and sniff. If the aroma is pleasant, the grappa is well made. Impurities in the grappa will come out in the vapor. This appealed to me and I was able to distinguish the pleasant scent of the grappa, choosing a small bottle for friends back home to drink and buying one for myself to use as an after dinner digestivo or a new perfume.

See and Savor More

Grappa is a wonderful way to end an Italian meal. You can drink it either as a shot on its own or added to an espresso in which case it's known in Italy as a *caffè coretto*, or a "corrected coffee". Salute!

Grappa glasses are designed to direct the flow of the wine onto parts of the palate and nose so that the flavors and aromas of the grappa can be enjoyed.

A well designed grappa spirit glass

Fans of Italian cycling will be interested to know that Bassano del Grappa is part of several cycling itinearies and the the starting point for Italy's *Gran Fondo del Monte Grappa*, a European style long distance cycling event where riders climb to the top of Monte Grappa.

In front of the *Ponte degli Alpini* in 2005

Chapter 36 Descended fromThe Doge

According to my cousin Mirna, the Trevisan side of our family was actually related to a 16th century Venetian Doge (*pronounced do jay*.) Doge, as in the chief magistrate and leader of the Most Serene Republic of Venice, Queen of the Adriatic, City of Light whose noble families ruled Venice for over a thousand years. Doge, who held office for life and was regarded as the ecclesiastical, civil and military leader of the Venetian republic which in those days extended into Dalmatia, further into Italy and across the Mediterranean and Aegean Seas. Doge, as in Duke of Venice whose Palazzo Ducale contains magnificent state rooms, a staircase of Giants and exqusite paintings including Tintoretto's massive "Paradise" said to be the largest oil painting on earth. Yes, descended from the Doges of Venice.
I know, it was hard for me to believe it too.

Our Nonna alluded to this relationship but only in the most secretive way and now it was confirmed but was being descended from the Doge such a good thing. I wondered. So I did a little research on the man behind the funny hat. The hat I am referring to is the *corno ducale*, the ducal hat. A stiff conical hat made of brocade encrusted with gems and worn over a linen cap called a *camauro*. It is said that an early abbess from the convent of San Zaccaria not far from St. Mark's Square created the now famous Doge hat. Every Easter Monday the Doge in procession from the Basilica of San Marco traveled to the Church of San Zaccaria where he was presented with a new *camauro* made by the nuns. This led me to wonder if the Doge was expected to wear the same linen cap all year long until the following year when he ceremoniously received another.

What the Doge was expected to do was to display the magnificence of Venice. His handlers made sure that his long sleeved gown known as a *vesta* and cape, *companoni,* were of the finest and most luxurious fabrics. Style, color and fabric were important to the political status of a Venetian Doge and he was expected to dress for success as was his wife. The Doge and Dogaressa would dazzle the citizens of the Republic with gowns of silk brocade, belts of gold, capes of ermine and necklaces of large pearls. Other members of the Doge's entourage would have dressed equally well although somewhat less ostentatiously wearing silk lined coats with silk bows and tassels, gold threaded fabrics and smaller pearls. That would have been easy to do in the Doge's Venice. Then as now Venice is known for exquisite silk and textiles and the blue of the Adriatic must have made the fabrics shimmer in the sunlight and dazzle in the moonlight.

As Venetians have been known to don masks to mingle without fear of recognition, one can only imagine scenes of Venetian life at the time of the Doge when opulence and intrigue combined to heighten every moment. You might meet Casanova walking along the *fondamenta* or hear a whisper from the Bridge of Sighs (*Ponte dei Sospiri*) that connected the Doge's Palace to the prison. People who were sentenced to death crossed this bridge (supposedly sighing) as they were brought to the *Piazzetta San Marco* for their execution. Today it is said that lovers will be granted everlasting love and bliss if they kiss on a gondola at sunset under the bridge.

So was it good to be the Doge? In some ways yes. Venice was one of the most important cultural and intellectual centers of the Middle Ages and Renaissance. It has been described as one of the most beautiful cities built by man and one of the most romantic cities in the world. The light reflected off the waters of the lagoon, the small lanes or *calle* that lead you to nowhere and everywhere and the exotic architecture all create a dreamlike atmosphere. During the Renaissance, Venice was a prosperous empire, a major port of trade and a market for craftsmen, glassmakers, painters, lace makers and all manner of decorative arts. Living in Venice during the time of the Doge certainly meant living large. But the Doge was under constant surveillance, his mail was censored and he was restricted as to where he could go. He was not allowed to own property or foreign land. When he was selected as Doge he was presented to the people with the following caveat "This is your Doge, if it pleases you". There were times when it did not. Three Doges were assassinated in the streets around San Zaccaria. Over the years Venetian Doges became little more than figure heads with a ruling Council designed to limit their power.

How did our Doge fare in all this? I really don't know, not much has been written about him. His name was Marcantonio Trevisan and he was Doge of Venice from 1553-1554, his reign was short. His name comes up on the Internet every so often in role playing fantasy games about 16th century Venice where he is described as "a religious firebrand who was decently well liked but went largely unmourned for his extremism". Whether or not this is based on fact is unknown although there is an account of his life before he became the Doge when it was said that an angel came to him while sleeping, asking,

264

"Why are you sleeping so soundly in your warm bed, while in the square there is a holy man, a poor pilgrim who needs your help?" Trevisan rushed downstairs to find Ignatius, founder of the Jesuit order, who became his house guest. Trevisan then helped to arrange funds that would allow Ignatius to continue his pilgrimage to Jerusalem. I imagined what our Doge would look like. Few pictures were found. There is an oil painting on canvas by Tintoretto in the Palazzo Ducale of *The Dead Christ Adored by Doges Pietro Lando and Marcantonio Trevisan.* It's a little hard to tell who is who in the painting as there is a lot going on. Trevisan is the Doge on the right wearing the funny hat. There is an official portrait of Doge Marcantonio Trevisan painted by Titian that bears a slight resemblance to our Nonna mostly around the nose. The family's physical resemblance is lost in the genetic recombant mix of hundreds of years but what remains is Trevisan's legendary kindness to strangers and desire to help in whatever way he could to assist a pilgrim on their way. Our Nonna was like that, a legacy from a 16th century Venetian Doge.

Modern day descendents of the Doges see and savor Italy at Venetian Bacari bars stopping for an *"ombra e cichelo"* a small glass of wine and snacks before dinner. Here you can taste typical Venetian appetizers like *sarde in saòr* (marinated sardines), *baccalà mantecato* (creamy dried cod), *folpeti* (baby octopus) and spicy, fried meat balls (*polpette*) with a glass of *Spriz* (a mixture of white wine, Campari and soda water) for an aperitivo from about 6 p.m. on. Or plan a Venetian pub crawl (*giro per bacari*) for a perfect way to experience the local color of Venice and taste a wide variety of local dishes inexpensively

265

in a relaxed atmosphere. Harry's Bar is a Venetian icon, peek in and if you decide enter and try the *Carpaccio*. Harry's Bar is said to be the birthplace of *Carpaccio*, the classic Italian dish of paper-thin slices of raw beef and the *Bellini*, the classic "pink cocktail" made with prosecco (an Italian sparkling wine) and white peach puree. Located on St. Mark's waterfront (from St Mark's Square take the 1st left down Calle Valleressa) legendary A-listers like Hemingway, Bogart and Chaplin as well as a host of famous writers, artists and royalty have dined and wined here. Giuseppe Cipriani, owner of Harry's Bar had a penchant for naming his food creations after artists. When Cipriani created *Carpaccio* in the 1950s he named his dish after the 15th century Italian painter Vittore Carpaccio who was noted for the use of red in his paintings while the *Bellini,* created in 1948, was named for the Renaissance painter Giovanni Bellini whose works were being exhibited in Venice that year.

The romantic ambience of Venice may make you forget all about eating as you arrive by *vaporetto* (motor launch) to a city with an evocative sense of time and place. But the food of Venice only heightens the experience of visiting *La Serenissima* . The scents and spices of the Middle East and tastes of the Mediterranean and beyond remind you that Venice was once a great commercial center and an important trading partner with far off exotic places. The Veneto is home to most of Italy's rice fields, so you're sure to find some of Italy's finest rice dishes served in Venice such as the famous *risi e bisi* (rice and peas) and the Venetian version of *risotto*. Venetian *risotto* is creamier and often served with fresh shellfish or blackened with the ink of tender *seppioline*, little squids. And because of Venice's

266

strategic position in the lagoons along the Adriatic, pasta dishes like *spaghetti alla vongole* (spaghetti with clams) and other seafood dishes are abundant. But for me, eating like a Doge means eating a Venetian specialty known as *fegato alla veneziana*, calves' liver with caramelized onions and herbs. Even if liver was your worst childhood food nightmare, you must try this dish. In his book, *La Cucina Veneziana*, Guiseppe Maffioli dates this dish back to Roman times with various recipes traced back to recipe books written in the 1790s. This dish combines the strong, spicy and sweet tastes of liver, onions and herbs and is generally served with creamy white Venetian style polenta.

See and Savor More

Doge Marcantonio Trevisan (1553-1554) (Titian)

Paint it Black. Venetian gondolas are said to be painted black because of sumptuary laws enacted in Venice during the 16th century. Before then gondolas could be painted any color and were lavishly decorated with silk brocades and velvets, a little too ostentatious and ambitious for the general public. So the Doge of Venice enacted a law that only gondole in the service of transporting important personages could be colored mandating that the gondole of Venice be painted black. Others say that the dark colored gondolas of Venice were due to the Black Death. Today gondolas are painted every color. However the influence of the Doge is still seen in the gondolas of Venice. At the front of the Venetian Gondola is a large piece of metal, the *ferro*, with a portion that is said to be in the shape of Doge's hat. At the *squero* (workshop) of San Trovaso in Dorsoduro you can still watch gondolas being made.

Gondola *ferro*. The six "teeth" of the *ferro* represent the six *sestieri* (administrative districts) of Venice

Chapter 37 The Villa of the Dwarfs

The northern Italian town of Vicenza has been designated a UNESCO World Heritage site yet it still is on the road less traveled for most Italian tourists unless you happen to be an architectural enthusiast. Then the city becomes your classroom and you become the pupil of Palladio. Andrea di Pietro della Gondola aka Palladio was the last great architect of the Renaissance. He was often commissioned to build summer residences for Venetian nobles in the countryside around Vicenza. Families would travel in barges along the Brenta Canal to their country estates to escape the heat of the Venetian summer. One Venetian summer my Italian cousins suggested we drive the A4 Autostrada from Milano to Vicenza to see some of o the most famous villas in Italy designed by Palladio, *Villa Capra* (also known as La Rotonda) and *Villa Valmarana ai Nani* (the Villa of the Dwarfs) stopping along the way eat *branzino* .

Vicenza flourished under the protection of La Serenissima's Republic of Venice and today reflects a tradition of art, architecture and dining that make it one of Northern Italy's most intriguing cities. Taste travelers can appreciate Vicenza's well earned reputation for Northern Italian cuisine with a diverse menu of flavors that includes *Baccalà alla vicentina*, dried cod, cooked in milk, served with polenta. My cousin Mirna makes this dish and she showed me how to cook it and graciously gave me the recipe. The tables of Vicenza are filled with wonderful dishes of the region making it a recommended stop on any taste and travel itinerary. Local *trattorie* and restaurants along the

Brenta Canal specialize in fresh fish and seafood and you can stop along the way to see the Palladian villas.

The scenic strand of coastline along the Brenta River that links Venice to Padua is known as the Brenta Riviera (*Rivera del Brenta*). Along the Brenta, architects, such as Palladio, designed summer residences *(villas)* for wealthy Venetians who were looking for a diversion from the heat of Venice. They would take "designer" barges known as *burchielli* and travel the Brenta Canal (*Naviglio Brenta*), stopping to party along the way. I wanted to follow the route of the party hardy Venetians and as we were driving by car and not *burchielli* we followed S11, a picturesque road that runs most of the canals length. My Italian cousins wanted to eat at *Trattoria Porto Menai dall' Antonia* (*Via Argine Destro 75*) along the canal in a town called Mira. We had a spectacular feast of *scampi giganti griglia* (giant grilled shrimp) and other assorted seafood. The other assorted seafood included my cousin Roberto's favorite dish, *branzino.* Also known as European sea bass, *branzino* has been enjoyed since Roman times. It is a white fish, sweet with a smooth texture that lends itself to the simplest of preparations. My preference is *alla griglia* as they do so well at *Trattoria Porto Menai dall' Antonia* .They also serve excellent pasta; spaghetti, gnochetti and risotto with seafood. Finding the fish of the Brenta is GPS mandatory and you are better off if you can speak a little Italian. This area is definitely off the tourist radar and may take a little doing but it is well worth it.

Our visit to to Villa Rotonda began with a typical Italy mishap, a wrong turn, a lost hubcap, unmapped roads and a exchange of Italian expletives about who was driving eventually settled into a panoramic view of the countryside of Vicenza with La Rotonda in the distance. Some architectural historians describe La Rotonda as a palazzo rather than a villa. They do so because of its close proximity to the city and for the fact that the building has no attachment to the land. Also La Rotonda was not a villa-farm but a "suburban mansion" where Paolo Almerico, the patron of La Rotonda would entertain his guests. Either way, it is as impressive as you would imagine.

The architecture of the Palladian villa was particularly pleasing to wealthy landowners. Architectural elements like pediments could be decorated with the owner's coat of arms to advertise a powerful presence across the countryside. Loggia, an open-sided, roofed or vaulted gallery along the front or side of the villa, offered an enjoyable place to eat, talk, or entertain and amuse in the shade. Kitchens, store-rooms, laundries and cellars were on the ground floor; and the space under the roof was used for storage. The main floor had a central axis with symmetrical suites of rooms, from large to mid-sized to small that were used for living space, studies or offices for administering the estate and for entertaining the owners' guests. This design was recapitulated over and over again as hundreds of thousands of houses, public buildings and churches with symmetrical fronts, halved pillars and gables were inspired by Palladio's design. The architecture of Palladio crossed the Atlantic to be interpreted in the classical style of architecture found in many of the United State's most famous buildings including Thomas Jefferson's Monticello. Jefferson, himself an amateur architect who designed the original buildings at the University of Virginia and his estate Monticello,

271

referred to Palladio's *il Quattro Libri dell' Architettura (the Four Books of Architecture)* as the Bible. Palladio was equally at home designing pleasure palaces for wealthy patricians as he was designing a church. If you happen to visit the central Piazza dei Signori in Vicenza you will see the Basilica Palladina redesigned by Palladio.

We walked around the outside of La Rotonda but did not go inside because the interior was only open 10:00am to noon on the day we were there (Wednesday). The current owner lives on site so I would advise checking with your hotel or calling in advance for scheduled hours of viewing as they are limited.

Down a walking path from La Rotonda is a jewel of a villa that although it may not be as impressive as Palladio's masterpiece is a delight. *Villa Valmarana ai Nani* (Villa at the Dwarfs) is the kind of villa I would have had Palladio design for me. Built by Antonio Muttoni and his son Francesco, Villa Valmarana is actually three buildings, the owner's residence, a guest house (*foresteria*) and stables (*scuderia*). There is a small internal garden and a pagoda in the woods. The walls alongside the Villa are decorated with whimsical figures of dwarfs and there is a legend about the design. The legend is reminiscent of Shrek but without the happy ending.

Once upon a time there was a nobleman who had a daughter who was a dwarf. To protect his daughter and to prevent her from feeling different from the rest of the world, he hired dwarfs from the countryside as servants to work for him. The nobleman's daughter fell in love with a knight in shining armor. Realizing she was different and could never have his love, the daughter threw herself to her death. The stone statues of the dwarfs on the walls alongside the villa represent the servants who were petrified (literally) upon seeing the beloved nobleman's daughter thrown to her death. I toured the villa. It is across the road and up the hill from Villa Rotonda but it is a fair walk. The inside of the villa is as delightful as the outside. The frescoed walls of the villa are attributed to the father and son Tiepolos and are considered to be among the greatest examples of the fresco art of the 18th century. The Valmarana family still lives in the villa so only the villa's *piano nobile* is open to the public.

Palladio designed 63 villas, most of them in the Veneto region. If you are interested in seeing and savoring the Veneto, visiting the Palladian villas would be a wonderful trip. Although La Rotonda is called the "magnificent one", there are 17 buildings on the UNESCO World Heritage List that were designed by Palladio in Vicenza that are very impressive. Others are located in Treviso, Padua, Rovigo, Verona and the famous Villa Foscari near Mira. The front of this villa overlooks the Brenta Canal while the back looks out on open green fields. It is breathtaking. So why is it also known as *La Malcontenta*, (dissatisfied in Italian). A romantic legend of the 1800's accounts for the name with a story about the wife of one of the Foscaris who was confined in the villa against her will, allegedly for a transgression involving her relationship with her husband. Another story talks about the frequent flooding along the Brenta and for this the villa owners would become dissatisfied. Either way living on the Brenta Riviera can have its draw backs even for the wealthiest of land owners.

273

See and Savor More

Among the 17 stone drawfs on the walls of *Villa Valmarana ai nani* are characters from Italy's *Commedia dell'arte* including the Soldier, the King, the Doctor, the Turk and the Guardian of the *Seraglio* (an enclosed or protected place, a sultan's palace).

Villa Valmarana ai Nani

Palladio received his name from his mentor, the poet Trissino, after a character in one of Tissino's poems who helped drive out the Goths from Italy.

The Barges of the Brenta were able to navigate through the shallow river and were pushed by oars from St. Venice (Piazza San Marco) through the Venetian lagoon to Fusina then pulled by horses along the Brenta.

Branzino has a delicate flavor with few bones and loaded with omega-3 fatty acids.

Chapter 38 The Magic of Gropparello

In the Food Valleys of Parma and Emilia Romanga, there lies one of the most ancient strongholds of the area, a castle that still preserves the fascination of a medieval fortress and the fantasy of a fairy tale. Castello di Gropparello is situated in a landscape of extraordinary beauty in an area that few know of. With origins that go back to the 8th century, the rugged beauty of the countryside that surrounds Castello di Gropparello creates breathtaking views with gorges and rock cliffs, woods with unique plants and geological formations that make it one of Italy's national treasures. Today's owners, Maria Rita Trecci Gibelli and her family have transformed it's wood into the first "emotional parc" of Italy, called the "*Parco delle Fiabe*" where the children discover the traces of fairies, gnomes, elves and witches, entering into a fairy-tale that leaves Disney far behind. Captivated by the experience, children and adults alike enter into the medieval world of a miracle play where lessons are learned through the characters of a white knight, a pilgrim and a wizard. Gropparello hosts a number of festivals and evocative medieval dinners. There is a famous Medieval Market which takes place in May and a seasonal Grape Festival in September where children are encouraged to take part in the production process, helping to tread the grapes, to produce what the Castle calls "*Vino dei Bambini*" (children's wine).

Over the last few years I have gotten to know Rita and her family and all I can say is that they are remarkable. I might even go so far as to say that Rita is the Italian version of Walt Disney. What she and her family have created at Castello Gropparello is nothing short of

275

magical. It begins with the landscape. The castle is grounded in the ancient rock of the 'Gole di Vezzeno' a deep gorge that cuts through the surrounding hills and on whose rocks an ancient Celtic stone altar stands. For the adventurous, you can hike into the gorge crossing a rope bridge over the river below on a narrow footpath that leads through a forest of trees and plants with ancient medicinal properties that evoke the gardens of fairies and witches. The Castle dates back to the time of Charlemagne and there are many artifacts and legends that have remained over the years. Ancient musical instruments, full sets of armor and swords, ceilings encrusted with gold to reflect the candle light and the legend of Rosania Fulgosio whose ghost is said to still inhabit the castle. Gianfranco Gibelli, Rita's husband writes of *la leggenda di Rosania Fulgosio* in his book Indagine. The ill fated Rosania, believed to have betrayed her husband with another, is walled up in a secret foundation in the castle, buried alive. Her apparition is said to be seen in the halls of the castle from time to time. We spent one evening touring the castle with Rita and Gianfranco's daughter Chiara. We walked through the rooms of the castle to see things that until now I had only read about in books or seen in glass display cases in museums or libraries. We climbed to the top of the turrets to the rooms where the soldiers that defended the castle stayed and climbed further to look out over a landscape that extended far into the distance for miles. You could imagine seeing troops advancing toward the Castle with their battle armor glistening in the sunlight. Chiara showed us the slits in the castle walls were the archers shot arrows and the defenders of the Castle poured boiling oil that spattered against the Castle walls acting like a giant atomizer to scorch the would be invaders. I had to pinch myself. Was I part of a

276

role playing medieval board game or was I living a part of history in the most evocative way? The experience of authentic travel is not easily forgotten especially when it is combined with world class food and wine. Gropparello Castle is part of the itinerary of *Strada dei Vini e dei Sapori Piacentini*, travel itineraries that allow you to taste and experience the food and wine of a particular region of Italy, in this case the region of Piacenza. I highly recommend these itineraries. They are found all over Italy and allow you to see and savor Italy at its best. Food and wines from artisan producers who are passionate about preserving the culinary traditions of Italy are showcased for taste travelers interested in an authentic experience. The gastronomic festivals and exceptional regional dishes prepared in the Gropparello Castle's Medieval Taverna reflect the great heritage of Emilia Romagna cooking at its best. You are expected to eat well at Gropparello. No pre packaged adventure park food here. I have eaten and cooked some remarkable meals at Gropparello. There is a cookery course at the castle where you can learn to cook regional Piacentini cuisine like pasta *maltagliati* and a sweet Placenza tart to be paired with Gutturnio and Malvasia DOC wines. After we left the Castle, Rita arranged for us to stay at the Locanda del Re Guerriero in the village of San Pietro in Cerro where the rarified atmosphere created by Gropparello continues on the grounds of the 15th century *Castello di San Pietro*. The locanda (inn) is on the grounds of an art park where the natural landscape becomes an open air museum in motion (MiM) with sculptures and installations one would expect to see at MOMA. The linden lined corso to the castle set the mood as we arrived and were greeted in a stunning reception area decorated in rustic chic Italian. Our room was spectacular. Muted

277

tones with dark wooden ceiling beams combined traditional with modern Italian design.

Castello Gropparello is an absolute must see if you will be visiting or touring the Northern region of Italy. It is close to the Lakes, Venice, Verona , Milano and Florence. I have the coordinates programmed into my Italian GPS but by now I can find it by heart.

See and Savor More

Emilia Romagna has over 13 *Strade dei vini e dei sapori* (Wine and Flavor Roads) that run along 2,000 km (over 1,240 miles) with over 1,000 destinations including commercial farms, wineries, milk and cheese factories, bed & breakfasts, agriturismos and artisan shops.

Educational, historical and architectural tours and re-enactments where fairy tales and medieval legends are brought to life are available at Castello Gropparello throughout the year. Most are interactive making the experience all the more delightful. Adventure travelers and nature enthusiasts can follow a steep path to the Vezzeno Gorge for a geological study of the region and there is a wonderful shop where kid travelers can bring the magic home with educational games and toys while their parents select a wine from the castle cellar or perhaps a perfume from the castle woods.

Taverna Medievale at Castello Gropparello

Near Gropparello is one of the most interesting and remote sites I have visited traveling in Italy, the Roman ruins in Veleia (*Veleja Romana*) near the town of Castell'Arquato near Parma. The site was discovered by chance in 1747 and I don't think many visitors have been by since. This place is off the radar. Without a GPS you won't have a chance of finding it but if you do it will be worth your while.

Roman ruins at Veleia

Chapter 39 Machiavelli's Hunting Lodge

If a total immersion into the Italian lifestyle is what you are looking for, brush up on your Italian, climb into your Fiat rental and stop at the COOP for groceries because seeing and savoring Italy takes on a whole new meaning when staying "in country" in a private Italian farmhouse or villa. Sleeping in your own bedroom (*la camera di letto*), cooking in your own Italian kitchen (*la cucina*), waking up to groves of olive trees and the scent of lavender with a view of the Chianti hills. For many people dreaming of Italy this is what it's all about.

Farmhouse and *agriturismo* accommodations are, by definition, outside the city Centro. Just how far outside a city can vary but in most cases you will need a car. Staying on this type of property allows you to plan your own schedule, coming and going as you please. Most are within driving distance of the artistic towns, villages, cultural sites, vineyards and attractions that define the region and day tripping is encouraged. If you don't have a car, ask if public transportation to the nearest town is available and how far it is from the property. You won't mind a short walk down the hill to the bus stop or train station but you will mind a 2 mile hike to the nearest road. Also ask where to buy your bus or train tickets as oftentimes they must be purchased in advance.

Although the *agriturismo* experience of staying in Tuscany is well publicized, accommodations of this type are found in every part of Italy. And for those of you who are wondering if staying in a rural farmhouse is the Italian version of Green Acres, well it can be but not necessarily. Some agriturismi are indeed working farms and do allow their guests to participate in some of the everyday activities of the farm like picking vegetables or feeding the animals. In others, everything is behind the scenes and you are the honored recipient of the fruits of their labors; their estate bottled wine and olive oil, organic produce, honey, jams and bountiful farmstead meals. Some *agriturismi* accommodations are simple and rustic, some are rural chic and some are as opulent as the country homes of the Medici. Some have pools, spas, gardens, libraries, music rooms and landscaped grounds to wander and enjoy. Many offer tours of local sites, wine tastings, cooking classes, horseback riding or mountain biking. You can decide how much or how little you want to do; feed me or cook, daytrip or relax, indulge your inner chef, read, write, paint, find time for yourself.

Did I have you back at hello? If so then drive to the village of San Casciano in Val di Pesa to experience *la bella Toscana* at the estate village of Castello Bibbione. Castello Bibbione is situated in the heart of the Chianti region along the Florence-Siena route near San Casciano in Val di Pesa not far from Florence (15km). Here you will be given the antique key that fits in the lock of the large wooden door to your own Tuscan farmhouse. As you step across the stone threshold you know that you are entering into another time and place of antique handmade terra cotta tiles, beamed wooden ceilings and stairways made of *pietra serena* (a typical Tuscan stone). This is why you travel beyond the beltway. You need to get in touch with your inner Italy, time to discover what makes your trip to Italy unique and special. Will it be the art, the architecture, the shopping and most definitely the food and wine but beyond that there is more.

In 1551 Niccolo Machiavelli knew he needed to get back in touch with himself. He had been involved with the politics and intrigue of Medici Florence and was looking for a diversion from the affairs of state. Machiavelli purchased Castello Bibbione and used it as a hunting lodge and country retreat. The current Marchioness Antonella Rangoni Machiavelli, the proprietor of the estate oversaw the renovation of the Castle and village which now consists of tastefully restored farm houses (*fattorie*) on the estate grounds that were originally built in the 13th century. The castello and grounds feature 14 apartments and cottages scattered among the fields and woods. Each house on the property has been restored in the traditional Tuscan style with modern conveniences and can accommodate from 2 to 12 people. All the houses enjoy a panoramic view of the Chianti hills and are decorated with family furniture and antique kilm carpets. This is the *agriturismo* experience[2].

On a recent trip I stayed in Le Ginestre, a two storied farmhouse with a private garden, Tuscan fireplace and an outside barbecue that cooked Ethan's famous Bistecca Fiorentina I wrote about earlier. Don't let the well appointed design and antique furnishings deter you from staying at Le Ginestre if you are a family traveling with children. Castello Bibbione has been described as a place to stay that will be "the joy of children and adults alike". It is very kid friendly and everyone does their utmost to ensure the quality of the accommodations and that your stay is most comfortable. We shopped at the nearby COOP, cooked in the farmhouse kitchen and when we turned the antique key in the lock of the large wooden farmhouse door and stepped across the stone threshold we felt like we were coming into our own Italian home in the heart of Tuscany. How wonderful!

See and Savor More

Castello di Bibbione farmlands extend over 100 hectares (approx. 200 acres) which are cultivated with vineyards, olive groves and some other crops.

Agriturismos can vary greatly in type and quality of accommodations from bucolic to bizarre. Recommendations are your best source when deciding if the agriturismo experience is right for you. There are several good books and web sites to look into but I would cross reference everything carefully. One fattoria my family stayed at had an appealing web site but when they arrived at the farm, the farmhouse itself was infested with bees that would come out every time they turned on the lights. Going agriturismo can be a wonderful experience especially for families and group travel since most of the accommodations can host four or more guests in a home like setting that tends to be more cost effective than a hotel but there are some things to consider. Here are five things to consider when choosing your *fattoria*

- Many agriturismos are off the beaten path on winding gravel roads so having a suitable car is mandatory

- Get detailed directions on the location, many farmhouse accommodations are REMOTE and isolated which of course adds to the charm of the location but makes them very difficult to find
- Even if you have driven in Italy using a GPS and/or MapQuest and touring atlas as well as a general conversational knowledge of the Italian language is advised
- Be aware that it may be difficult to get to town quickly because of the location - that is why I like Castello Bibbione because it is rural yet near a major town and not far from Florence
- Some agriturismos have spectacular meals offering food and wine typical of the region, others have kitchens that allow you to cook in your villa, some offer no meals and you may have to drive a distance to a town to eat
- Some do not take credit cards

Whats a COOP? COOP stands for an Italian cooperative which operates the largest supermarket chain in Italy. An IPERCOOP (*ipermercato*) is a combination of a supermarket and a department store; a hypermarket.

Le Ginestre at Castello Bibbione

Chapter 40 Eugenia and the Kids

Radda is one of my favorite places to visit in Chianti and it's all about location. Radda is located in the heart of the Chianti hills 50 km southeast of Florence and 30 km north of Siena. On the see and savor map it is well placed for day trips throughout the region, visiting some of Chianti's most traveled towns and villages. Castellina in Chianti, Greve, Gaiole, Castelvecchi, Volpaia, Certaldo are only a few of the many postcard stops you can make along the way eating the food and drinking the wine that connects you to a historical landscape of medieval villages, still intact, set on hilltops with ancient walls that overlook the woods and vineyards of Chianti. On my mind map Radda is a place that connects me to artisan producers that are still committed to preserving the handcrafted traditions of the region.

L'Azienda Agricola La Pensiola in Radda in Chianti is one of those places. It is here is that Eugenia and "the kids" live and work.The "kids" I'm referring to are a herd of Cashmere goats husbanded by Nora, the owner. In an era that has marked the destruction of the small farm and lessened the ability of artisan producers to remain true to their traditions *L'Azienda Agricola La Pensiola* remains a model for small-scale agricultural enterprise and a guarantee that MADE IN ITALY means all fine things Italian. With meticulous care and attention, Nora oversees the entire process that transforms the raw materials of wool into finished cashmere yarn used to make hand woven shawls and scarves of unsurpassed quality. Italian weavers using handlooms, some of them dating from as far back as the 18th

285

century, create one of a kind scarves, shawls, blankets and throws from the wool of the goats of uncommon beauty. Unique skin care products are made from the milk of the goats. Goat's milk is thought to be one of the most natural and effective skin care ingredients on the planet and no fossil fuels, chemicals, feed or hormones are used in the entire production process. *Capra* (*goat* in Italian) Eugenia and her family freely roam the Tuscan hillsides busily producing the milk and wool used to make the skin care products and hand woven shawls and scarves. I spent an afternoon in the farm house kitchen at *La Pensiola* discussing the craftsmen and artisan producers behind the brand. Over *un caffe'* Nora and I shared our thoughts on small business enterprises in the States and in Italy and what it was like to take a dream and a passion and make it into a life's work.

The story of Nora Kravis, creator and founder of the Chianti Cashmere Company is nothing short of remarkable. Leaving Long Island, New York in 1972, she traveled to Italy with a Fine Arts Degree and a love for animals. She ended up studying Veterinary Medicine at the Univerisita of Pisa, bought a "under the Tuscan sun" farm house and developed a company with worldwide distribution. She also raises what she refers to as "expat dogs". Visitors to *La Pensiola* are often so taken up by the joyous, buoyant nature of her family of Bolognese that they want to take one home with them. One of the few true Italian breeds, the small white compact Bolognese was the favorite companion dog of nobility during the Renaissance (and a popular court gift among the royal families of Spain, Russia, Italy and France) but became nearly extinct by the end of the 19th century. They are

286

very intelligent, eager to please, affectionate and compatible and should you like to visit Eugenia and the "kids", you can spend an Italian farm holiday at La Pensiola. There is a very nice self catering farmhouse for weekly rental with views of the Volpaia valley, an outdoor loggia terrace, beamed ceilings, terra cotta tile floors complete with visits from some friendly Bolognese dogs and Chianti goats.

See and Savor More

La Pensiola Chianti Cashmere Goat   Italian Bolognese Dogs

Cashmere is the fine, fluffy, downy undercoat produced by a Cashmere goat, a fiber of 11-18 microns in thickness, 10 times lighter and warmer than wool.

Chapter 41 Saints, Sinners, Pilgrims and Kings

The gastronomic landscape of Italy has always been populated by saints, sinners, pilgrims and kings. From the ancient Etruscans to Artusi's Science of Cookery and the Art of Eating Well, the food of Italy has a tradition that cannot be denied. The generational recipes of our grandparents are forever written in stone and the collected works of Hazan and Bastianich are deemed essential. The orange Crocs worn by Mario Batali are firmly planted on the *terra firma* of Italian culinary soil and even the contemporary Italian cooking of Chef Michael White doesn't stray too far from the tables of history. White's *Pesto Shrimp Mac and Cheese* still relies on Parmigiano Reggiano, the undisputed "king of cheeses" and Italian *pinoli* (pine nuts), the richly flavorful nut from the Italian Stone Pine tree of the Northern Mediterranean. I gathered some of these nuts walking down a neighborhood street in Perugia with my friend Luca. The trees are beautiful, stately; valued both for their edible nuts and as ornamental trees.

When I look back at all the Italian food I've eaten I can see a bloodline that is both ancient and new with contributors from every part of Italian society. Whether you were a Medici princess or pilgrim on the *Via Francigena* the foods you favored were proudly made following traditional recipes. So who were the caretakers and custodians of Italy's food traditions.The first foods of Italy, bread, wine, cheese and olive oil were mainly for family consumption, cultivated and curated *alla casa*. But there were many who were without a family to feed them; orphans, widows and weary travelers who often looked to the

Church as a source of spiritual and physical nourishment. Monasteries and abbeys were places where whatever was on the table could be shared with the needy. As part of a religious community, monasteries and abbeys had a complex of buildings that included dining rooms, kitchens, bakeries and barns for animals and storage, a granary, gardens and land with vineyards and orchards. There was a hierarchy and an infrastructure that fostered the growing and making of food to feed the community so it was only natural that many food traditions were born and nurtured here.

I have visited many monasteries and abbeys in Italy on a parallel journey of art, history, spirituality and food. Some abbeys have been commercially re-purposed and are no longer used as a religious site like Badia a Coltibuono, "the abbey of the good harvest". I stopped here on one of my first trips to Italy. Located 2½ miles from Gaiole in Chianti, Badia a Coltibuono is not a religious site as the name might imply (*badia* being the Italian word for abbey) but the site of an almost religious experience for those who come to this former 11th century Benedictine abbey seeking culinary inspiration. The former abbey is now a wine estate and mecca for food enthusiasts. There is a residential cooking school, where parts of the abbey once stood and gardens to visit. Cooking classes are offered under the auspices of Lorenza de' Medici, well known author of cookbooks on authentic Tuscan cooking. Her photographic Tuscany the Beautiful, a tabletop cookbook, has interesting anecdotes about eating and cooking in Tuscany with inspiring pictures of regional Tuscan food. However the vibe of this place is "touristy" and can be expensive. Even if you don't come here to participate in the cooking classes, it is worth a trip. The setting is beautiful. The abbey is surrounded by forests of chestnut, oak and fir. There is an estate shop that sells various products and a restaurant attached to the estate. Make sure to arrange reservations well in advance because it is a popular place for tours coming to experience Tuscan cuisine. Reservations are also needed to visit the winery and do a tasting. Some people describe Badia a Coltibuono as a "wine resort". It is definitely more upscale with "designer cellars" and modern technology but the remaining part of the abbey's old Romanesque church dedicated to San Lorenzo is still standing.

Abbazia di Monte Oliveto Maggiore was the first monastery I visited in Italy. My cousin Lidia suggested I stop there on my way to Siena to see the Great Cloister (*Chiostra Grande*) with 36 frescos that line the inner courtyard. The frescos depict the life of St. Benedict including Benedict giving CPR to a monk who has fallen off a wall and a self portrait of one of the artists, with his pet badger. Monte Oliveto Maggiore is one of the most renowned monasteries in Italy.The abbey is 20 miles from Siena driving through an area of Tuscany called the Crete Senesl, "Tuscan Desert". After driving through the stark rolling landscape of the *crete* (*crete* means "clay" in Italian), the abbey emerges high on a hill surrounded by cypress and olive trees. Be prepared for a climb as all monasteries are remote and off the beaten track. The farm, vineyard and olive groves at Monte Oliveto Maggiore Abbey are now state of the art and the Abbey's wine cellar can be visited and their wine and oil tasted at no charge. Spelt (*farro* in Italian), an unhybridized ancestor of modern wheat with a hearty nutty flavor, continues to be cultivated at Monte Oliveto and you can buy

290

Farro dei Colli from the store at the Abbey. *(i prodotti del lavoro monastico sono venduti nel negozio dell'Abbazi)* You can also buy teas, elixirs, honey, religious articles and a liqueur known as *La Flora di Monteoliveto* infused with 23 herbs made according to an ancient formula from the monastery pharmacy. Monte Oliveto Maggiore Abbey is an active Benedictine monastery with monks who work and pray daily. Although open to tourists, there are certain features of the monastery that are private spaces. The historical library and pharmacy can only be seen by special arrangement. Gregorian chants are sung at the Abbey after 6.00pm and at 11.00am mass on Sunday and there are guest rooms located in the Abbey farm house that can be rented at a most reasonable cost.

A monastery road less traveled is one that leads to the forest and mountain sanctuary of La Verna, *Santuario San Francesco*, the Sanctuary of St. Francis. It is a place *"ricca bellezze naturali e di opere d'arte"*, rich in the beauty of nature and works of art. La Verna is the site imaged in the famous garden statues of St. Francis surrounded by birds whirling with delight. The monastery is built on the edge of a mountain cliff (4160 ft) which means driving and walking on long, winding roads, so you will need to be prepared with comfortable walking shoes to enjoy the journey. As you walk to the *Santuario* at La Verna you will see chapels and places to sit and reflect on the beauty and spirituality of this place. The monastery at La Verna together with Assisi are spiritual centers for the followers of St. Francis. These sacred sites have been visited by pilgrims for hundreds of years. The chapels, buildings and grounds of La Verna tend to envelope you in a mysticism that is palpable. It is here where

291

Francis received the Stigmata. I can remember visiting La Verna with my family and 2 year old grandson, Ethan. He and I were standing along the side of a long hallway in the monastery watching the friars walking along the corridor in procession. The friars, in their brown robes, were chanting and contemplative and Ethan was holding on tight because the whole setting was solemn and imposing. Then one of the friars, stepping out of line, came over to us and put his hand on Ethan's head and with a big smile gave him a blessing. Ethan was filled with wonder and immediately at ease. In the Refectory (dining room) a traditional lunch of *ribollita*, *tagliatelle*, meat and fish was served. The food of Francis and his brothers was simple and wholesome and the monastic practice of extending food and hospitality is an Italian tradition that is still followed today.

Abbazia Sant' Antimo, in Tuscany's stunningly beautiful Val d' Orcia, has a monastic myth attached to it that will appeal to the wine lover. I traveled there to see the site of a legend and to experience the spiritual clarity of Abbazia di Sant'Antimo where around the year 800 the Emperor Charlemagne on his return to Rome made camp. His army was suffering from the plague and an angel advised him to collect a particular kind of grass and infuse it with Brunello wine (not bad medicine). The army was cured and Charlemagne built an abbey on the site dedicated to the martyred Saint Antimo. Only 9 km from the Brunellos of Montalcino you can easily see how myth becomes reality when you are surrounded by the vineyards of the region. The abbey stands in solitary splendor against the open fields where olive orchards go on for miles and Chianina cattle graze. One of Italy's most beautiful Romanesque churches, Sant'Antimo is like a laser

292

beam concentrating all the history and mysticism of centuries of saints, sinners, pilgrims and kings that have traveled through its doors and eaten of its fields.

See and Savor More

Abbazia Sant' Antimo

Chapter 42 The Festival of the Squeak

One thing I've learned about traveling in Italy is that Italians are always ready for a celebration. Getting together at the homes of their family and friends, at their favorite local trattoria or in the piazza with several hundred like minded party goers, Italians enjoy a spirit of conviviality. It doesn't take much for them to plan a *festa*; a party or festival that celebrates or commemorates anything from the food and wine of the region to frogs, wild boar and pine nuts. A cross between a country fair, open air market and block party these festivals, or *sagras* as they are called in Italy, often combine seasonal foods of the region, entertainment and traditional folklore that attracts all ages. In fact, if you are taste traveling in Italy, look for posters advertising local sagras. They are great for families and a casual, inexpensive way to taste authentic Italian food in the company of everyday Italians, learning about the history and culture of the region.

Although there are many sagras in Italy that celebrate what we might consider to be an unusual food or event, one of the most curious I know about is the *Festa dello Scricchio*, festival of the squeak. The festival is held every year in the village of San Giovanni d' Asso, 25 miles southeast of Siena. On the road less traveled, among the clay hills of the Crete Senesi, most travelers would need to think outside the box to visit here. The unique nature of this small (938 inhabitants) medieval village, named after the Asso River is near some of my favorite places in Tuscany as well as those that most Tuscan tourists want to visit. The wines of Montalcino with its famous Brunello and the Vin Nobile of Montepulciano are waiting to be tasted and Siena,

Pienza, Buonconvento and the thermal spa town of San Quirico d'Orcia are a short distance away. The abbeys of Monte Oliveto Maggiore and Sant' Antimo are all within driving distance and Florence is 80 km. There is a popular cyclist's itinerary that passes through San Giovanni d' Asso and a wonderful locanda with a ristorante that is at the top of my see and savor Italy list but more about that later.The unique nature and spirit of San Giovanni d'Asso is reflected in the 14th century Church of San Giovanni Battista where the Festival of the Squeak is held. In the church on the high altar is a cabinet with wooden painted shutters that house the relics of various saints, including Saint Peter the Apostle. The cabinet is opened every year on the Saturday after Easter. A name of a saint is then raffled and the following Sunday his relic is carried in procession. The relic is then returned to the cabinet and by the squeak the shutters make when the cabinet is closed one can supposedly foretell a good or bad harvest.

From the well known Palio in Siena to the Pisa Rock Festival; from the *Festa del Nocciolo* (hazelnuts) in Panzano to the *Sagra Della Lumacia* (Festival of the Snail) near Arezzo; from the wine barrel rolling race of Montepulciano to the cheese rolling competition in Pienza, Italians just want to have fun and enjoy good food. This brings me back to San Giovanni d'Asso. Each November in San Giovanni d'Asso, Italian truffle hunters and their dogs take to the nearby woods in search of the *tartufo bianco* "white diamonds of Italy" to bring to S. G. d'Asso's Annual Fall Truffle Festival. Held the 2nd and 3rd weekends in November, you can buy local products, eat local dishes made with truffles and arrange to watch truffle hunters at work. You can also visit

295

Italy's first truffle museum located in a medieval castle in the center of the town where you can get up close and personal with truffles and take in the heady, earthy aroma of one of the most expensive foods on the planet.

See and Savor More

Another unusual Italian festival is the *Aria di Festa*, a *sagra* that takes place in San Daniele del Friuli at the end of June each year celebrating the air that cures the famous raw ham known as Prosciutto di San Daniele.

A sagra poster announcing a fair that showcases the ancient flavors of the sea and land in the town of Cattolica in Rimini.

296

Chapter 43 Truffle and Termes in Tuscany

There's more to Tuscany than wine. After many years of traveling the wine roads of Chianti on SS222 under the looming gaze of the Black Rooster, Gallo Nero (symbol of the Chianti Wine League) I was ready for a change. Don't get me wrong, there's nothing more thrilling than traveling along the twisting Via Chiantigiana (SS222). Fields of sunflowers and hillsides of vineyards and olive trees pass by and the glow of burnt umber, olive green and red wine color the landscape with breathtaking beauty. You can easily spend a week wandering down the winding roads from this town to the next eating salumi, crostini and wild boar, searching for the perfect ribollito, stopping to sample the classic wines of the region, developing what I refer to as that "Tuscan Glow". But on my last trip to Chianti I vowed that I would search out another Tuscan treasure, the aromatic white truffle (tartufo bianco) found in the woods near the town of San Giovanni d'Asso and along the way pay a visit to a terme, one of the many natural hot springs that can be found In the Tuscan countryside.

The village of San Giovanni d' Asso is in the heart of the Crete Senesi. The Crete Senesi (pronounced KREH-teh seh-NEH-seh) is a rolling panorama of windswept hills and isolated farmhouses south of Siena. It is the parallel universe of Chianti and attracts travelers seeking the elemental Tuscan experience. Driving through the rolling hills and woods that straddle the Crete and the Val d'Orcia is a solitary experience. You can drive for miles without seeing a soul and then come upon a group of avid cyclists who find the rise and fall of the road less traveled the ultimate ride.

297

The Museo di Tartufo in San Giovanni d' Asso is the Italian version of Alice in Wonderland, a visual-sensory journey of discovery to learn about the prized fungus. There's even an "odorama" exhibit that allows visitors to experience the heady aromas of dozens of different kinds of truffles. Located in a 13th century castle, the museum is next to La Locanda del Castello, a country inn with an equally powerful effect on your senses. Selvana, the owner, her son Massimo and innkeeper, Fiorella make you stay at the inn very special. They are most attentive and the accommodations a traveler's delight. My room was decorated with 19th century Italian country furniture combined with touches of French toile fabric to create what I would imagine to be the style of day when traveling from *locanda* to *locanda*.

You arrive at the locanda piazza where a series of contemporary sculptures are on display then walk through the Castello drawbridge and into the castle courtyard. There is a *ristorante* downstairs from the inn (very convenient) decorated in rustic-Italian chic with a private veranda that overlooks the town and valley below. When ordering, I would willingly take the advice of chef Enrico whose Nouveau Tuscan cuisine and artful presentation were *fantastici*. My fellow taste travelers and I were treated to a delicious plate of pici pasta with *cacio e pepe* (cheese and pepper) one night and another night a wild boar ragu' that defined the dish. The ravioli with truffles is a must and the caprese salad was another favorite. There is also an antipasti of assorted salumi included Lardo di Colonnata, a protected Tuscan delicacy that should not be missed. Staying in one of the suites in this *locanda,* dining at the *ristorante* and taste traveling through the region could be one of the best see and savor experiences you can have in

298

Tuscany. When surrounded by the aphrodisial aroma of truffles, the heady wines of Tuscany and stark landscape of the Crete, an afternoon spent at a Tuscan terme is *benessere*.

Terme is the Italian word for thermal waters. Popes, pilgrims, princes and everyday Italians have traveled to these natural hot springs seeking the beneficial virtues of the waters to regenerate the body and mind since ancient times. On last year's trip I got "my feet wet" at Bagno Vignoni, a small medieval town south of Siena. The town itself is built around a central thermal pool with a thermal stream you can walk through. The ancient Etruscans and Romans knew about these hot springs and pilgrims traveling the Via Francigena Road on their way to Rome stopped to rest in the waters. Pope Pius II, St. Caterina of Siena and Lorenzo Medici all bathed here. But now it is very casual, with mostly Italians on holiday taking the waters at one of the two thermal centers in town. Not yet ready to take the plunge, I took off my sandals and felt the warm, rich volcanic water run across my tired feet and for a moment knew what it must have been like to be weary pilgrim on their way to Rome. This year after tasting truffles in San Giovanni d'Asso, I was ready to get my terme on and decided the best place to loss my inhibitions would be at Terme Antica Querciolaia near the town of Rapolano Terme. There are other popular termes in Italy, Montecatini and Saturnia come to mind, but to see and savor Italy I like to travel like an Italian and I find Antica Querciolaia the type of *terme* that appeals to me. It is small, family oriented (yes, Italian children come with their parents) with 3 large pools rich in minerals such as calcium, magnesium, sodium and potassium. I spent one memorable afternoon in September languishing in the thermal waters

299

of Antica Querciolaia under the Tuscan sun knowing that this was another reason why Italy is the best place on earth.

See and Savor More

The restaurant at La Locanda del Castello alone is worth a trip to this region of Italy. Tastefully decorated with equally tasteful food like

- Tagliolini freschi al Tartufo "Marzuolo delle Crete senesi" prezzo secondo la quotazione del giorno
- Pici al ragù di Cinghiale
- Pappardelle al ragù di Chianina
- Ribollità della Crete Senesi
- Ravioli al Tartufo "Marzuolo delle Crete senesi"

The Italian White Truffle

Chapter 44 The Ice Man

There's a lot for seeing and savoring Italy with a sense of adventure. You can travel in Northern Italy, Tuscany and Umbria to experience hiking, mountain biking, horseback riding, rock climbing, skiing, sailing, ballooning, snowboarding, truffle hunting, pizza making and tomb raiding. An Italian dude ranch in the Maremma, the road to the monastery at La Verna, caving the wells of Umbria, the secret underground passages of Bologna, hang gliding in the Dolomites. Did you know that Italy has some of the most extreme golfing in Europe? Although it has been described technically as moderate, the Molino del Pero Golf Club in the Emilia Romagna Apennines is situated on such a steep rise from the Savena Valley that the first few holes have been called "the stairway to Heaven". When I was there most golfers were carrying their own bags over the hilly, 18 hole course with its sloping fairways which I thought was pretty extreme. I on the other hand made my way to the clubhouse for a panino and a cold drink.

Your sense of adventure can be satisfied through a variety of activities and on a trip to the Alto-Adige region of Northern Italy my cousin Lidia suggested we spend an afternoon at the South Tirol Museum of Archeology to visit one of the world's best known and important mummies, the Iceman. The Iceman was discovered in the Ötztal Alps of Italy's South Tirol. In 1991 two hikers found the back of a human figure jutting out of the ice and melt water in a rocky gully. Excavation and recovery efforts further uncovered leather and hide remnants, grasses, string, pieces of skin, muscle fibers, hair, a fingernail and a section of a broken longbow as well as a bearskin cap. The location and climatic conditions preserved the body of the Iceman virtually intact protecting it from predators and decomposition so that it was naturally mummified creating what is called a "wet mummy", one in which humidity is retained in individual cells. That meant that the body tissue remained elastic and was suitable for performing detailed scientific analysis. Finding and recovering the Iceman with his clothing and equipment intact provided a natural diorama over 5000 years old. On display in the museum were grass mating, pieces of a goat skin coat, a leather loincloth, a bearskin cap, leggings and shoes that are of the oldest kind in the world, a belt and pouch with flint tools, a copper bladed ax and a dagger made of flint from the quarries in the Lessini Mountains north of Verona. Seeing all this was amazing but there was more. There was a yew bow and quiver of arrows, part of a net, a backpack and a blackened birch bark container with various plant remains and traces of charcoal. A Copper Age first aid kit had a type of preserved fungus with known antibiotic properties but this could not prevent the death of the Iceman. X-ray studies revealed a foreign body wound in the Iceman's left shoulder caused by a flint arrowhead which was the probable cause of his death. Today a sealed refrigerated chamber exhibits and conserves the mummy of the Iceman. Visitors file through a darkened room to view the Iceman through a small window that measures 40 x 40 cm. A larger opening would result in excessive temperature fluctuations inside the controlled cell that would cause the mummy to be destroyed.

Traveling through Italy is an adventure. Seeing Italy's art, architecture and historical monuments outside the pages of a book is like traveling in a time machine. The food and wine are stimulating and interacting with the Italian people can be a cultural exchange of ideas that introduces you to another lifestyle. Italy is both familiar and exotic with few constructed attractions as compared to the United States. Perhaps it's because Italy IS the attraction. The castles are real with towers and turrets, armor and weaponry. The palaces of princes and dukes are still standing and open to the public. The art and architecture of the Renaissance can be found around every corner and Rome remains eternal. On my trip to Italy I've stayed in castles in the Umbrian hills of Perugia that were built in 1384AD and visited fortresses that still stand from the time of Charlemagne. Italians refer to these types of accommodations as "residenza d'epoca" a period residence and custodian of age old memories.

It doesn't take much of an imagination to begin to immerse your self in the wonders found in every Italian city, town and village and children especially are intrigued by the magic and fantasy they can conjure up when visiting Italy. So use the magic and adventure of Italy to your advantage. Don't look for the same type of attractions and amusements that are typically found back home. See and savor the Italian adventure and for you extreme travelers although you won't be able to go shark diving I hear there is a dive site somewhere deep in the waters of Riviera di Levante near Portofino called Il Christo degli Abissi where a 2.5 m statue of Christ protects the people of the sea.

Chapter 45 Est, Est, Est

Umbria has been called the land of mysticism where the lives of saints like Francis and Clare of Assisi combine with vestiges of Etruscan, Roman, Medieval and Renaissance art and history to create a setting where a gastronomic palate is rich with layers of food and wine from Italy's Green Heart. In Umbria you can taste and travel among the rolling green plains of the River Tiber or on the edge of the tufa cliffs of Orivieto. The food will always be exceptional. Although one of the smallest regions of Italy, Umbrian food is big on flavor with bold and rustic dishes and rare ingredients hidden in the shadows of ancient forests.

Taste travelers in the know have always been drawn to this region of Italy. 899 years ago German Bishop Johann DeFuk was on his way to Rome. The Bishop's steward was sent ahead in search of local inns and producers that served the best wine so that the oenophilic Bishop could be alerted as to where he might taste the most exceptional wines of the region. Any places found to be particularly good were to be marked with the Latin word "Est" meaning "Here it is ". As the Bishop followed the route of his steward, he stopped at each place marked with "Est". As legend has it, just past Orvieto, at an inn near the town of Montefiascone the superlative "Est! Est! Est!" appeared on the door of a local wine grower and the Bishop traveled no further. Some say he dropped dead on the spot after drinking too much of a good thing. Others say that he lived out his days in the town of Montefiascone happily drinking his favorite wine until the time of his death when he was then buried in the church of San Flaviano, outside the walls of Montefiascone with the following inscription on his tomb

Est, Est, Est. Propter nimium est,
(hic) Jo(hannes) De Fuk. D(ominus) meus mortuus est.

Roughly translated to mean "My Lord, Johnannes died here because of too much "Est". According to some accounts DeFuk willed all his belongings to the town council on the condition that each year a barrel of wine be poured over his tomb, a practice observed until about a century ago. The contemporary version of Est, Est Est wine from Monttefiascone has been described by diwinetaste as a "crisp white wine, excellent as an aperitif" with a clear pleasant taste and "hints of pear, broom and pineapple followed by aromas of apple and almond". DeFuk's steward was most likely one of the earliest wine critics giving the wine a superlative rating. Robert Parker takes it down a few notches to 89, the Wine Spectator slightly less and Garyvee (Gary Vaynerchuk) from the hugely popular on line wine video blog, Wine Library TV, and author of Crush It, to the best of my knowledge doesn't mention it. What does all this mean? Nothing. All three experts would be the first to say you should drink what you like and although DeFuk was enthralled with Est, Est, Est; I wasn't. When I'm in Umbria, I look for a red Sagrantino from Montefalco. I've written about this wine before. Many believe that it is one of the finest expressions of Italian wine making. Cultivated only on the hills around Montefalco, the grapes produce a wine that is garnet red with a faint scent of violet petals and an aroma reminiscent of blackberries. For me, seeing and savoring Umbria begins with a glass of Sagrantino

305

and continues with pork and pici. Pork occupies a special place in the hearts, minds and bellies of Umbrians especially pork from Norcia, a small town high in the Sibillini Mountains. Here pork is so skillfully prepared that the word norcino (meaning someone from Norcia) is now synonymous with the Italian word for butcher. According to the Insituto Valorizzazione Salumi Italiani, a Consortium that provides information on Italian charcuterie products, between the 12th and 17th century Italian butchers started to organize themselves into specialized guilds or confraternities. It was also during this time that pork received the blessings of popes when Pope Paul V recognized the Confraternity of Pork Butchers dedicated to Saints Benedetto and Scholastica of Nursia (ancient name of Norcia). In 1677, Pope Gregorius XV elevated this group of pork lovers to an Archconfraternity which was later joined by the University of Norcia and Cascia Pork Butchers and Empirical Pork Physicians (types of sorcerers). Pork, popes and patronage led to delicious sausages, salami and cured meats that were highly sought after especially Umbrian capocollo, made with prime cuts of pork neck flavored with wild fennel seeds, black pepper, garlic and wine. Although found in other regions of Italy (i.e. Emilia Romagna and Campania) capocollo from Umbria has been described as the most characteristic of its type.

The skill of the norcini of Umbria is further justified by the distinctive flavors of sausages, salami and other delicacies such as *corallina di Norcia* (a finely ground pork salami scented with garlic, smoked over juniper wood and aged up to 5 months) *mazzafegati* (fresh pork sausages made from pig's livers; if sweet they are flavored with orange zest, pine nuts, raisins, and sugar), *barbozza* (aged guanciale or pig cheeks) and *coppa Umbra* (an Umbrian head cheese flavored with orange zest). *Prosciutto di montagna di Norcia*, prosciutto from the mountains of Norcia, has been called the king of Umbrian delicacies. The high mountain ridges and chalk formations of this region of Umbria create a prosciutto with a unique nutty taste, slightly spicy, more savory than salty. Ordering *affetato misto*, an assortment of sliced cured meats and sausages as an antipasti, is a good way to sample the unique selection of pork from Umbria but it doesn't stop there. A pantheon of pork products awaits you including the whole hog. Porchetta, a whole young pig, deboned, flavored with wild fennel and garlic and spit roasted in a wood-burning oven is a signature Umbrian dish. As in other parts of Italy, porchetta is often served panino style from food stalls or "porchetta trucks" at local markets. Always ask for a little of the pork's crispy skin. It has a lot of flavor.

The closeness of Umbria to Tuscany has resulted in a culinary crossover of sorts. Both regions of Italy are known for the earthy, robust flavors of rustic cooking and therefore share similarities in food preparation. And between them, as in most of Italy, there are a lot of border crossings. Foods slip across the border only to be reinterpreted according to local recipes using regional ingredients. In the Geography of Italian Pasta , David Alexander writes that "short of asking each household in Italy what the family tradition in pasta making is, there is no way to establish precise regional boundaries of each species of pasta". A good example of this is the Tuscan/Umbrian pasta known as pici, a hand rolled, long round, thick, chewy, fat sphaghetti. I have had this pasta in the Val d'Orcia in Tuscany as well as at the Umbrian home of my friends in Perugia. Often the only difference is the type of sauce (*sugo*) used and for a taste traveler in Italy that makes for many a culinary adventure in good eating. I personally subscribe to the Shakespearian theory of pasta, that is to say, would pasta by any other name be less tasty. I don't think so, at least not in Italy.

In the end the Est of seeing and savoring Umbria would be driving from Tuscany by way of Lake Trasimeno into Perugia then following the towns and villages into the Green Heart of Italy, stopping along the way to buy linens and ceramics for which Umbrian artisan producers are well known. Begin your trip with a night or two at Hotel Tiferno in Citta'di Castello for a perfect balance of historic Italian tradition with innovative Italian design. Artwork and paintings by Albert Burri, a native of Citta', complement the monastic architecture resulting in a unique space. Or stay at Castello dell'Oscano in the Umbrian countryside near the town of Perugia for a Cinderella like experience that begins when you drive through the wooded hillsides and come upon what must be an illusion. Castello dell' Oscano's park like setting with turrets and towers and arched porticos was just as I imagined a castle to be. Many of the furnishings and fittings in the castle are original to the 1700's but with very little signs of age, it was as if time had stood still. Curious, I know. I visited this castle on one of my first trips to Italy and have a picture of me sitting at a writing desk in the library castle that I keep on my desk at home to this day to remind me of that fairy tale experience. There are two other residences associated with Oscano but I would definitely try to stay in room 202 at the Castle that looks out over the courtyard and into a dream.

So although it may be difficult for you to the get out from under the Tuscan sun, the food and wine of Umbria, Tuscanys's "gentler sister", has emerged from the shadows of its neighbor and offers the taste traveler yet another opportunity to experience to see and savor Italy.

See and Savor More

A *norcineria* is a shop that sells pork products such as sausages, hams, salami and cured meats. Look for these establishments in your travels throughout Italy, as they produce top-quality pork products. Some shops also sell fresh bread so you have the makings for a great picnic lunch. But be prepared. You are likely to run into a stuffed boar's head amid the hunks of hanging prosciutti, shelves of salami and piles of fragrant cheese.

Depending on the region of Italy pici pasta is also known as *pinci, stringozzi, bigoli* (in the Veneto), *ciriole* or *ombrichelli* (which is actually a big handmade sphaghetti).

Pici pasta may be difficult to find in the States. Mario Batali has a recipe for homemade pici pasta that is easy to make and doesn't require an expensive pasta machine. The hand rolled pasta should be slightly thinner than a pencil and will vary in thichness due to the rustic preparation. Pici is a great pasta to make with kids.

Chapter 46 My Friend Lui

Once when I was seeing and savoring Italy with a group of fellow taste travelers, someone asked me who my friend "Louie" was. They said I talked about him a lot. Not knowing the Italian language they didn't realize that my friend "Louie" was actually spelled "Lui" and referred to the Italian personal pronoun for he or him. So when I would say "Lui mi piace" or "Mi piace Lui", I wasn't saying "I like Louie" as in a person by name but rather I was referring to someone of the male gender not necessarily named Louie.

Confusing? All the more reason for you to know a little Italian when seeing a savoring Italy. But knowing a little Italian can be a dangerous thing. Phrase book Italian is confining and is a little like speaking from a script. Learning vocabulary is good but limited. What does this mean? It means that no matter what anyone has told you there is no "quick, easy, instant" way to learn the Italian language. A language has many dimensions and language without grammar and conjugation is a meaningless shell. Although an Italian phrase book is a good starting point for your first trip to Italy you will need to build on these rout sayings and idioms to carry on a conversation.

My study of the Italian language began on my first trip to Italy. My cousin Lidia, who is a teacher, began my "Italian education" in a very simple way. I call it experiential learning, in other words, relating the study of the language to what you are doing at the time whether it was cooking, buying food at the COOP, ordering a meal in a restaurant, shopping for clothes or on a road trip in Tuscany. I soon realized that learning the language to suit the occasion was effective for the occasion but limiting. When I returned to the States I began to study Italian grammar, tenses and verb conjugations with la maestra, Gina, my patient and long-suffering Italian teacher. In the dedication of this book, I have included a special note of thanks to Gina saying I am grateful to her in the present, past, future, imperfect and conditional tenses although I continue to struggle with the last two. But grammar need not be the big bad wolf of language. Find a way to learn some basic grammar; nouns, pronouns, adjectives, adverbs, number, gender, tenses; then you can manage. There is more than one way to get your idea across but speaking in the infinitive doesn't leave much room for that. So if you are serious about seeing and savoring Italy take some time and make an effort to learn the language. Of course, many Italians do speak English but if you will be traveling to little known places in Italy, outside of the tourist "comfort zone" you will need to understand and speak some Italian. That way you can experience all that Italy has to offer and interact with the Italian people speaking the language of their country. Italians appreciate it when "*tu parli l'italiano*" and are more than happy to help you with pronunciation. They also like to practice their English with "*gli americani*"! A word about speaking with Italians who are speaking English. Italians who speak English generally still retain their Italian accent. That is to say that sometimes they pronounce an English word using the vowel sounds from the Italian language which is very phonetic. I became aware of this at a dinner party when my friend Luca, who was spending the summer with us at our home in the

311

States, began to tell a story about his father and Rinaldo. Luca and his family are from Umbria, a region of Italy whose winding hills and valleys still retain the rugged landscape of medieval fortresses, Roman aqueducts and Etruscan ruins. Hunting in Umbria is part of a tradition as deep as the garnet ruby color of a glass of Umbrian Sagrantino and whether you're hunting for *funghi* (mushrooms), truffles, wild boar or game birds, there are rituals and rites that are followed. Luca's father, Antonio, hunts game birds and has an aviary on his property where he keeps birds that are trained to attract the prey as live decoys. Rinaldo is one of these decoy birds and enjoys a decidedly good life as he prepares for the fall hunting season. Antonio is very kind and good to his birds and trains and feeds them well. When the birds are "working", they are attached by a short tether to a long pole and taken out into the field. They flap their wings and fly only so far and in doing so attract the wild game birds to the hunt. At the dinner table, Luca told the story about how Antonio's keeper of the birds was feeding Rinaldo one day. Luca said he took mice and chewed the mice in his mouth and then gave a piece of mice to Rinaldo. As you can imagine all the dinner guests were shocked and disgusted by this feeding practice especially as I asked if they would like another helping of *tagliatelle alla Bolognese*. Luca continued on with his story saying how much Rinaldo liked the ground up mice and how Rinaldo was his father's prize bird. Finally I interrupted Luca and said that maybe this conversation wasn't appropriate for Americans eating at the dinner table. Luca turned to me with a puzzled look and mentioned that we had been talking earlier about eating mice and said the mice grown in our area was especially good. I then realized that we were talking about corn and Luca was talking about maize, which is what Italians call corn and with his Italian accent the word maize sounded like the word mi- a -ze which sounded like mice! This was of course a lesson in language I would not forget. Listen carefully when Italians speak and remember that they pronounce every vowel, like in the word veg-e-ta-bl-es.

You will also need to remember that there are many dialects in Italy, variations of the standard language. Standard, classical Italian is based on the Tuscan dialect which at one time was only spoken by Florentine high society. Dante Alighieri is credited with standardizing the Italian language and the dialect of Tuscany making it the basis for what would become the official language of Italy. That's not to say that everyone agreed with him. There was much debate over the centuries on what criteria should govern the establishment of a modern Italian literary and spoken language but Dante prevailed and is credited for being the "Father of the Italian Language".

So how should you begin to learn to speak Italian? Learn it in the context of whatever interests you; art and architecture, ancient history, fashion and design. Use your interest as a starting point with related vocabulary and grammar that will keep you engaged and then branch out from there. I decided that since my trips to Italy centered on culinary traditions and cooking what better way to learn the Italian language than through learning words and phrases associated with food. I consider food to be the universal language of all cultures and learning the Italian language in courses is a perfect way to see and savor Italy because at least 3 times a day your conversations will center around food. For example you will need to know that breakfast is la colazione or prima colazione, lunch is il pranzo or seconda colazione and dinner is la cena. In addition, you will be learning ideas and concepts associated with food like time, place, greetings, utensils, money, directions and transportation. After all you need to know how to make a dinner reservation, ask for directions to the trattoria or ristorante, how to order from il menu, compliment the chef and pay for you meal. I soon learned that studying the Italian language in this context was practical as well as being a springboard for other areas of conversation, like shopping.

However you decide to find your friend Lui; audio, video, textbook, flash cards or formal classes, begin and keep at it. As I mentioned before, when I was complaining to my Italian cousin, Ornella, about how difficult it was to study the Italian language she laughed and told me about the building of Milan's Cathedral, the Duomo. The Duomo, one of the largest churches in the world, with its 135 spires and 3,400 statues was commissioned in 1386, by Gian Galeazzo Visconti, the first Duke of Milan. The Duomo was not finished until the early 1800s. Ornella explained that because of the centuries needed to complete the Duomo, if anything looks like it will take forever, the Milanese often use the term *"la fabbrica del Duomo"* (the building of the Duomo) to describe an extremely long, complex task, maybe even impossible to complete. I sometimes feel that studying the Italian language is my duomo but then again how else would I have found my friend Lui.

314

See and Savor More

Seeing and savoring Umbria includes lentils from the mountain town of Castelluccio and black truffles from the Umbrian forests. EuroChocolate, one of Europe's largest chocolate festivals, takes place in Perugia and draws nearly one million tourists and Italian natives each year. For nine days you can live like Wille Wonka with tastings, exhibitions, workshops and events on all things chocolate.

The Umbrian town of Gubbio, 40 km NE of Perugia is one of my favorite taste and travel locations. It contains a hidden treasure with linguistic importance as Egypt's Rosetta Stone. On display in the civic museum of Gubbio are the Eugubine (Iguvine) Tablets, sheets of bronze inscribed in ancient Umbrian using a modified Etruscan alphabet and the Latin alphabet. They date from the 3rd to the 1st century BC and were discovered in 1444 and are the longest texts so far found written in the extinct Umbrian language. They report about religious practices and sacred rites, information about places and about the government system of the town.

Source Information

Most of the information in this book has come from first hand accounts, interviews and dialogues with my Italian family and friends that have been part of my ongoing taste travels in Italy. Additional information is from the following sources.

Amherst, David. "The Geography of Italian Pasta". Professional Geographer. January 1999, 52(3) p 553-566.

Anderson, Burton. *The Foods of Italy*. New York: The Italian Trade Commission, 2007.

Anderson, Burton. *The Wines of Italy*. New York: The Italian Trade Commission, 2004.

Artusi, Pellegrino. *Science in the Kitchen and the Art of Eating Well*. Toronto: University of Toronto Press, 2004.

Associazione Verace Pizza Napoletana.
http://www.verapizzanapoletana.org

Boccaccio, Giovanni and G.H. McWilliam (ed.,translator). *The Decameron*. New York:Penguin Classics, 2003.

Batali, Mario. *Molto Italiano*. New York: Ecco Press, 2005.

Barker,Gaeme and Tom Rasmussen. *The Etruscans (The Peoples of Europe)*. New Jersey: Wiley-Blackwell, 2000.

Bastianich, Joseph and David Lynch. *Vino Italiano: The Regional Wines of Italy*. New York: Clarkson Potter, 2005.

Brivio, Ernesto. *The Duomo*. Milan: Veneranda Fabbrica del Duomo di Milano, 2003.

Cappitelli, Francesca, Joshua D. Nosanchuk, Arturo Casadevall, Lucia Toniolo, Lorenzo Brusetti, Sofia Florio, Pamela Principi, Sara Borin, Claudia Sorlini "Synthetic Consolidants Attacked by Melanin Producing Fungi: Case Study of the Biodeterioration of Milan (Italy) Cathedral Marble Treated with Acrylics". Applied and

<u>Environmental</u> <u>Microbiology.</u> Jan. 2007, p. 271-277, Vol. 73 No.1

Clark, Oz and Marc Millon. *Oz Clarke's Wine Companion:Tuscany.* De
Agostini Editions. London: Websters International Publishers,1997.

De'Medici, Lorenza. *Tuscany the Beautiful Cookbook.* New York:
Harper Collins,1996.

Editoriale Domus. *The Silver Spoon.* New York: Phaidon Press, 2006.

Folengo, Teofilo and Anne E. Mullaney (translator). *Baldo,* Vol.1:
Books I-XII. (I Tatti Renaissance Library). Cambridge, Mass: Harvard
University Press, 2007.

Gibelli, Gianfranco Giorgio. *Indagine: la leggenda di Rosania Fulgosio.*
Piacenza, Italy: Tep:S.r.l, 2004.

Hazan, Marcella. *Essentials of Classic Italian Cooking.* New York:
Alfred A. Knopf, 1992.

Johnson, Hugh. *Tuscany and Its Wines.* San Francisco: Chronicle
Books, 2000.

Krasner, Deborah. *The Flavors of Olive Oil: A Tasting Guide and
Cookbook.* New York: Simon and Schuster, 2002.

Lawrence, D.H. *D.H. Lawrence and Italy:Twlight in Italy, Sea and
Sardinia, Etruscan Places.*London: Penguin Classics, 1997.

Luongo, Pino, Angela Hederman, Barbara Raives. *A Tuscan in
The Kitchen: Recipes and Tales from My Home.* New York:
Clarkson Potter,1988.

Mandelbaum, Allen, Anthony Oldcorn, Charles Ross. *Lectura Dantis:
Purgatorio. A Canto-by-Canto Commentary.* Berkeley: University of
California Press, 2008.

McGovern. Patrick E. *Ancient Wine.* Princeton, New Jersey:
Princeton University Press, 2003.

Norwich, John Julius. *A Short History of Byzantium.* New York:
Vintage Books, Random House, 1997.

Peniakoff, Vladmir. *Popski's Private Army.* UK: Cassell ,2002.

Piras, Claudia, ed. *Culinaria Italy.* Cologne: KONEMAN, 2004.
317

Plumb, J.H. *The Italian Renaissance*. New York: Mariner Books, 2001.

Romer, Elizabeth. *The Tuscan Year: Life and Food in an Italian Valley*. New York: Antheneum Publishers, North Point edition, 1996.

Root, Waverly. *The Food of Italy*. New York: Vintage Books, 1992.

Ruskin, John. Ed. by J.G. Links.*The Stones of Venice*. Cambridge Massachusetts: Da Capo Press, 1985.

Seed, Diane. *The Top One Hundred Italian Rice Dishes*. Berkeley, CA: Ten Speed Press,2004.

UNESCO World Heritage http://whc.unesco.org/en/statesparties/it

Urban Square Initiative http://www.urbansquares.com hosted by Aleksander Janicijevic

"World's Best Awards Readers Survey".Travel + Leisure Magazine. 2006-2007-2008.

Wiel, Althea. *The History of Venice*. New York: Barnes & Noble Books, 2006.

Index

321

322